Deep Learning Approaches to Text Production

Synthesis Lectures on Human Language Technologies

Editor
Grame Hirst, *University of Toronto*

Synthesis Lectures on Human Language Technologies is edited by Graeme Hirst of the University of Toronto. The series consists of 50- to 150-page monographs on topics relating to natural language processing, computational linguistics, information retrieval, and spoken language understanding. Emphasis is on important new techniques, on new applications, and on topics that combine two or more HLT subfields.

Deep Learning Approaches to Text Production

Shashi Narayan and Claire Gardent

ISBN: 978-3-031-01045-3 paperback
ISBN: 978-3-031-02173-2 ebook
ISBN: 978-1-68173-821-5 epub
ISBN: 978-3-031-00184-0 hardcover

DOI 10.1007/978-3-031-02173-2

A Publication in the Springer series
SYNTHESIS LECTURES ON ADVANCES IN AUTOMOTIVE TECHNOLOGY

Lecture #44
Series Editor: Grame Hirst, *University of Toronto*
Series ISSN
Print 1947-4040   Electronic 1947-4059

Deep Learning Approaches to Text Production

Shashi Narayan
University of Edinburgh

Claire Gardent
CNRS/LORIA, Nancy

SYNTHESIS LECTURES ON HUMAN LANGUAGE TECHNOLOGIES #44

ABSTRACT

Text production has many applications. It is used, for instance, to generate dialogue turns from dialogue moves, verbalise the content of knowledge bases, or generate English sentences from rich linguistic representations, such as dependency trees or abstract meaning representations. Text production is also at work in text-to-text transformations such as sentence compression, sentence fusion, paraphrasing, sentence (or text) simplification, and text summarisation. This book offers an overview of the fundamentals of neural models for text production. In particular, we elaborate on three main aspects of neural approaches to text production: how sequential decoders learn to generate adequate text, how encoders learn to produce better input representations, and how neural generators account for task-specific objectives. Indeed, each text-production task raises a slightly different challenge (e.g, how to take the dialogue context into account when producing a dialogue turn, how to detect and merge relevant information when summarising a text, or how to produce a well-formed text that correctly captures the information contained in some input data in the case of data-to-text generation). We outline the constraints specific to some of these tasks and examine how existing neural models account for them. More generally, this book considers text-to-text, meaning-to-text, and data-to-text transformations. It aims to provide the audience with a basic knowledge of neural approaches to text production and a roadmap to get them started with the related work. The book is mainly targeted at researchers, graduate students, and industrials interested in text production from different forms of inputs.

KEYWORDS

text production, text generation, deep learning, neural networks, meaning-to-text, data-to-text, text-to-text, recurrent neural networks, sequence-to-sequence models, attention, copy, coverage, AMR generation, RDF generation, verbalise, simplification, compression, paraphrasing, dialogue generation, summarisation, content selection, adequacy, input understanding, sentence representation, document representation, communication goals, deep generators, reinforcement learning, evaluation, grammatical, fluent, meaning-preserving, BLEU, ROUGE, relevant, coherent

To my family.

– Shashi

A mes trois rayons de soleil, Jennifer, Gabrielle, et Caroline.

– Claire

Contents

List of Figures

List of Tables

Preface

Neural methods have triggered a paradigm shift in text production by supporting two key features. First, recurrent neural networks allow for the learning of powerful language models which can be conditioned on arbitrarily long input and are not limited by the Markov assumption. In practice, this proved to allow for the generation of highly fluent, natural sounding text. Second, the encoder-decoder architecture provides a natural and unifying framework for all generation tasks independent of the input type (data, text, or meaning representation). As shown by the dramatic increase in the number of conference and journal submissions on that topic, these two features have led to a veritable explosion of the field.

In this book, we introduce the basics of early neural text-production models and contrast them with pre-neural approaches. We begin by briefly reviewing the main characteristics of pre-neural text-production models, emphasising the stark contrast with early neural approaches which mostly modeled text-production tasks independent of the input type and of the communicative goal. We then introduce the encoder-decoder framework where, first, a continuous representation is learned for the input and, second, an output text is incrementally generated conditioned on the input representation and on the representation of the previously generated words. We discuss the attention, copy, and coverage mechanisms that were introduced to improve the quality of generated texts. We show how text-production can benefit from better input representation when the input is a long document or a graph. Finally, we motivate the need for neural models that are sensitive to the current communication goal. We describe different variants of neural models with task-specific objectives and architectures which directly optimise task-specific communication goals. We discuss generation from text, data, and meaning representations, bringing various text-production scenarios under one roof to study them all together. Throughout the book we provide an extensive list of references to support further reading.

As we were writing this book, the field had already moved on to new architectures and models (Transformer, pre-training, and fine-tuning have now become the dominant approach), and we discussed these briefly in the conclusion. We hope that this book will provide a useful introduction to the workings of neural text production and that it will help newcomers from both academia and industry quickly get acquainted with that rapidly expanding field.

We would like to thank several people who provided data or images, and authorization to use them in this book. In particular, we would like to thank *Abigail See* for the pointer-generator model, *Asli Celikyilmaz* for the diagrams of deep communicating paragraph encoders, *Bayu Distiawan Trisedya* for graph-triple encoders, *Bernd Bohnet* for an example from the 2018 surface realisation challenge, *Diego Marcheggiani* for graph convolutional network (GCN) diagrams, *Jiwei Tan* for hierarchical document encoders and graph-based attention mechanism using them,

Jonathan May for an abstract meaning representation (AMR) graph, *Laura Perez–Beltrachini* for an extended RotoWire example, *Linfeng Song* for graph-state long short-term memories (LSTMs) for text production from AMR graphs, *Marc'Aurelio Ranzato* for exposure bias and curriculum learning algorithm diagrams, *Qingyu Zhou* for selective encoding figures, *Sam Wiseman* for a corrected RotoWire example, *Sebastian Gehrmann* for the bottom-up summarization diagram, *Tsung-Hsien Wen* for an alternative coverage mechanism plot, *Xingxing Zhang* for reinforcement learning for sentence simplification, and *Yannis Konstas* for AMR-to-text and data-to-text examples. Huge thanks to *Emiel Krahmer, Graeme Hirst,* and our anonymous reviewer for reviewing our book and providing us with detailed and constructive feedback. We have attempted to address all the issues they raised. All the remaining typos and inadequacies are entirely our responsibility. Finally, we would like to thank Morgan & Claypool Publishers for working with us in producing this manuscript. A very special thanks goes to *Michael Morgan* and *Christine Kiilerich* for always encouraging us and keeping us on track.

Shashi Narayan and Claire Gardent
March 2020

CHAPTER 1

Introduction

In this chapter, we outline the differences between text production and text analysis, we introduce the main text-production tasks this book is concerned with (i.e., text production from data, from text, and from meaning representations) and we summarise the content of each chapter. We also indicate what is not covered and introduce some notational conventions.

1.1 WHAT IS TEXT PRODUCTION?

While natural language understanding [NLU, Bates, 1995] aims to analyse text, text production, or natural language generation [NLG, Gatt and Krahmer, 2018, Reiter and Dale, 2000], focuses on generating texts. More specifically, NLG differs from NLU in two main ways (cf. Figure 1.1). First, unlike text analysis, which always takes text as input, text production has many possible input types, namely, text [e.g., Nenkova and McKeown, 2011], data [e.g., Wiseman et al., 2017], or meaning representations [e.g., Konstas et al., 2017]. Second, text production has various potential goals. For instance, the goal may be to summarise, verbalise, or simplify the input.

Correspondingly, text production has many applications depending on what the input (data, text, or meaning representations) and what the goal is (simplifying, verbalising, para-phrasing, etc.). When the input is text (text-to-text or T2T generation), text production can be used to summarise the input document [e.g., Nenkova and McKeown, 2011], simplify a sentence [e.g., Shardlow, 2014, Siddharthan, 2014] or respond to a dialogue turn [e.g., Mott et al., 2004]. When the input is data, NLG can further be used to verbalise the content of a knowledge [e.g., Power, 2009] or a database [e.g., Angeli et al., 2010], generate reports from numerical [e.g., Reiter et al., 2005] or KB data [e.g., Bontcheva and Wilks, 2004], or generate captions from images [e.g., Bernardi et al., 2016]. Finally, NLG has also been used to regenerate text from the meaning representations designed by linguists to represent the meaning of natural language [e.g., Song et al., 2017].

In what follows, we examine generation from meaning representations, data, and text in more detail.

1.1.1 GENERATING TEXT FROM MEANING REPRESENTATIONS

There are two main motivations for generating text from meaning representations.

First, an algorithm that converts meaning representations into well-formed text is a nec-essary component of traditional pipeline NLG systems [Gatt and Krahmer, 2018, Reiter and Dale, 2000]. As we shall see in Chapter 2, such systems include several modules, one of them

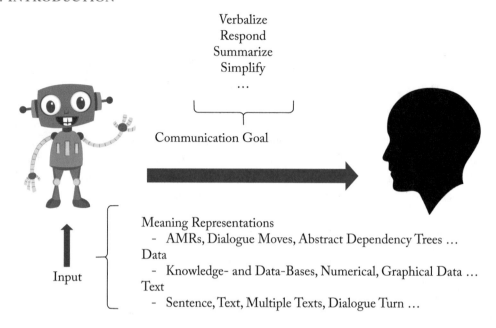

Figure 1.1: Input contents and communicative goals for text production.

(known as the surface realisation module) being responsible for generating text from some abstract linguistic representation derived by the system. To improve reusability, surface realisation challenges have recently been organised in an effort to identify input meaning representations that could serve as a common standard for NLG systems, thereby fueling research on that topic.

Second, meaning representations can be viewed as an interface between NLU and NLG. Consider translation, for instance. Instead of learning machine translation models, which directly translate surface strings into surface strings, an interesting scientific challenge would be to learn a model that does something more akin to what humans seem to do, i.e., first, understand the source text, and second, generate the target text from the conceptual representation issued from that understanding (indeed a recent paper by Konstas et al. [2017] mentions this as future work). A similar two-step process (first, deriving a meaning representation from the input text, and second, generating a text from that meaning representation) also seems natural for such tasks as text simplification or summarisation.

Although there are still relatively few approaches adopting a two-step interpret-and-generate process or reusing existing surface realisation algorithms, there is already a large trend of research in text production which focuses on generating text from meaning representations produced by a semantic parser [May and Priyadarshi, 2017, Mille et al., 2018] or a dialogue manager [Novikova et al., 2017b]. In the case of semantic parsing, the meaning representations capture the semantics of the input text and can be exploited as mentioned above to model a

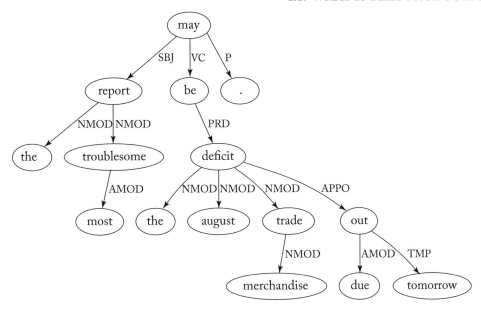

Figure 1.2: Input shallow dependency tree from the generation challenge surface realisation task for the sentence "*The most troublesome report may be the August merchandise trade deficit due out tomorrow.*"

two-step process in applications such as simplification [Narayan and Gardent, 2014], summarisation [Liu et al., 2015] or translation [Song et al., 2019b]. In the case of dialogue, the input meaning representation (a dialogue move) is output by the dialogue manager in response to the user input and provides the input to the dialogue generator, the module in charge of generating the system response.

While a wide range of meaning representations and syntactic structures have been proposed for natural language (e.g., first-order logic, description logic, hybrid logic, derivation rather than derived syntactic trees), three main types of meaning representations have recently gained traction as input to text generation: meaning representations derived from syntactic dependency trees (cf. Figure 1.2), meaning representations derived through semantic parsing (cf. Figure 1.3), and meaning representations used as input to the generation of a dialogue engine response (cf. Figure 1.4). All three inputs gave rise to shared tasks and international challenges.

The Surface Realisation shared task [Belz et al., 2012, Mille et al., 2018] focuses on generating sentences from linguistic representations derived from syntactic dependency trees and includes a deep and a shallow track. For the shallow track, the input is an unordered, lemmatised syntactic dependency tree and the main focus is on linearisation (deriving the correct word order from the input tree) and morphological inflection (deriving the inflection from a lemma and a set of morphosyntactic features). For the deep track, on the other hand, the input is a de-

Meaning Representation	Text
```(a / and :op1 (r / remain-01 :ARG1 (c / country :wiki "Bosnia_and_Herzegovina" :name (n / name :op1 "Bosnia")) :ARG3 (d / divide-02 :ARG1 c :topic (e / ethnic))) :op2 (v / violence :time (m / match-03 :mod (f2 / football) :ARG1-of (m2 / major-02)) :location (h / here) :frequency (o / occasional)) :time (f / follow-01 :ARG2 (w / war-01 :time (d2 / date-interval :op1 (d3 / date-entity :year 1992) :op2 (d4 / date-entity :year 1995)))))```	Following the 1992-1995 war, Bosnia remains ethnically divided and violence during major football matches occasionally occurs here.

Figure 1.3: Example input from the SemEval AMR-to-Text Generation Task.

Meaning Representation	Text
name[Loch Fyne] eatType[restaurant] food[French] priceRange[less than £20] familyFriendly[yes]	Loch Fyne is a family-friendly restaurant providing wine and cheese at a low cost.

Figure 1.4: E2E dialogue move and text.

pendency tree where dependencies are semantic rather than syntactic and function words have been removed. While the 2011 shared task only provided data for English, the 2018 version is multilingual and includes training data for Arabic, Czech, Dutch, English, Finnish, French, Italian, Portuguese, Russian, and Spanish (shallow track), and English, French, and Spanish (deep track).

In the SemEval-2017 Task 9 Generation Subtask [May and Priyadarshi, 2017], the goal is to generate text from an Abstract Meaning Representation (AMR, cf. Figure 1.3), a semantic representation which includes entity identification and typing, PropBank [Palmer et al., 2005] semantic roles, entity grounding via wikification, as well as treatments of modality and negation. The task and the training data are restricted to English.

Finally, following on previous work targeting the generation of a system response from a meaning representation consisting of a speech act (e.g., instruct, query, recommend) and a set of attribute-value pairs [Mairesse and Young, 2014, Wen et al., 2015], the E2E challenge [Novikova et al., 2017b] targets the generation of restaurant descriptions from sets of attribute-value pairs.[1]

1.1.2 GENERATING TEXT FROM DATA

Data is another common source of input for text production with two prominent data types, namely table and knowledge-base data.[2] For instance, Angeli et al. [2010] show how generation can be applied to sportscasting and weather forecast data [Reiter et al., 2005]. Konstas and Lapata [2012a,b] generate text from flight booking data, Lebret et al. [2016] from Wikipedia, and Wiseman et al. [2017] from basketball games box- and line-score tables. In those cases, the input to generation are tables containing records with an arbitrary number of fields (cf. Figure 1.5).

There has also been much work on generating text from knowledge bases. Bontcheva and Wilks [2004] generate patient records from clinical data encoded in the RDF format (Resource Description Framework). Power [2009] generates text from whole knowledge bases encoded in OWL or description logic. And, more recently, Perez-Beltrachini and Lapata [2018] have investigated the generation of sentences and short texts from RDF-encoded DBPedia data.

Whereas in generation from AMRs and dependency-based meaning representations, there is often an almost exact semantic match between input and output, this is not the case in data-to-text generation or generation from dialogue moves. As illustrated by the examples shown in Figure 1.5, there is no direct match between input data and output text. Instead, words must be chosen to lexicalise the input KB symbols, function words must be added, ellipsis and coordination must be used to avoid repetitions, and sometimes, content selection must be carried out to ensure that the output text adequately resembles human produced text.

1.1.3 GENERATING TEXT FROM TEXT

The third main strand of research in NLG is text-to-text generation. While for meaning representations and data-to-Text generation the most usual communicative goal is to verbalise the input, text-to-text generation can be categorised into three main classes depending on whether the communicative goal is to summarise, simplify, or paraphrase.

Text summarisation has various possible inputs and outputs. The input may consist of multiple documents in the same [Dang, 2006, Hachey, 2009, Harman and Over, 2004] or multiple languages [Filatova, 2009, Giannakopoulus et al., 2017, Hovy and Lin, 1997, Kabadjov et al., 2010, Lloret and Palomar, 2011]; a single document [Durrett et al., 2016]; or a single (complex) sentence [Chopra et al., 2016, Graff et al., 2003, Napoles et al., 2012]. The latter task is often also referred to as "Sentence Compression" [Cohn and Lapata, 2008, Filippova and

---

[1]In this case, the speech act is omitted as it is the same for all inputs namely, to recommend the restaurant described by the set of attribute-value pairs.

[2]Other types of input data have also been considered in NLG such as numerical, graphical and sensor data. We omit them here as, so far, these have been less often considered in neural NLG.

(a)

(b)

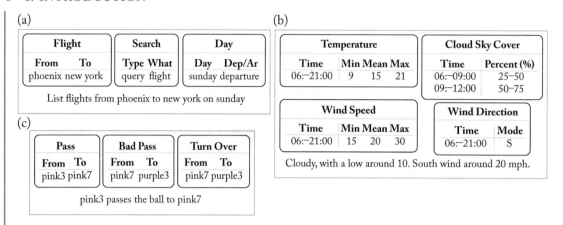

(c)

Figure 1.5: **Data-to-Text example input and output** (source: Konstas and Lapata [2012a]).

Strube, 2008, Filippova et al., 2015, Knight and Marcu, 2000, Pitler, 2010, Toutanova et al., 2016] while a related task, "Sentence Fusion", consists of combining two or more sentences with overlapping information content, preserving common information and deleting irrelevant details [Filippova, 2010, McKeown et al., 2010, Thadani and McKeown, 2013]. As for the output produced, research on summarisation has focused on generating either a short abstract [Durrett et al., 2016, Grusky et al., 2018, Sandhaus, 2008], a title [Chopra et al., 2016, Rush et al., 2015], or a set of headlines [Hermann et al., 2015].

Text paraphrasing aims to rewrite a text while preserving its meaning [Bannard and Callison-Burch, 2005, Barzilay and McKeown, 2001, Dras, 1999, Mallinson et al., 2017, Wubben et al., 2010], while text simplification targets the production of a text that is easier to understand [Narayan and Gardent, 2014, 2016, Siddharthan et al., 2004, Woodsend and Lapata, 2011, Wubben et al., 2012, Xu et al., 2015b, Zhang and Lapata, 2017, Zhu et al., 2010].

Both paraphrasing and text simplification have been shown to facilitate and/or improve the performance of natural language processing (NLP) tools. The ability to automatically generate paraphrases (alternative phrasings of the same content) has been demonstrated to be useful in several areas of NLP such as question answering, where they can be used to improve query expansion [Riezler et al., 2007]; semantic parsing, where they help bridge the gap between a grammar-generated sentence and its natural counterparts [Berant and Liang, 2014]; machine translation [Kauchak and Barzilay, 2006]; sentence compression [Napoles et al., 2011]; and sentence representation [Wieting et al., 2015], where they help provide additional training or evaluation data. From a linguistic standpoint, the automatic generation of paraphrases is an important task in its own right as it demonstrates the capacity of NLP techniques to simulate human behaviour.

Because shorter sentences are generally better processed by NLP systems, text simplification can be used as a pre-processing step which facilitates and improves the performance of parsers [Chandrasekar and Srinivas, 1997, Jelínek, 2014, McDonald and Nivre, 2011, Tomita, 1985], semantic role labelers [Vickrey and Koller, 2008], and statistical machine translation (SMT) systems [Chandrasekar et al., 1996]. Simplification also has a wide range of potential societal applications as it could be of use for people with reading disabilities [Inui et al., 2003] such as aphasia patients [Carroll et al., 1999], low-literacy readers [Watanabe et al., 2009], language learners [Siddharthan, 2002], and children [De Belder and Moens, 2010].

1.2 ROADMAP

This book falls into three main parts.

Part I sets up the stage and introduces the basic notions, motivations, and evolutions underlying text production. It consists of three chapters.

Chapter 1 (this chapter) briefly situates text production with respect to text analysis. It describes the range of input covered by text production, i.e., meaning representations, data, and text. And it introduces the main applications of text-production models which will be the focus of this book, namely, automatic summarisation, paraphrasing, text simplification, and data verbalisation.

Chapter 2 summarises pre-neural approaches to text production, focusing first on text production from data and meaning representations, and second, on text-to-text generation. The chapter describes the main assumptions made for these tasks by pre-neural approaches, setting up the stage for the following chapter.

Chapter 3 shows how deep learning introduced a profound change of paradigm for text production, leading to models which rely on very different architectural assumptions than pre-neural approaches and to the use of the encoder-decoder model as a unifying framework for all text-production tasks. It then goes on to present a basic encoder-decoder architecture, the sequence-to-sequence model, and shows how this architecture provides a natural framework both for representing the input and for generating from these input representations.

Part II summarises recent progress on neural approaches to text production, showing how the basic encoder-decoder framework described in Chapter 3 can be improved to better model the characteristics of text production.

While neural language models demonstrate a strong ability to generate fluent, natural sounding text given a sufficient amount of training data, a closer look at the output of text-production systems reveals several issues regarding text quality which have repeatedly been observed across generation tasks. The output text may contain information not present in the input (weak semantic adequacy) or, conversely, fail to convey all information present in the input (lack of coverage); repetitions (stuttering) frequent (diminished grammaticality and fluency); and rare or unknown input units may be incorrectly or not at all verbalised. Chapter 4 discusses these issues and introduces three neural mechanisms standardly used in text production to address them, namely, attention, copy, and coverage. We show how integrating these additional features in the encoder-decoder framework permits generating better text by improving the *decoding* part of NLG systems. We also briefly mention alternative methods that were proposed in the literature.

In contrast to Chapter 4, which shows how to improve the decoding part of the encoder-decoder framework, Chapter 5 focusing on *encoding* and shows how encoders can be modified to better take into account the structure of the input. Indeed, relying on the impressive ability of sequence-to-sequence models to generate text, most of the earlier work on neural approaches to text production systematically encoded the input as a sequence. However, the input to text production often has a non-sequential structure. In particular, knowledge-base fragments are generally viewed as graphs, while the documents which can make up the input to summarisation systems are hierarchical structures consisting of paragraphs which themselves consist of words and sentences. Chapter 5 starts by outlining the shortcomings arising from modelling these complex structures as sequences. It then goes on to introduce different ways in which the structure of the input can be better modelled. For document structure, we discuss hierarchical long short-term memories (LSTMs), ensemble encoders, and hybrid convolutional sequence-to-sequence document encoders. We then review the use of graph-to-sequence, graph-based triple encoders and graph convolutional networks as means to capture the graph structure of e.g., knowledge-based data and Abstract Meaning Representations (AMRs).

Chapter 6 focuses on ways of guiding the learning process so that constraints stemming from the communication goals are better captured. While the standard encoder-decoder framework assumes learning based on the ground truth, usually using cross-entropy, more recent approaches to text production have started investigating alternative methods such as reinforcement learning and multi-task learning (the latter allows signal from other complementary tasks). In Chapter 6, we review some of these approaches, showing for instance how a simplification system can be learned using deep reinforcement learning with a reward of capturing key features of simplified text such as whether it is fluent (perplexity), whether it is different from the source (SARI metrics), and whether it is similar to the reference (BLEU).

Finally, Part III reviews some of the most prominent data sets used in neural approaches to text production (Chapter 7) and mentions a number of open challenges (Chapter 8).

1.3 WHAT'S NOT COVERED?

While natural language generation has long been the "parent pauvre" of NLP, with few researchers, small workshops, and relatively few publications, "the effectiveness of neural networks and their impressive ability to generate fluent text"[3] has spurred massive interest for the field over the last few years. As a result, research in that domain is progressing at high speed, covering an increasingly large number of topics. In this book, we focus on introducing the basics of neural text production, illustrating its workings with some examples from data-to-text,

---

[3]http://karpathy.github.io/2015/05/21/rnn-effectiveness/

text-to-text, and meaning-representations-to-text generation. We do not provide an exhaustive description of the state of the art for these applications, however, nor do we cover all areas of text production. In particular, paraphrasing and sentence compression are only briefly mentioned. Generation from videos and image, in particular caption generation, are not discussed,[4] as is the whole field of automated creative writing, including poetry generation and storytelling. Evaluation is only briefly discussed. Finally, novel models and techniques (e.g., transformer models, contextual embeddings, and generative models for generation) which have recently appeared are only briefly discussed in the conclusion.

1.4   OUR NOTATIONS

We represent words, sentences, documents, graphs, word counts, and other types of observations with Roman letters (e.g., x, w, s, d, W, S, and D) and parameters with Greek letters (e.g., α, β, and θ). We use bold uppercase letters to represent matrices (e.g., $\mathbf{X}, \mathbf{Y}$, and $\mathbf{Z}$), and bold lowercase letters to represent vectors (e.g., $\mathbf{a}, \mathbf{b}$, and $\mathbf{c}$) for both random variables x and parameters θ. We use $[\mathbf{a}; \mathbf{b}]$ to denote vector concatenation. All other notations are introduced when they are used.

---

[4]See Bernardi et al. [2016], Gatt and Krahmer [2018] for surveys of automatic description generation from images and of the Vision-Language Interface.

PART I

Basics

CHAPTER 2

Pre-Neural Approaches

In this chapter, we briefly review the main architectures that were prevalent in pre-neural text generation. These architectures focus on modelling multiple, interacting factors and differ depending on the NLG task they address. More specifically, three main types of pre-neural NLG architectures can be distinguished depending on whether the task is to generate from data from meaning representations or text.

This chapter sets up the stage for the following chapters where early neural approaches will be shown, usually to model text production as a single end-to-end process independently of the specific NLG task being considered and of the number of factors being involved. As we shall see, contrary to pre-neural approaches which use distinct architectures for different NLG tasks, early neural NLG models mostly consist of two sub-modules: an encoder which maps the input into a continuous representation and a decoder which incrementally generates text based on this continuous representation and on the representation of previously generated words.

2.1 DATA-TO-TEXT GENERATION

Generating text from data is a multiple-choice problem. Consider, for instance, the example input data and the associated text shown in Figure 2.1.

Generating this text involves making the following choices.

- *Content Selection:* deciding which parts of the input data should be realised by the text. For instance, in our example, the pass from "purple6" to "purple3" is not mentioned. More generally, a generation system needs to decide which parts of the input should be realised in the output text and which information can be omitted.

- *Document Planning:* finding an appropriate text structure. In our example, the text structure is simple and consists of a single sentence. When the input data is larger however, document planning requires making decisions regarding the number of sentences to be generated, their respective ordering, and the discourse relations holding between them.

- *Lexicalisation:* determining which words should be chosen to realise the input symbols. For instance, the input symbol "badPass" is lexicalised by the verbal phrase "to make a bad pass".

- *Referring Expression Generation:* determining which referring expression (pronoun, proper name, definite description, etc.) should be used to describe input entities. In our example,

Input Data	Output Text
pass(arg1=purple6,arg2=purple3) kick(arg1=purple3) badPass(arg1=purple3,arg2=pink9) turnover(arg1=purple3,arg2=pink9)	purple3 made a bad pass that was picked off by pink9

Figure 2.1: A Robocup input and output pair example.

all entities are referred to by identifiers which directly translate into proper names. In more complex settings, however, particularly when the generated text is longer and contains multiple references to the same entity, it is necessary to decide whether to use, a pronoun or a definite description. Furthermore, when using a definite description (e.g., "the man"), the content of the description needs to be determined: should it be, e.g., "the man with the hat", "the tall man with a hat", or "the president"?

- *Aggregation:* using anaphora, ellipsis, coordination, and generally any convenient syntactic means of avoiding repeating the verbalisation of data fragments which occur multiple times in the input. For instance, the use of the subject relative clause in the example above ("purple3 made a bad pass that was picked off by pink9") permits generating a more compact text than the alternative "purple3 made a bad pass to pink9. There was a turnover from pink3 to pink9".

- *Surface Realisation:* deciding which syntactic constructs should be exploited to combine the selected lexical items into a well-formed output text. For instance, in the example above, surface realisation determined the use of two verbs, one in the passive voice, the other one in the active voice, both verbs being connected by a subject relative clause.

Figure 2.2 shows how these different sub-tasks can be modeled in a pipeline architecture. As discussed in Gatt and Krahmer [2018], alternative architectures have been explored reflecting different levels of division between modules. Modular approaches maintain a strict division between each sub-task, implementing the interactions between them using either a pipeline, a revision, or a constrained architecture. Planning-based approaches view language production as a goal-driven task (following a "language as action" paradigm) and provide a unifying framework where all modules are implemented by a given set of actions. Finally, integrated or global approaches cut across task divisions, implementing all modules via a single unifying mechanism (e.g., probabilistic context-free grammar or discriminative classifiers) and jointly optimising the various generation sub-tasks.

Overall, though, distinct generation sub-tasks are implemented separately. For instance, even in global, joint optimisation approaches such as Konstas and Lapata [2012a], different rule

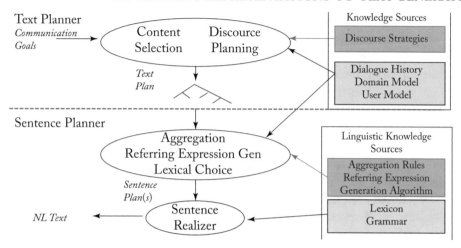

Figure 2.2: Data-to-Text: A pipeline architecture (source: Johanna Moore).

sets are defined to implement content selection, text planning, and surface realisation. Similarly, in Angeli et al. [2010], three distinct classifiers are used to implement each of these components.

2.2   MEANING REPRESENTATIONS-TO-TEXT GENERATION

For meaning representation to text (MR-to-text) generation, two main types of approaches can be distinguished depending on the nature of the input, the amount of training data available, and on the type of text to be produced: grammar-centric *vs.* statistical.

Grammar-centric approaches are used when the generation task mainly involves surface realisation, i.e., when the gap between input MR and output text is small and the generation task mainly consists of linearising and inflecting some input structure (usually a graph or an unordered tree) whose nodes are decorated with lemmas or words. In that case, a grammar can be used to define a mapping between input MR and output text. Additional heuristic or statistical modules are usually added to handle the ambiguity induced by the strong non-determinism of natural-language grammars.

Statistical approaches often provided a more robust solution compared to grammar-centric approaches. They used machine learning to handle a wider range of choices, going beyond just handling syntactic ambiguity resolution.

2.2.1   GRAMMAR-CENTRIC APPROACHES

In a grammar-centric approach, a grammar describing the syntax of natural language is used to mediate between meaning and text. The grammar can be handwritten [Gardent and Perez-

Beltrachini, 2017] or automatically extracted from parse trees [Gyawali and Gardent, 2014, White, 2006]. Because natural language is highly ambiguous, grammar-centric approaches additionally integrate heuristics or statistical modules for handling non-determinism. Three main types of disambiguation filters have been used: filters that reduce the initial search space (often called hypertaggers), filters that eliminate unlikely intermediate structures, and filters that select the best solution from the set of output solutions (usually referred to as rankers).

Pruning the Initial Search Space.   Bottom-up grammar-based approaches first select the set of lexical entries/grammar rules which are relevant given the input. For instance, if the input contains the predicate "book", the lexical entries for "book" will be selected. Because the grammar and the lexicon of a natural language are highly ambiguous, this first step (lexical selection) yields a very large input space where the number of possible combinations to be considered is the cartesian product of the number of entries/rules selected for each input token. For instance, if the input consists of 10 tokens and each token selects an average of 5 entries, the number of possible combinations to be explored is 5^{10}.

To reduce this initial search space, Espinosa et al. [2008] introduced hypertagging, a technique adapted from the supertagging method first proposed for parsing by Bangalore and Joshi [1999]. In essence, a hypertagger is a classifier which was trained to select for each input token, the n most probable grammar rules/lexical entries, with n a small number. Gardent and Perez-Beltrachini [2017] present an interesting application of hypertagging which shows that hypertagging can be used to support the generation of well-formed natural language queries from description logic formulae. In that case, the hypertagger is shown not only to reduce the initial search space, but also to make choices that correctly capture the interactions between the various micro-planning operations (lexicalisation, referring expression generation, sentence segmentation, aggregation, and surface realisation).

Other techniques used to filter the initial search space include polarity filtering, a technique which rules out any combination of grammar rules such that the syntactic requirements of verbs are not exactly satisfied [Gardent and Kow, 2007], and hybrid bottom-up, top-down filtering, where the structure of the input is used both top-down—to constrain the selection of applicable rules—and bottom-up, to filter the initial search space associated with local input trees [Narayan and Gardent, 2012].

Filtering out Intermediate Structures.   Carroll and Oepen [2005] present a subsumption-based local ambiguity factoring and a procedure to selectively unpack the generation forest according to a probability distribution given by a conditional, discriminative classifier to filter out unlikely, intermediate structures.

To address the fact that there are $n!$ ways to combine any n modifiers with a single constituent, White [2004] proposes to use a language model to prune the chart of identical edges representing different modifier permutations, e.g., to choose between "fierce black cat" and "black fierce cat." Similarly, Bangalore and Rambow [2000] assumes a single derivation tree that encodes a word lattice ("a {fierce black, black fierce} cat") and uses statistical knowledge to select the best linearisation while Gardent and Kow [2007] propose a two-step surface realisation algorithm for FB-LTAG (Feature-Based Lexicalised Tree-Adjoining Grammar) where, first, substitution is applied to combine trees together and, second, adjunction is applied to integrate modifiers and long-distance dependencies.

Ranking.   Two main approaches have been used to rank the output of grammar-based sentence generators. Early approaches simply apply language model n-gram statistics to rank alternatives [Bangalore and Rambow, 2000, Langkilde, 2000, Langkilde-Geary, 2002]. Discriminative disambiguation models were later proposed which used linguistically motivated features, often additionally using language model scores as an additional feature [Nakanishi et al., 2005, Velldal and Oepen, 2006].

2.2.2   STATISTICAL MR-TO-TEXT GENERATION

Because they permit modelling a wider range of transformations than grammars such as, for instance, aggregation, document planning, and referring expression generation, statistical approaches are generally favoured when the input meaning representation is deeper, i.e., when it abstracts away from surface differences and involves more complex MR-to-text transformations. They are, in particular, prevalent when the input MR is an Abstract Meaning Representation (AMR) or a deep unordered dependency tree.

For AMR-to-text generation, Flanigan et al. [2016] convert input graphs to trees by splitting reentrencies (nodes with multiple parents), and then translating the trees into sentences using a tree-to-string transducer. Song et al. [2017] use a synchronous node replacement grammar to simultaneously parse input AMRs and generate sentences. Pourdamghani et al. [2016] first linearise input graphs by breadth-first traversal, and then use a phrase-based machine translation (MT) system to generate text from the resulting linearised sequences. Castro Ferreira et al. [2017] frame generation as a translation task, comparing two different Machine Translation (MT) approaches (phrase-based and neural MT) and providing a systematic study of the impact of 3 AMR pre-processing steps (delexicalisation, compression, and linearisation) applied before the MT phase.

For deep dependency trees, Bohnet et al. [2010] uses a cascade of support vector machine (SVM) classifiers whereby an initial classifier decodes semantic input into the corresponding syntactic features, while two subsequent classifiers first linearise the syntax and then perform morphological realisation to inflect the input lemmas.

Statistical approaches have also been used to generate from shallow dependency trees. For instance, Filippova and Strube [2007, 2009] propose a two-step linearisation approach using maximum entropy classifiers, first determining which constituent should occupy sentence-initial position, then ordering the constituents in the remainder of the sentence.

Complex Sentence	In 1964 Peter Higgs published his second paper in Physical Review Letters, describing Higgs mechanism, which predicted a new massive spin-zero boson for the first time.
Simplified Sentence	Peter Higgs wrote his paper explaining Higgs mechanism in 1964. Higgs mechanism predicted a new elementary particle.

Figure 2.3: Simplifying a sentence.

2.3 TEXT-TO-TEXT GENERATION

Just like data- and MR-to-text production usually decompose the generation task into several sub-tasks, pre-neural Text-to-Text generation focuses on modelling several operations and their interactions. Simplification, compression, and paraphrasing are generally viewed as involving all or some of four main operations: sentence splitting, phrase rewriting, phrase reordering, and phrase deletion, while summarisation is generally decomposed into a three-step process involving content selection (selecting the key information in the input), aggregation (grouping together related information), and generalisation (abstracting from the input document to produce a better text).

2.3.1 SENTENCE SIMPLIFICATION AND SENTENCE COMPRESSION

Sentence Simplification. As illustrated in Figure 2.3, sentence simplification maps a sentence to a simpler, more readable text approximating its content. Typically, a simplified text differs from the original version in that it involves simpler words, simpler syntactic constructions, shorter sentences, and fewer modifiers. In pre-neural approaches, simplification has thus often been modeled using four main operations:

- *splitting* a complex sentence into several simpler sentences;

- *deleting* words or phrases;

- *reordering* phrases or constituents;

- *substituting* words/phrases with simpler ones.

As for data-to-text generation, existing approaches vary in whether they capture all or some of these operations and on how these operations are integrated (pipeline vs. joint approach).

Earlier work on sentence simplification focused mostly on splitting and rewriting, relying on handcrafted rules to capture syntactic simplification, e.g., to split coordinated and subordinated sentences into several, simpler clauses or to model active/passive transformations [Bott et al., 2012, Canning, 2002, Chandrasekar and Srinivas, 1997, Siddharthan, 2002, 2011].

Sentence	Britain's Ministry of Defense says a British soldier was killed in a roadside blast in southern Afghanistan.
Compression	A British soldier was killed in a blast in Afghanistan.

Figure 2.4: A Sentence/Compression pair.

A large strand of work has focused on developing machine learning approaches to sentence simplification and used the parallel data set formed by Simple English Wikipedia (SWKP)[1] and traditional English Wikipedia (EWKP)[2]. Zhu et al. [2010] learned a simplification model inspired by *syntax-based* machine translation techniques [Yamada and Knight, 2001], which encodes the probabilities for the four rewriting operations (substitution, reordering, splitting, and deletion) on the parse tree of the input sentence. It is combined with a language model to improve grammaticality and the decoder translates sentences into simpler ones by greedily selecting an output sentence with the highest probability. Woodsend and Lapata [2011] learn a quasi-synchronous grammar [Smith and Eisner, 2006] describing a loose alignment between parse trees of complex and simple sentences. Following Dras [1999], they then generate all possible rewrites of a source tree and use integer linear programming to select the best simplification. In Coster and Kauchak [2011], Wubben et al. [2012], simplification is viewed as a monolingual translation task where a complex sentence is the source and a simpler one is the target. To account for deletions, reordering and substitution, Coster and Kauchak [2011] trained a phrase-based machine translation system on the PWKP corpus while modifying the word alignment output by GIZA++ in Moses to allow for empty alignments. Similarly, Wubben et al. [2012] train a phrase-based machine translation system augmented with a post hoc reranking procedure designed to rank the outputs based on their dissimilarity from the source. Finally, Narayan and Gardent [2014] present a hybrid approach combining a probabilistic model for sentence splitting and deletion with a statistical machine translation system trained on PWKP for substitution and reordering.

Sentence Compression.   Most work on sentence compression is extractive.[3] That is, the generated compressions are composed of sub-sequences of the input sentence. As a result, work on sentence compression mainly focuses on deletion. However, syntax is often used to optimise the well-formedness of the compressed output. This partially captures syntactic transformations that may result from extractive compression.

---

[1]SWKP (http://simple.wikipedia.org) is a corpus of simple texts targeting children and adults who are learning English Language and whose authors are requested to use easy words and short sentences.

[2]http://en.wikipedia.org

[3]There are some exceptions. For example, the task of title generation [Filippova and Altun, 2013b] or sentence summarisation [Rush et al., 2015] can be treated as abstractive sentence compression.

Dorr et al. [2003], Jing and McKeown [2000], Zajic et al. [2007] rely on rule-based approaches to determine which words should be kept and which should be deleted. Galanis and Androutsopoulos [2010], Gillick and Favre [2009], Knight and Marcu [2000], Turner and Charniak [2005] developed supervised models trained on parallel data. Finally, Clarke and Lapata [2006], Filippova and Strube [2008], Woodsend and Lapata [2011], Woodsend et al. [2010] present unsupervised approaches which rely on integer linear programming and a set of linguistically motivated constraints to infer globally optimal compressions.

Sentence Paraphrasing. Unsurprisingly, work on paraphrasing has mainly been concerned with modelling phrase reordering and substitution. Pre-neural approaches include rule-based approaches, drawing on linguistic resources and approaches based on statistical machine translation (SMT).

Thus, McKeown [1983] present a rule-based method for deriving a paraphrase from the input sentence and its syntactic tree. Bolshakov and Gelbukh [2004] use WordNet and internet statistics of stable word combinations (collocations) to generate paraphrases: words or expressions are substituted with WordNet synonyms only if the latter form valid collocations with the surrounding words according to the statistics gathered from internet.

Paraphrase generation can be viewed as a monolingual machine translation task. Building on this intuition, Quirk et al. [2004] train a paraphrasing SMT system on large volumes of sentence pairs automatically extracted from clustered news articles available on the World Wide Web. Zhao et al. [2008] use SMT and multiple resources to generate paraphrases. Specifically, a phrasal paraphrase table and a feature function are derived from each resource, which are then combined in a log-linear SMT model for sentence-level paraphrase generation. Similarly, Napoles et al. [2016] provide a black-box machine translation model which uses the PPDB paraphrase database and a statistical machine translation model to generate paraphrases.

Grammar-based models of paraphrases have also been explored. For instance, Narayan et al. [2016] introduces a grammar model for paraphrase generation which is trained on the Paralex corpus, a large monolingual parallel corpus, containing 18 million pairs of question paraphrases.

2.3.2 DOCUMENT SUMMARISATION

Intuitively, humans perform summarisation by extracting the key information contained in the input document, aggregating this information, and abstracting from the resulting aggregated text. That is, humans create a summary by *abstracting* over its content. In practice, however, much of the pre-neural work on automatic text summarisation has focused on *extractive* summarisation, an approach which simply extracts key sentences from the input document and combines them to form a summary. The difference is illustrated in Figure 2.5. While abstractive summarisation reformulates the selected content, extractive approaches simply stitch together text fragments selected by the extraction step.

There is a vast literature on pre-neural text summarisation. For an overview of this work, we refer the reader to Mani [1999], Nenkova and McKeown [2012], Nenkova et al. [2011].

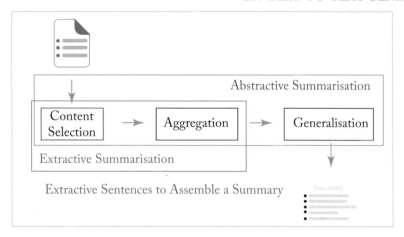

Figure 2.5: Abstractive vs. extractive summarisation.

Here, we briefly survey some key techniques used in the three main steps usually involved in extractive summarisation, namely:

- creating an intermediate representation of the sentences contained in the input text;

- scoring these sentences based on that representation; and

- creating a summary by selecting the most relevant sentences [Nenkova et al., 2011].

Representing Sentences.   Work on extractive summarisation has explored two main ways of representing text: topic and indicators representations.

In *topic-based approaches*, an input document is assigned a topic representation which captures what the text is about. This topic representation is then used to extract from the input those sentences that are strongly topic-related. Several approaches have been proposed to derive these topic representations.

Frequency-based approaches use counts to identify those words that represent a document topic. Luhn [1958] used a frequency threshold to identify frequent content words in a document as descriptive of the document's topic. Similarly, Conroy et al. [2006] used the log-likelihood ratio to extract those words that have a likelihood statistic greater than what one would expect by chance. Other approaches have used tf.idf ratio and word probability [Goldstein et al., 2000, Luhn, 1958, Nenkova and Vanderwende, 2005].

Latent semantic analysis (LSA) [Dumais et al., 1988, Gong and Liu, 2001] and Bayesian topic models [Celikyilmaz and Hakkani-Tur, 2010, Daumé III and Marcu, 2006, Haghighi and Vanderwende, 2009, Wang et al., 2009] exploit word co-occurrences to derive an implicit representation of text topics.

Document	**AFL star blames vomiting cat for speeding**
	Adelaide Crows defender Daniel Talia has kept his driving license, telling a court he was speeding 36 km over the limit because he was distracted by his sick cat. The 22-year-old AFL star, who drove 96km/h in a 60km/h road work zone on the South Eastern expressway in February, said he didn't see the reduced speed sign because he was so distracted by his cat vomiting violently in the back seat of his car. In the Adelaide magistrates court on Wednesday, Magistrate Bot Trap fined Talia $824 for exceeding the speed limit by more than 30km/h. He lost four demerit points, instead of seven, because of his significant training commitments.
Summary	• Adelaide Crows defender Daniel Talia admits to speeding but says he didn't see road signs because his cat was vomiting in his car. • 22-year-old Talia was fined $824 and four demerit points, instead of seven, because of his "significant" training commitments.

Figure 2.6: A document/summary pair from the CNN/DailyMail data set.

Finally, lexical chains [Barzilay and Elhadad, 1997, Galley and McKeown, 2003, Silber and McCoy, 2002] have been proposed to capture the intuition that topics are expressed not by single words but by sets of related words. For example, the words "asana", "pranayama", "breathing", "body", "soul" indicate a clear topic, even if each of the words is not by itself very frequent. Based on the lexical relations (synonymy, antonymy, part-whole, and general-specific) contained in WordNet, lexical chains track the prominence of different topics discussed in the input by measuring the occurrence of words that are lexically related to each of these topics.

In contrast to topic-based approaches, *indicators approaches* do not rely on a single topic representation, but on different text-based indicators such as the position of a sentence in the input document or its similarity with the document title [Kupiec et al., 1995]. Two main types of indicator methods can be distinguished: graph-based and vectorial.

In the graph-based approach [Erkan and Radev, 2004, Mihalcea and Tarau, 2004], an input text is represented as a graph whose vertices represent sentences and where edge labels indicate sentence similarity. Sentences that are related to many other sentences are likely to be central and have high weight for selection in the summary.

Vectorial approaches represent input sentences as feature vectors which can then be exploited by classifiers to determine whether or not a given input sentence should be part of the extracted summary [Hakkani-Tur and Tur, 2007, Leskovec et al., 2005, Lin and Hovy, 2000, Louis et al., 2010, Osborne, 2002, Wong et al., 2008, Zhang et al., 2013, Zhou and Hovy, 2003]. In addition to the topic features that are classically derived by topic-based approaches, common features include the position of the sentence in the document (in news articles, first sentences are almost always informative), position in the paragraph (first and last sentences are often important), sentence length, similarity of the sentence with the document title or headings, weights of the words in a sentence determined by any topic representation approach, presence of named entities or cue phrases from a predetermined list, etc.

Scoring Sentences.   Based on whichever text representation has been created, each sentence is then assigned a score indicating its importance. For topic representation approaches, the importance of a sentence is usually computed as the number or the proportion of topic words it contains. For vectorial methods, the weight of each sentence is determined by combining the evidence from the different indicators using machine learning techniques to discover feature weights. In the multi-document summarisation LexRank system, the weight of each sentence is derived by applying stochastic techniques to the graph representation of the text [Erkan and Radev, 2004].

Selecting Summary Sentences.   The last step consists of selecting the best combination of important sentences to form a paragraph length summary. The extracted summary should obey three main constraints: It should not exceed a given length, it should contain all relevant information, and it should avoid repetitions.

Most summarisation approaches choose content greedily by incrementally selecting the most informative (highest-scoring) sentences until the length limit is reached. A common strategy for greedily constructing a summary one sentence at a time is maximal marginal relevance (MMR) [Carenini et al., 2007], where, at each step, the algorithm is constrained to select a sentence that is maximally relevant and minimally redundant with sentences already included in the summary. Relevance and novelty are measured separately and then combined using some linear combination to produce a single score determining the importance of a sentence at a given stage of the selection process.

Sentence selection global optimisation algorithms have also been proposed to jointly maximise informativeness, minimise repetition, and conform to summary length restrictions [Gillick et al., 2009, Riedhammer et al., 2008].

2.4   SUMMARY

In this chapter, we briefly reviewed pre-neural approaches to text-production. We saw that these approaches typically decompose the text-production task into several interacting subtasks which vary depending on the specific text-production task being considered. Figure 2.7 illustrates this intuition.

Data-to-text production typically involves text planning (selecting and structuring content) and sentence planning (choosing words, syntactic structures, and means of avoiding repetitions as well as choosing appropriate referring expressions to describe input entities). Simplification, paraphrasing, and compression involve modelling all or some of four operations, namely, phrase rewriting, reordering and deletion, and sentence splitting. Finally, summarisation can be

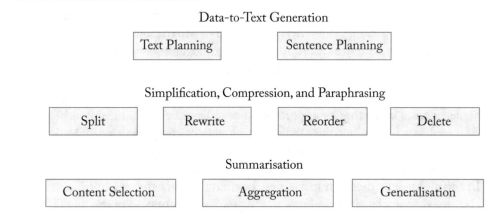

Figure 2.7: Key modules in pre-neural approaches to text production.

viewed as encompassing three main modules: content selection (identifying key information), aggregation (structuring key information into a coherent text plan), and generalisation (using linguistic means to generate a naturally sounding, fluent summary).

In Chapter 3, we will see that initial neural approaches to text production markedly differ from these pre-neural approaches in that they provide a single, unifying framework, moving away from a decomposition of the text-production task into multiple subtasks. In Chapters 6 and 8, we will then see how more recent work focuses on integrating key ideas from these pre-neural approaches back into the novel deep learning paradigm.

C H A P T E R   3

Deep Learning Frameworks

In recent years, deep learning, also called the neural approach, has been proposed for text production. The pre-neural approach generally relied on a pipeline of modules, each performing a specific subtask. The neural approach is very different from the pre-neural approach in that it provides a uniform (end-to-end) framework for text production. First the input is projected on a continuous representation (**representation learning**), and then, the generation process (**generation**) generates an output text using the input representation. Figure 3.1 illustrates this high-level framework used by neural approaches to text production.

One of the main strengths of neural networks is that they provide an amazing tool for representation learning. Representation learning often happens in a continuous space, such that different modalities of input, e.g., text (words, sentences, and even paragraphs), graphs, and tables are represented by dense vectors. For instance, given the user input "I am good. How about you? What do you do for a living?" in a dialogue setting, a neural network will first be used to create a representation of the user input. Then, in a second step—the generation step—this representation will be used as the input to a decoder which will generate the system response, "Ah, boring nine to five office job. Pays for the house I live in", a text conditioned on that input representation. Representation learning aims at encoding relevant information from the input that is necessary to generate the output text. Neural networks have proven to be effective in representation learning without requiring directly extracting explicit features from the data. These networks operate as complex functions that propagate values (linear transformation of input values) through non-linear functions (such as the sigmoid or the hyperbolic tangent function) to get outputs that can be further propagated the same way to upper layers of the network.

This chapter introduces current methods in deep learning that are common in natural language generation. The goal is to give a basic introduction to neural networks in Section 3.1, and discuss the basic encoder-decoder approach [Cho et al., 2014, Sutskever et al., 2014] which has been the basis for much of the work on neural text production.

3.1   BASICS

Central to deep learning is its ability to do representation learning by introducing representations that are expressed in terms of other simpler representations [Goodfellow et al., 2016].[1] Typically, neural networks are organised in layers; each layer consists of a number of intercon-

---

[1] *Deep Learning*; An MIT Press book. Ian Goodfellow, Yoshua Bengio, and Aaron Courville (https://www.deeplearningbook.org/).

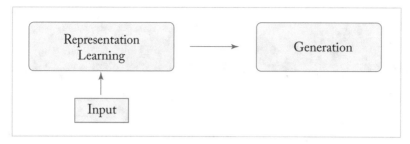

Figure 3.1: Deep learning for text generation.

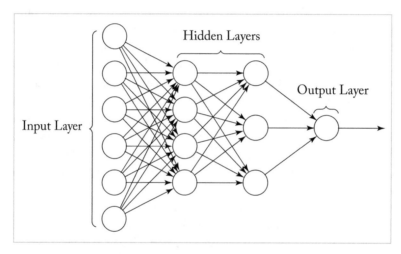

Figure 3.2: Feed-forward neural network or multi-layer perceptron.

nected nodes; each node takes inputs from the previous layer and applies linear transformation followed by a nonlinear *activation function*. The network takes an input through the *input layer* which communicates with one or more *hidden layers* and finally produces model predictions through the *output layer*. Figure 3.2 illustrates an example deep learning system. A key characteristic of deep learning systems is that they can learn complex concepts from simpler concepts through the use of nonlinear activation functions; the activation function of a node in a neural network defines the output of that node given an input or set of inputs. Several hidden layers are often stacked to learn more and more complex and abstract concepts, leading to a *deep* network.

What we just explained here is essentially a *feed-forward neural network* or *multi-layer perceptron*. Basically, it learns a function mapping a set of input values from the input layer to a set of output values in the output layer. The function is formed by composing many linear functions through nonlinear activations.[2] Such networks are called feed-forward because information always flows forward from the input layer to the output layer through the hidden layers in between. There is no autoregressive connection in which outputs of a layer are fed back to itself. Neural networks with autoregressive connections are often called *recurrent neural networks* (RNNs), they are widely explored for text production. We will discuss them later in this section.

3.1.1 CONVOLUTIONAL NEURAL NETWORKS

Another type of neural networks, called convolutional neural networks, or CNNs [Lecun, 1989], are specialised for processing data that has a known grid-like topology. These networks have turned out to be successful in processing image data which can be represented as 2-dimensional grids of image pixels [Krizhevsky et al., 2012, Xu et al., 2015a], or time-series data from automatic speech recognition problems [Abdel-Hamid et al., 2014, Zhang et al., 2017]. In recent years, CNNs have also been applied to natural language. In particular, they have been use to effectively learn word representations for language modelling [Kim et al., 2016] and sentence representations for sentence classification [Collobert et al., 2011, Kalchbrenner et al., 2014, Kim, 2014, Zhang et al., 2015] and summarisation [Cheng and Lapata, 2016, Denil et al., 2014, Narayan et al., 2017, 2018a,c]. CNNs employ a specialised kind of linear operation called *convolution*, followed by a *pooling* operation, to build a representation that is aware of spatial interactions among input data points. Figure 3.3 from Narayan et al. [2018a] shows how CNNs can be used to learn a sentence representation. First of all, CNNs require input to be in a grid-like structure. For example, a sentence s of length k can be represented as a dense matrix $\mathbf{W} = [\mathbf{w}_1 \oplus \mathbf{w}_2 \oplus \ldots \oplus \mathbf{w}_k] \in R^{k \times d}$ where $\mathbf{w}_i \in R^d$ is a continuous representation of the ith word in s and $\oplus$ is the concatenation operator. We apply a one-dimensional convolutional filter $\mathbf{K} \in R^{h \times d}$ of width h to a window of h words in s to produce a new feature.[3] This filter is applied to each possible window of words in s to produce a feature map $\mathbf{f} = [f_1, f_2, \ldots, f_{k-h+1}] \in R^{k-h+1}$, where f_i is defined as:

$$f_i = \text{ReLU}(\mathbf{K} \circ \mathbf{W}_{i:i+h-1} + b) \tag{3.1}$$

where $\circ$ is the Hadamard product, followed by a sum over all elements, ReLU is a rectified linear activation and $b \in R$ is a bias term. ReLU activation function is often used as it is easier to train and often achieves better performance than sigmoid or tanh functions [Krizhevsky et al., 2012]. A max-pooling over time [Collobert et al., 2011] is applied over the feature map f to get $f_{\max} = \max(f)$ as the feature corresponding to this particular filter $\mathbf{K}$. Multiple filters $\mathbf{K}_h$ of width h are often used to compute a list of features $\mathbf{f}^{\mathbf{K}_h}$. In addition, filters of varying widths

---

[2]We ask the reader to work out the role of nonlinear activation functions. What happens if nonlinear activations are replaced by linear activations? Without the nonlinear activation, the neural network will essentially reduce to a simple linear function and it will fail to learn complex and abstract concepts.

[3]For image or time series data, higher-dimensional convolutional filters are often utilised to capture complex spatial interactions among data points. In NLP, one-dimensional convolution is commonly used to capture sequential interactions among words or characters.

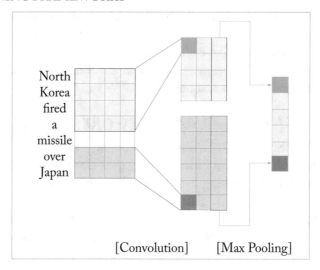

Figure 3.3: Convolutional neural network for sentence encoding.

are applied to learn a set of feature lists ($\mathbf{f}^{\mathbf{K}_{h_1}}$, $\mathbf{f}^{\mathbf{K}_{h_2}}$, ...). Finally, all feature lists are concatenated to get the final sentence representation.

We describe in Chapter 5 how such convolutional sentence encoders can be useful for better input understanding for text production. Importantly, through the use of convolutional filters, CNNs facilitate sparse interactions, parameter sharing and equivariant representations. We refer the reader to Chapter 9 of Goodfellow et al. [2016] for more details on these properties.

3.1.2   RECURRENT NEURAL NETWORKS

Feed-forward and CNNs fail to adequately represent the sequential nature of natural languages. In contrast, RNNs provide a natural model for them.

RNNs updates its state for every element of an input sequence. Figure 3.4 presents an RNN on the left and its application to a natural language text "How are you doing?" on the right. At each time step t, it takes as input the previous state s_{t-1} and the current input element x_t, and updates its current state as:

$$\mathbf{s}_t = \tanh(\mathbf{U}\mathbf{s}_{t-1} + \mathbf{V}\mathbf{x}_t)$$

where $\mathbf{U}$ and $\mathbf{V}$ are model parameters. At the end of an input sequence, it learns a representation, encoding information from the whole sequence.

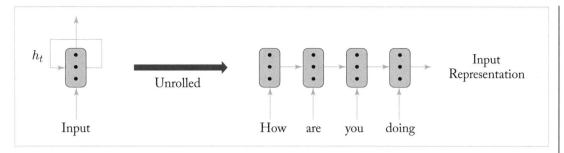

Figure 3.4: RNNs applied to a sentence.

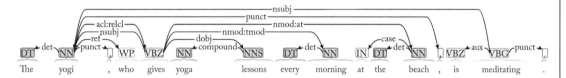

Figure 3.5: Long-range dependencies. The shown dependency tree is generated using the Stanford CoreNLP toolkit [Manning et al., 2014].

Most work on neural text production has used RNNs due to their **ability to naturally capture the sequential nature of the text** and to **process inputs and outputs of arbitrary length**.

3.1.3   LSTMS AND GRUS

RNNs naturally permit taking arbitrary long context into account, and so implicitly capture long-range dependencies, a common phenomenon frequently observed in natural languages. Figure 3.5 shows an example of long-range dependencies in a sentence "*The yogi, who gives yoga lessons every morning at the beach, is meditating.*" A good representation learning method should capture that "*the yogi*" is the subject of the verb "*meditating*" in the sentence.

In practice, however, as the length of the input sequence grows, RNNs are prone to losing information from the beginning of the sequences due to vanishing and exploding gradients issues [Bengio et al., 1994, Pascanu et al., 2013]. This is because, in the case of RNNS, back propagation applies through a large number of layers (the multiple layers corresponding to each time step). Since back propagation updates the weights in proportion to the partial derivative (the gradients) of the loss, and because of the sequential multiplication of matrices as the RNN is unrolled, the gradient may become either very large, or (more commonly), very small, effectively causing weights to either explode or never change at the lower/earlier layers. Consequently, RNNs fail to adequately model the long-range dependencies of natural languages.

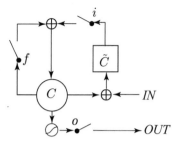

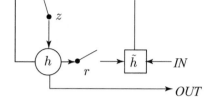

(a) Long Short-Term Memory   (b) Gated Recurrent Unit

Figure 3.6: Sketches of LSTM and GRU cells. On the left, i, f, and o are the input, forget, and output gates, respectively. c and $\tilde{c}$ represent the memory cell contents. On the right, r and z are the reset and update gates, and h and $\tilde{h}$ are the cell activations.

Long short-term memory (LSTM, [Hochreiter and Schmidhuber, 1997]) and gated recurrent unit (GRU, [Cho et al., 2014]) have been proposed as alternative recurrent networks which are better prepared to learning long-distance dependencies. These units are better in learning to memorise only the part of the past that is relevant for the future. At each time step, they dynamically update their states, deciding on what to memorise and what to forget from the previous input.

The LSTM cell (shown in Figure 3.6, left) achieves this using input (i), forget (f), and output (o) gates with the following operations:

$$f_t = \sigma(\mathbf{W}_f \cdot [\mathbf{h}_{t-1}, \mathbf{x}_t] + b_f) \tag{3.2}$$
$$i_t = \sigma(\mathbf{W}_i \cdot [\mathbf{h}_{t-1}, \mathbf{x}_t] + b_i) \tag{3.3}$$
$$o_t = \sigma(\mathbf{W}_o \cdot [\mathbf{h}_{t-1}, \mathbf{x}_t] + b_o) \tag{3.4}$$
$$\tilde{\mathbf{c}}_t = \tanh(\mathbf{W}_c \cdot [\mathbf{h}_{t-1}, \mathbf{x}_t] + b_c) \tag{3.5}$$
$$\mathbf{c}_t = f_t * \mathbf{c}_{t-1} + i_t * \tilde{\mathbf{c}}_t \tag{3.6}$$
$$\mathbf{h}_t = o_t * \tanh(\mathbf{c}_t) \tag{3.7}$$

where $\mathbf{W}_*$ and b_* are LSTM cell parameters. The input gate (Eq. (3.3)) regulates how much of the new cell state to retain, the forget gate (Eq. (3.2)) regulates how much of the existing memory to forget, and the output gate (Eq. (3.4)) regulates how much of the cell state should be passed forward to the next time step. The GRU cell (shown in Figure 3.6, right), on the other hand, achieves this using update (z) and reset (r) gates with the following operations:

$$z_t = \sigma(\mathbf{W}_z \cdot [\mathbf{h}_{t-1}, \mathbf{x}_t]) \tag{3.8}$$
$$r_t = \sigma(\mathbf{W}_r \cdot [\mathbf{h}_{t-1}, \mathbf{x}_t]) \tag{3.9}$$
$$\tilde{\mathbf{h}}_t = \tanh(\mathbf{W} \cdot [r_t * \mathbf{h}_{t-1}, \mathbf{x}_t]) \tag{3.10}$$
$$\mathbf{h}_t = (1 - z_t) * \mathbf{h}_{t-1} + z_t * \tilde{\mathbf{h}}_t \tag{3.11}$$

where $\mathbf{W}_*$ are GRU cell parameters. The update gate (Eq. (3.8)) regulates how much of the candidate activation to use in updating the cell state, and the reset gate (Eq. (3.9)) regulates how much of the cell state to forget. The LSTM cell has separate input and forget gates, while the GRU cell performs both of these operations together using its reset gate.

In a vanilla RNN, the entire cell state is updated with the current activation, whereas both LSTMs and GRUs have the mechanism to keep memory from previous activations. This allows recurrent networks with LSTM or GRU cells to remember features for a long time and reduces the vanishing gradient problems as the gradient back propagates through multiple bounded non-linearities.

LSTMs and GRUs have been very successful in modelling natural languages in recent years. They have practically replaced the vanilla RNN cell from recurrent networks.

3.1.4   WORD EMBEDDINGS

One of the key strengths of neural networks is that representation learning happens in a continuous space. For example, an RNN learns a continuous dense representation of an input text by encoding the sequence of words making up that text. At each time step, it takes a word represented as a continuous vector (often called a *word embedding*). In sharp contrast to pre-neural approaches, where words were often treated as symbolic features, word embeddings provide a more robust and enriched representation of words, capturing their meaning, semantic relationships, and distributional similarities (similarity of context they appear in).

Figure 3.7 represents two-dimensional representation of word embeddings. As can be seen, words that often occur in a similar context (e.g., "battery" and "charger") are mapped closer to each other compared to words that do not occur in a similar context (e.g., "battery" and "sink"). Word embeddings give a notion of similarity among words that look very different from each other in their surface forms. Due to this continuous representation, neural text-production approaches lead to a robust model and better generalisation compared to pre-neural approaches that use symbolic representations, making them brittle. Mikolov et al. [2013] further show that these word embeddings demonstrate compositional properties in distributional space, e.g., one could start from the word "queen" and get to the word "woman" following the direction from the word "king" to the word "man".

Given a vocabulary V, we represent each word $w \in V$ by a continuous vector $\mathbf{e}_w \in R^d$ of length d. We define a word embedding matrix $\mathbf{W} \in R^{|V| \times d}$, representing each word in the vocabulary V. Earlier neural networks often used pre-trained word embeddings such as Word2Vec [Mikolov et al., 2013] or Glove [Pennington et al., 2014]. Using these approaches, the word embedding matrix $\mathbf{W}$ is learned in an unsupervised fashion from a large amount of raw text. Word2Vec adapts a predictive feed-forward model, aiming to maximise the prediction probability of a target word, given its surrounding context. Glove achieves this by directly re-

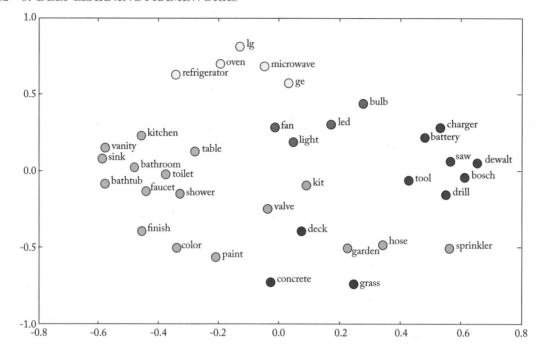

Figure 3.7: Two-dimensional representation of word embeddings (based on `https://shanel ynnwebsite-mid9n9g1q9y8tt.netdna-ssl.com/wp-content/uploads/2018/01/word-vector-space-similar-words.png`).

ducing the dimensionality of the co-occurrence counts matrix. Importantly, embeddings learned from both approaches capture the distributional similarity among words. In a parallel trend to using pre-trained word embeddings, several other text-production models have shown that word embeddings can first be initialised randomly and then trained jointly with other network parameters; these jointly trained word embeddings are often fine tuned and better suited to the task.

More recently, there is a growing trend of contextualised word embeddings such as ELMo [Peters et al., 2018], BERT [Devlin et al., 2019], and GPT [Radford et al., 2018, 2019].[4] ELMo embeddings are learned functions of the internal states of a traditional deep bidirectional language model. BERT representations are learned using bidirectional encoder representations from Transformers [Vaswani et al., 2017] through a language modelling objective. Finally, GPT embeddings are an outcome of unsupervised pre-training of Transformer language models. All three types of embeddings are pretrained on a very large text corpus. These models have achieved groundbreaking performances for various NLP tasks, e.g., part-of-speech (POS) tagging, semantic role labelling, named entity extraction, sentiment analysis, and textual entailment, and

---

[4]These embeddings are not covered in this book. Please check Section 8.5 on "Recent Trends in Neural NLG" for a brief description of them.

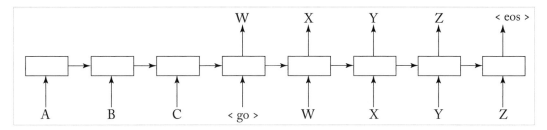

Figure 3.8: Sequence-to-sequence learning using RNN-based encoder-decoder architecture.

have recently begun to be explored for text production. Section 8.5 briefly discusses this more recent trend in neural NLG.

3.2   THE ENCODER-DECODER FRAMEWORK

Much of the work on neural text production adopts the encoder-decoder approach that was first advocated and shown to be successful for machine translation by Sutskever et al. [2014] and Cho et al. [2014]. First the input is encoded into a continuous representation, using an RNN called the encoder. Then the text is produced using a second RNN, the decoder. The decoder essentially operates as a language model conditioned on the input sequence and the previously generated tokens. Figure 3.8 illustrates this encoder-decoder framework to text production. This network is often referred to as a *sequence-to-sequence* model as it takes as input a sequence, one element at a time, and then outputs a sequence, one element at a time.

RNNs are natural models for natural language for at least two reasons. First, they naturally capture the sequential nature of text and, second, they can process input of arbitrary length. Thus, Sutskever et al. [2014] and Cho et al. [2014] showed impressive results using RNNs both to encode the source sentence and decode the target sentence, and since then, RNNs have become a standard framework for text-to-text production. Similarly, even though RNNs fail to adequately capture the non-sequential structure of complex input forms such as graphs, tables, or trees, they have also been successfully applied to data- and MR-to-text generation due to their simplicity in the way they process the input and their ability to learn complex functions. In these cases, complex input forms are linearised before passing them to the network.

3.2.1   LEARNING INPUT REPRESENTATIONS WITH BIDIRECTIONAL RNNS

Earlier encoders often use RNNs to process the input sequence from left to right to build an input representation that is then passed to the decoder. For instance, given the input sentence, "How are you doing?" in a dialogue setting, the same operation will be applied to each word of that sentence in a left-to-right fashion to generate a representation for this dialogue turn.

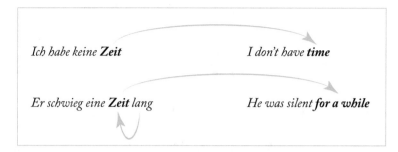

Figure 3.9: The German word "*zeit*" with its two translations.

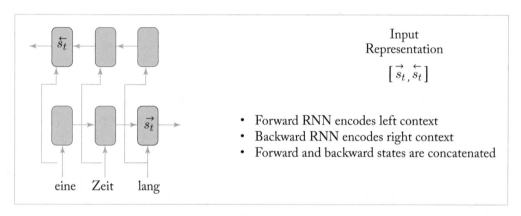

Figure 3.10: Bidirectional RNNs applied to a sentence.

Such encoders are, of course, intuitive, but a better input representation can be learned by not only processing the input sequence from left to right but also looking into the future. The later representation will reflect the fact that when we write or speak, it is not only driven by what has already been written or spoken, but also what we plan to write or speak. A more concrete example is shown in Figure 3.9, which shows why such representation could be useful for natural language applications. In machine translation, the German word "Zeit" has two forms in English "time" and "for a while". For the correct translation for the word "Zeit", it is necessary to look into its right context. Bidirectional recurrent neural networks (BiRNNs) address this issue; they permit creating word representations which take into account information from the whole input sequence, not just the preceding words.

BiRNNs, shown in Figure 3.10, combine a forward recurrent layer with a backward recurrent layer. The forward recurrent layer processes the input from left to right and generates an input representation $\overrightarrow{s_t}$. The backward recurrent layer processes the input from right to left and generates an input representation $\overleftarrow{s_t}$. The final representation $[\overrightarrow{s_t} ; \overleftarrow{s_t}]$ concatenates both of these representations and is passed to the decoder.

3.2.2   GENERATING TEXT USING RECURRENT NEURAL NETWORKS

The decoder RNN takes the encoder output as input and starts generating text, one token at a time, conditioned on the input representation and the previously generated tokens. At each time step t, it takes as input the previous decoder state s'_{t-1} and the last predicted token x'_t and performs two operations: first, it updates its current state as

$$s'_t = \tanh(U's'_{t-1} + V'x'_t)$$

where, U' and V' are model parameters, and second, it uses this updated representation of the decoder context to produce a probability distribution over a target vocabulary V of possible output tokens:

$$y'_t = \mathrm{softmax}(W's'_t)$$

where, W' are model parameters. Figures 3.11 and 3.12 present an example generation of the response "Fine, and you?" for the input sentence "How are you doing?" in a dialogue setting. In the beginning, the decoder takes the input representation from the encoder and a special start symbol "<s>" as input and produces a probability distribution over the vocabulary V with "Fine" being the most probable token. The next step takes a continuous representation for "Fine" as input and produces the comma token. The decoder repeats this generation process in the recurrent fashion (i.e., updating its state and generating a new token) until it produces a special end-of-the-sentence "<eos>" symbol. In the example shown, the RNN decoder generates "Fine, and you?" as a response.

The decoder essentially works as a classifier where it predicts a token from a fixed vocabulary distribution. However, at each time step, the network is aware of the whole input and the previously predicted sequence. As such, the token prediction at each step is conditioned over the input and the text generated so far. Figure 3.13 presents the graphical representation of this conditional generation process.

Given the input sequence $X = x_1, \ldots, x_n$, the model generates the output sequence $Y = y_1, \ldots, y_m$ using a parameterised classifier $p(y_i|y_1, \ldots, y_{i-1}, X; \theta)$, where θ are the model parameters. Hence, the probability of generating the output sequence Y is:

$$p(Y|X; \theta) = \prod_{i=1}^{m} p(y_i|y_1, \ldots, y_{i-1}, X; \theta). \tag{3.12}$$

Does this objective sound familiar to the reader? It is very similar to learning a statistical language model. A **language model** is a probability distribution over a sequence of words or given a sequence of words; it assigns a probability to the whole sequence. Similarly, sequence-to-sequence models to text productions operate as language models.

Neural language models differ from traditional phrase-based language models. Phrase-based language models or n-gram models rely on the Markov assumption, i.e., the

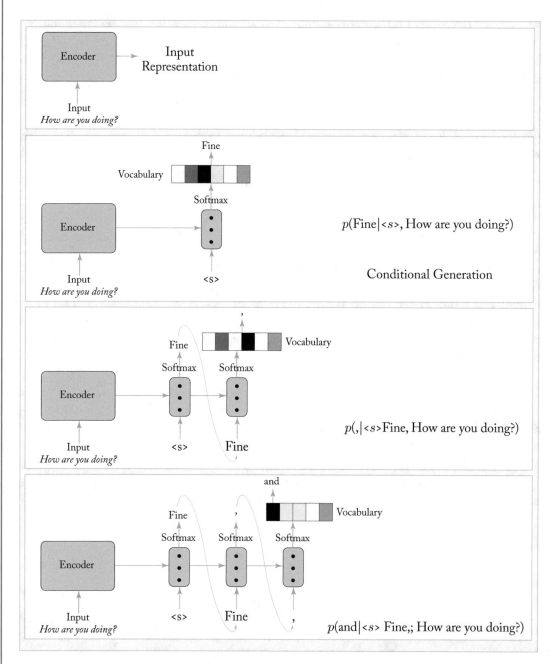

Figure 3.11: **RNN** decoding steps. (*Continues.*)

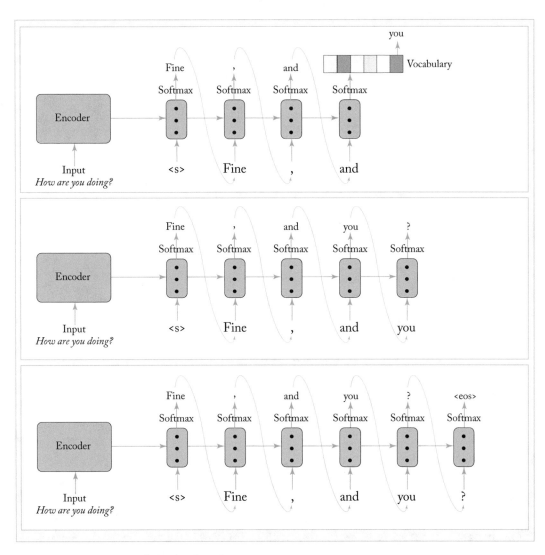

Figure 3.12: (*Continued.*) RNN decoding steps.

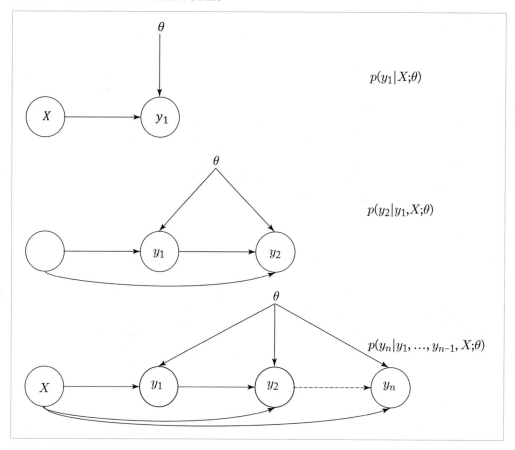

Figure 3.13: **RNN** decoding: conditional generation at each step.

prediction of next token is only dependent on the last few predicted tokens. For example, a bigram language model assumes that the prediction of next token is only dependent on the last predicted token. According to the bigram language model, the probability of a sequence Y can be calculated as: $p(Y) = p(y_m|y_{m-1})p(y_{m-1}|y_{m-2})\ldots p(y_2|y_1)p(y_1)$. One of the key strengths of neural language models is that they do not have the Markov assumption; they are able to predict the next token which is conditioned on the whole previously predicted sequence. As a result, neural language models are much better in capturing the phenomenon of **long-range dependencies** in natural languages.

In sequence-to-sequence models, like neural language models, the prediction of next token is conditioned on all previously predicted tokens. In addition, with the use of the encoder in sequence-to-sequence models, it is also conditioned on the input. As such, sequence-to-sequence models aim to generate text which is consistent with the input and fluent in the target distribution.

In short, sequence-to-sequence models are essentially input-conditioned neural language models without any Markov assumptions.

3.2.3 TRAINING AND DECODING WITH SEQUENTIAL GENERATORS

Training. Sequential generators are often trained in a supervised setting with a *cross-entropy loss*. Given an input sequence $X^{(i)} = \{x_1^{(i)}, \ldots, x_n^{(i)}\}$, the generator is trained to maximise the likelihood of producing the gold output sequence $\hat{Y}^{(i)} = \{\hat{y}_1^{(i)}, \ldots, \hat{y}_m^{(i)}\}$. This is achieved by minimising the negative log-likelihood over the training set[5]:

$$L(\theta) = \frac{1}{N} \sum_{i=1}^{N} -\log p(\hat{Y}^{(i)} | X; \theta) \tag{3.13}$$

$$= -\frac{1}{N} \sum_{i=1}^{N} \sum_{j=1}^{m} \log p(\hat{y}_j^{(i)} | \hat{y}_1^{(i)}, \ldots, \hat{y}_{j-1}^{(i)}, X; \theta) \tag{3.14}$$

where N is the number of input and output sequence pairs in the training set, and θ the model parameters to learn. Gradient descent algorithms are used to minimise the loss function by moving in the direction of the negative of the gradient of the loss function; in particular, the *stochastic gradient descent* algorithm (Algorithm 3.1) is applied, which permits calculating the loss function over a sample of the training set and not the whole training set, making the training feasible.

It is often very challenging to choose a reliable learning rate ℓ. It determines how fast we want to update our model parameters and as a results significantly affects model performance. There has been a lot of interest in modifying the stochastic gradient descent algorithm with an adaptive learning rate for more stable training. We encourage the reader to check for algorithms with adaptive learning rates, e.g., AdaGrad [Duchi et al., 2011], AdaDelta [Zeiler, 2012], Adam [Kingma and Ba, 2014] and AMSGrad [Reddi et al., 2018]. The $\nabla_\theta L(\theta)$ is the gradient or the first-order partial derivative of $L(\theta)$ estimated using the *Back Propagation* algorithm [Rumelhart et al., 1986].

Several other optimisation techniques are applied to make the learning stable and the model deeper and more robust including *dropout* [Srivastava et al., 2014], *residual connections* [He et al., 2016], *batch normalisation* [Ioffe and Szegedy, 2015] and *layer normalisation* [Ba et al., 2016].

We refer the reader to the respective publications and to Chapter 8 of Goodfellow et al. [2016] for further details on how to optimise deep neural networks.

---

[5]Maximising the likelihood is the same as maximising the log-likelihood, which is the same as minimising the negative log-likelihood. It is also the same as minimising the cross-entropy between the gold and the predicted distribution.

Algorithm 3.1 Stochastic gradient descent algorithm inspired by Goodfellow et al. [2016]

Input : Training set $\{(x^{(1)}, y^{(1)}, \ldots, (x^{(n)}, y^{(n)}\}$, initial model parameter θ and learning rate ℓ
Output : Final model parameter θ

1: $k \leftarrow 1$
2: **while** $\ell > \ell_{min}$ **do**
3:      Sample a minibatch of m examples from the training set.
4:      Compute gradient estimate: $\hat{g} \leftarrow \frac{1}{m} \nabla_{\theta} \sum_i L(f(x^{(i)}; \theta), y^{(i)})$
5:      Update model parameters: $\theta \leftarrow \theta - \ell \times \hat{g}$
6:      Decay the learning rate linearly until iteration k'.
7:      $k \leftarrow k + 1$
8: **end while**

Decoding.   During test time, we generate text as described earlier in Section 3.2.2. Given an input sequence $X = \{x_1, \ldots, x_n\}$, we basically pass the most likely token predicted with $p(y_i | y_1, \ldots, y_{i-1}, X; \theta)$ at the previous step as input to the next step. This method of generating text at the test time is called *greedy decoding*.

Greedy decoding provides a natural way to produce text. However, if a trained model makes a small error and produces a wrong word, then it will affect the entire sequence that follows. *beam search decoding* [Ranzato et al., 2015, Rush et al., 2015] provides a better way of decoding without affecting the model training.

At each step of the decoding, the decoder keeps track of not only the most likely token, but the k-best hypotheses that have been produced so far. k is also referred to as the beam size. The next decoding step take these k-best hypotheses and produces k-best tokens for each. Then, only the k-best ones among these are kept, and so on.

Beam search decoding has shown to be very useful when generating a long sequence. It is very common to find a beam search decoder in recent text-production systems [Ranzato et al., 2015, Rush et al., 2015, See et al., 2017].

3.3   DIFFERENCES WITH PRE-NEURAL TEXT-PRODUCTION APPROACHES

Neural approaches to text production provide a new perspective to text generation problems which is very different from pre-neural approaches. It has addressed some problems that existed in pre-neural approaches, but also brought some of the interesting problems that did not exist before. We will go through some of these differences between neural and pre-neural approaches below.

One of the main strengths of neural approaches is that they often do not require directly extracting explicit task-specific features from the data. As such they provide a uniform framework for different text-production problems. For example, the sequence-to-sequence model discussed above has been successfully applied to various data-to-text, text-to-text, and MR-to-text productions [Konstas et al., 2017, See et al., 2017]. Neural approaches facilitate ways for multi-task learning, multi-modal learning, domain adaptation, transfer learning, and unsupervised learning. In contrast, pre-neural text-production approaches are often task-specific; they rely on modelling task-specific features from the data.

Pre-neural text-production approaches use symbolic representations which often make them brittle. For example, sentence simplification methods in Narayan and Gardent [2014] will fail to simplify a word if it has never occurred in the training data. These representations are also an obstacle for better generalisation. In contrast, the representation learning in neural networks happens at a continuous space, such that different modalities of input are represented by dense, relatively short, vectors. Due to this continuous representation learning, neural approaches lead to a robust model and better generalisation. BiRNNs can utilise the surrounding contexts to build a good representation for unseen words using the words with similar contexts.

Neural approaches to text production have brought numerous advantages over earlier approaches. It is no surprise that they have taken the field by storm. However, they have also brought new challenges that were not encountered before. These approaches are very good in representation learning; however, the sequential decoders or generators essentially function as conditional language models which learn to predict from a fixed vocabulary distribution. In particular, they are prone to generating text which is not consistent with the input (the generated text either contains information not present in the input or misses information present in the input); their performance decreases with the length of the input and they often fall short of appropriately capturing the structure of the input.

3.4   SUMMARY

In this chapter, we briefly reviewed neural approaches to text production. We saw that these early approaches provide a single, unifying framework, doing away with a decomposition of the text-production task into subtasks as is often done in pre-neural approaches.

Chapters 4, 5, and 6 look into more advanced techniques for neural text production. In Chapter 4, we show how sequential decoders can be improved using attention, copy, and coverage mechanisms to better control the quality of generated text. Chapter 5 describes better input representation learning, which takes into account the input structure to improve text production. In Chapter 6, we will then go on to see how later work focused on integrating key ideas from pre-neural approaches into the novel deep learning paradigm. Chapter 8 briefly discusses how more recent trend in neural NLG depart from the simple end-to-end models proposed by early neural NLG (NNLG) approaches.

PART II

Neural Improvements

CHAPTER 4

Generating Better Text

In the previous chapter, we saw how encoder-decoder networks could be used to model text production. The input (a meaning representation, a text, or some data), is first encoded into a continuous representation. This representation is then input to the decoder, which predicts output words, one step at a time, conditioned both on the input representation and on the previously predicted words.

One of the first NLP applications which showed the power of this encoder-decoder model was machine translation. In particular, Sutskever et al. [2014] showed that a sequence-to-sequence model including deep long short-term memories (LSTMs) with a limited vocabulary could outperform a standard SMT-based system whose vocabulary is unlimited. The sequence-to-sequence model was then applied to other text-production tasks.

For text-to-text production, Zhang and Lapata [2014] proposed character-based RNNs to generate Chinese poetry. Rush et al. [2015] were the first to apply the encoder-decoder approach to abstractive text summarisation, achieving state-of-the-art performance on DUC-2004 and Gigaword, two sentence-level summarisation data sets. Nallapati et al. [2016] provided the first neural baselines for abstractive summarisation on the CNN/Daily Mail data set.

For MR-to-text generation, Wen et al. [2015] introduced a semantically controlled LSTM recurrent network to generate dialogue turns from dialogue moves; Konstas et al. [2017] applied sequence-to-sequence models to the task of AMR generation; five out of the seven systems participating in the Surface Realisation shared task (generating text from dependency trees) include a sequence-to-sequence model [Mille et al., 2018].

Similarly, sequence-to-sequence models have been used to generate from databases [Wiseman et al., 2017] and RDF data [Gardent et al., 2017a].

While these approaches showed that, given a sufficient amount of training data, neural models were impressively good at generating fluent text, they also repeatedly highlighted a number of issues regarding the quality of the generated output. Four main issues can be identified.

- Accuracy: The output text sometimes contains information that is not present in the input.

- Repetitions: The output text sometimes contains repetitions.

- Coverage: The output text sometimes fail to cover all the information contained in the input.

- Rare or unknown words: As in machine translation or speech recognition, entities not or rarely seen during training fail to be appropriately verbalised.

These issues cut across all text-production tasks and arise independent of the input type and of the communication goal. Figure 4.1 shows some example output for MR-to-text and summarisation. It shows how the generated texts sometimes fail to express important information and contain added material, repetitions, and UNK (unknown) symbols for rare words.

In order to address these recurring issues, three neural mechanisms were introduced: attention, copy, and coverage.[1] Attention is geared at improving accuracy by focusing decoding on the part of the input that is most relevant to each decoding step. The copy mechanism targets handling of rare or unknown input items. It is also useful for text-to-text applications where much of the generated text needs to be copied from the input. Finally, coverage helps ensure that the output text covers all the input and only the input.

In what follows, we focus on these three mechanisms, showing how they help address the quality issues listed above. We also briefly mention alternative methods that were proposed in the literature.

4.1   ATTENTION

In a standard encoder-decoder framework, the input is compressed into a fixed-length vector independent of its length. In other words, no matter the size of the input, its content will be compressed to a single-size vector. Intuitively, this puts long input at a disadvantage in that more information must be crammed into the same number of vector dimensions. And indeed, Bahdanau et al. [2014] show that performance decreases with the length of the input.

The attention mechanism targets this shortcoming. Instead of taking as input a single, global representation of the input, an attention-based decoder takes into account an input representation (usually called the "context vector") which builds on the similarity of the current decoder hidden state with each of the input words based on the corresponding encoder hidden states. More formally, the difference with a standard decoder is that the attention-based decoder generates predictions based not only the previous state s_{t-1} and the previously generated token y_{t-1}, but also on a weighted average of the encoder outputs or the context vector. This context vector depends on the decoder state and therefore changes at each decoding step. It defines a probability distribution over the input words. Intuitively, it is meant to capture those parts of the input that are most relevant for prediction at each decoding step.

Figures 4.2 and 4.3 sketch the decoding step of a decoder with attention which is formalised in Eqs. (4.1) to (4.5). First, the current decoder state s_{t-1} is compared with each encoder hidden state h_j and a score is computed for each encoder state (Eq. (4.1)). This score is then turned into a probability (Eq. (4.2)) which will be used to create the context vector. Equation (4.3) shows how this context vector is created. It is the sum of the encoder states weighed by their probability. The next state is produced taking into account the previous state s_{t-1}, the

---

[1]Note that the term "coverage" refers both to an observed phenomena (text generated by neural NLG models often fails to verbalise all the input) and a neural mechanism (designed to combat the observed phenomena). We nevertheless adopt this terminology as it is frequently used in the literature.

Example from MR-to-Text Generation (E2E Challenge)

MR   inform(name='the in san francisco';address='943 s van ness ave'; phone='4156410188')

Text   **the the sun** in san francisco's address is 943 s van ness ave . their phone number is 4156410188

MR   inform(name='straits restaurant';price range=expensive;**food=singaporean;** good for meal=dinner)

Text   straits restaurant is expensive and is good for dinner

---

Example from Text-to-Text Generation (Summarisation)

Document   (truncated): lagos, nigeria (cnn) a day after winning nigeria's presidency, muhammadu buhari told cnn's christiane amanpour that he plans to aggressively fight corruption that has long plagued nigeria and go after the root of the nation's unrest. buhari said he'll "rapidly give attention" to curbing violence in the northeast part of nigeria, where the terrorist group boko haram operates. by cooperating with neighboring nations chad, cameroon and niger, he said his administration is confident it will be able to thwart criminals and others contributing to nigeria's instability. for the first time in nigeria's history, the opposition defeated the ruling party in democratic elections. buhari defeated incumbent goodluck jonathan by about 2 million votes, according to nigeria's independent national electoral commission. the win comes after a long history of military rule, coups and botched attempts at democracy in africa's most populous nation.

Summaries   **UNK UNK** says his administration is confident it will be able to destabilise nigeria's economy. UNK says his administration is confident it will be able to thwart criminals and other nigerians. he says the country has long nigeria and nigeria's economy.
muhammadu buhari says he plans to aggressively fight corruption in the northeast part of nigeria. he says he'll "rapidly give attention" to curbing violence in the northeast part of nigeria. he says his administration is confident it will be able to thwart criminals.

Figure 4.1: Example input/output. Boldface indicates missing, added, or repeated information.

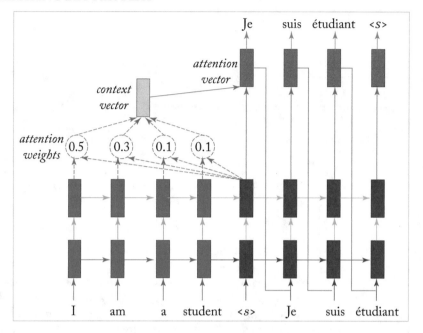

Figure 4.2: Focusing on the relevant source word: An example of neural machine translation. At the first decoding step, the context vector gives highest probability to the source word "I", thereby favoring the generation of the corresponding french word "Je" (source: `https://medi um.com/syncedreview/a-brief-overview-of-attention-mechanism-13c578ba9129`).

previously generated token y_{t-1}, and the context vector $\mathbf{c}_t$ (Eq. (4.4)).[2] Finally, a softmax layer is applied to the new state in order to generate a probability distribution over the target vocabulary (Eq. (4.5)).

$$\mathbf{e}_{t,j} = a(\mathbf{s}_{t-1}, \mathbf{h}_j) \tag{4.1}$$

$$\boldsymbol{\alpha}_{t,j} = \frac{\exp(\mathbf{e}_{t,j})}{\sum_{k=1}^{T_X} \mathbf{e}_{t,k}.\mathbf{h}_j} \tag{4.2}$$

$$\mathbf{c}_t = \sum_{j=1}^{T_X} \boldsymbol{\alpha}_{t,j}.\mathbf{h}_j \tag{4.3}$$

$$\mathbf{s}_t = f(\mathbf{s}_{t-1}, \mathbf{y}_{t-1}, \mathbf{c}_t) \tag{4.4}$$

$$\mathbf{y}_t = \text{softmax}(\mathbf{W} * \mathbf{s}_t). \tag{4.5}$$

In practice, most current text-production models use attention as it regularly produces better results than models without the attention mechanism. As we shall see in Chapters 5, 6,

[2]In Eq. (4.4), f stands for the transformation applied by the specific network being used, e.g., an RNN, LSTM or GRU.

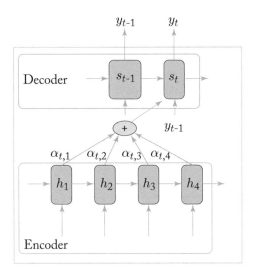

Figure 4.3: Sketch of the attention mechanism.

and 8, other types of more sophisticated attention mechanisms can also be used. For instance, in hierarchical models of extractive summarisation, attention has been used to focus on specific sentences rather than words [Celikyilmaz et al., 2018]. To improve semantic adequacy in text summarisation, Cao et al. [2018b] enrich the input with open information extraction (OpenIE)-style triples. They then use a dual attention mechanism which attends to the encoding of both the input sentence and the extracted information extraction triples. Similarly, Tan et al. [2017] propose a summarisation approach in which the input text is represented as a graph and the attention mechanism is modified to take into account the lexRank score of each input sentence. The underlying intuition is that sentences with a high lexRank score contain key information and should therefore be focused on when generating the summary.

There are also different means of computing the similarity between decoder and encoder states. A simple way is to use the dot product (Eq. (4.6)) or a dot product mediated by a learned matrix determining how much weight to put on each part of the dot product (Eq. (4.7)). A third possibility is to use the initial [Bahdanau et al., 2014]'s proposal. Encoder and decoder states are concatenated and rescaled using a single-layer neural network and multiplying the result by a learned vector (Eq. (4.8)).

$$a(\mathbf{s}_{t,j}, \mathbf{h}_j) = \mathbf{s}_{t,j}{}^{\top}\mathbf{h}_j \tag{4.6}$$
$$a(\mathbf{s}_{t,j}, \mathbf{h}_j) = \mathbf{s}_{t,j}{}^{\top}\mathbf{W}_a\,\mathbf{h}_j \tag{4.7}$$
$$a(\mathbf{s}_{t,j}, \mathbf{h}_j) = \mathbf{V}_a{}^{\top}\tanh(\mathbf{W}_a[\mathbf{s}_{t,j}; \mathbf{h}_j]). \tag{4.8}$$

4.2   COPY

At decoding time, RNNs predict each output token based on a fixed-size background vocabulary usually derived from the training and development data. Since each decoding step involves computing a probability distribution over this vocabulary, the size of this background vocabulary is necessarily restricted. For instance, in neural machine translation, the n most frequent tokens will be used, and all other tokens will be replaced with a special token "UNK", resulting in UNK also being generated at inference time. Moreover because it is derived from the training data (i.e., not taking into account the test data), not all tokens necessary to generate text at test time will necessarily be available in that vocabulary. In short, tokens that do not occur in this background vocabulary (rare or unknown words such as dates or proper names) will not be generated.

To address this shortcoming, Vinyals et al. [2015] introduced a novel pointer mechanism which repurposes the attention mechanism to create pointers to input elements and generates text by copying the input token whose attention weight is highest. Since it can be used not only for handling rare or unknown words but also for copying input words to the output, Vinyals et al. [2015]'s copy mechanism is highly relevant for text production. In extractive compression and summarisation, for instance, much of the words in the generated text can be copied over from the input.

In text production, the copy mechanism is usually combined with the standard generation mechanism to allow for hybrid architectures in which words can either be generated from the background vocabulary using the standard generation step or copied from the input using a pointer mechanism. That is, in addition to sampling words from the target vocabulary, the decoder can also select words directly from the input sequence and copy them into the output text. We focus here on See et al. [2017]'s proposal, which involves two main steps. First, a generation probability p_{gen} is computed based on the current context. Second, this probability is used to define a mixture model that specifies for each token; the probability $P_{final}(w)$ of generating this word based on (i) the probability of sampling it from the background vocabulary, and (ii) the probability of copying it from the input.

The generation probability p_{gen} represents the probability of generating vs. copying. It is calculated as shown in Eq. (4.9), based on the current context vector $\mathbf{c}_t$, the current decoder hidden state $\mathbf{s}_t$ and the previously generated word $\mathbf{y}_{t-1}$.[3]

$$p_{gen} = \sigma(\mathbf{w}_c * \mathbf{c}_t + \mathbf{w}_s * \mathbf{s}_t + \mathbf{w}_y * \mathbf{y}_{t-1}). \tag{4.9}$$

At each decoding step, the probability $P_{final}(w)$ of generating word w is then defined as shown in Eq. (4.10).

$$P_{final}(w) = p_{gen} * P_{vocab}(w) + (1 - p_{gen}) * \sum_{i:w=w_i} \alpha_{t,i}. \tag{4.10}$$

---

[3]Recall that the σ function returns a scalar value between 0 and 1. Hence p_{gen} can be viewed as defining a probability.

That is, the probability of generating a word is defined by a mixture model combining the probability of generating that word and the probability of copying it. Note that when a word w is out of vocabulary (OOV), i.e., is not in the vocabulary then $P_{\text{vocab}}(w)$ will be null, and therefore the probability of generating w will depend entirely on its attention score $\alpha_{t,w}$. Conversely, when a word is not in the input, its attention score will be null, and therefore its generation probability will depend entirely on the probability $P_{\text{vocab}}(w)$ of sampling that word from the standard probability distribution $\mathbf{y}_t$ created at each time step by the decoder.

The copy mechanism is widely used in text-production approaches where it is relevant both for handling rare tokens and for copying from the input. Thus, Cheng and Lapata [2016], Gu et al. [2016], Miao and Blunsom [2016], Nallapati et al. [2016], See et al. [2017], Zeng et al. [2016] exploit copying for text summarisation, Cao et al. [2017] to generate paraphrases, and He et al. [2017] to generate answers.

Alternative Approaches

Two main alternative approaches have been proposed to handle rare words, namely, delexicalisation and subword encoding.

Delexicalisation consists of replacing rare items with placeholders while keeping a record of which placeholder has been substituted for which item. Delexicalisation is applied to both input and output on the whole data set (development, train, and test) and the models are trained on these delexicalised data. The generated text is then post-processed to replace placeholders with their original values. Figure 4.4 shows some example input/output pairs from the E2E and the WebNLG data with and without delexicalisation.

While delexicalisation is a popular technique for handling rare named entities in data- or MR-to-text generation,[4] it also suffers from various shortcomings [Goyal et al., 2016]. First, it requires an additional pre- and post-processing step which must be re-implemented for each new application. Second, the matching procedure needed to correctly match a rare input item (e.g., Alexis Dupont) with the corresponding part in the output text (e.g., the head of Caroline's school) may be quite complex, which, in turn, may result in incorrect or incomplete delexicalisations. Third, it loses important information that is relevant for sentence planning. The examples in Figure 4.5 illustrates this last point. While the value of an attribute value (french, seafood) can be inserted as is in the output text in some cases (Sentences s1 and s2.2), the insertion can also result in ill-formed output as shown in Sentence s2.2 [Nayak et al., 2017]. The impact of copying and delexicalisation on two data-to-text generation tasks (E2E and WebNLG) is studied in detail in Shimorina and Gardent [2018] and shows that rare items strongly impact performance, that combining delexicalisation and copying yields the strongest improvement, that copying underperforms for rare and unseen items, and that the impact of these two mech-

---

[4]It was used for instance by six submissions to the E2E and WebNLG challenge [Chen et al., 2018, Davoodi et al., 2018, Juraska et al., 2018, Puzikov and Gurevych, 2018, Trisedya et al., 2018, van der Lee et al., 2017].

E2E	
Input	name[Midsummer House], customer_rating[average], near[The Bakers]
Output	Customers gave Midsummer House, near The Bakers, a 3 out of 5 rating.
Delexicalised Input	name[NAME], customer_rating[average], near[NEAR]
Delexicalised Output	Customers gave NAME , near NEAR , a 3 out of 5 rating.
WebNLG	
Input	(Abilene_Regional_Airport cityServed Abilene), (Abilene isPartOf Texas)
Output	Abilene is in Texas and is served by the Abilene regional airport.
Delexicalised Input	(X cityServed Y), (Y isPartOf Z)
Delexicalised Output	Y is in Z and is served by the X.

Figure 4.4: Example delexicalisations from the E2E and WebNLG data sets.

1	recommend(restaurant name= Au Midi, neighborhood = midtown, cuisine = **french**
s1	✓ Au Midi is in Midtown and serves **French** food.
2	recommend(restaurant name= Loch Fyne, neighborhood = city centre, cuisine = **seafood**)
s2.1	★Loch Fyne is in the City Center and serves **seafood** food.
s2.2	✓ There is a **seafood** restaurant in the City Centre called Loch Fyne.

Figure 4.5: Interactions between slot values and sentence planning.

Input	Title: Almond-raspberry thumbprint cookies Ingredients: 1 cup butter or margarine softened, 1 cup sugar, 1 can solo almond filling, 2 egg yolks, 1 tsp almond extract, 2 1/2 cups all-purpose flour, 1/2 tsp baking powder, 1/2 tsp salt, 1 can solo raspberry filling
Output	In a large bowl, beat butter and sugar until light and fluffy. Add eggs, one at a time, beating well after each addition. Blend in flour, baking powder, baking soda, salt, and baking soda. Add to creamed mixture and mix well. Stir in nuts and vanilla. Drop dough by rounded table spoonfuls 2" apart onto ungreased cookie sheets. Bake 8 to 10 minutes or until edges are lightly browned. Cool on wire racks.

Figure 4.6: Example of generated text containing repetitions (the recipe is generated from the title and a list of ingredients Kiddon et al. [2016]).

anisms greatly varies depending on how the data set is constructed and on how it is split into train, dev, and test.

Character-based Models. Inspired by work toward tackling the problem of rare words in neural machine translation [Ling et al., 2015], character-based models have also been used for dealing with rare entities in text production [Agarwal and Dymetman, 2017, Goyal et al., 2016, Jagfeld et al., 2018]. In these approaches, both the input and the output are encoded as character strings. One advantage is that data sparsity is much reduced as the model works over a small vocabulary (around 50 symbols after lower-casing for English). When combined with a copy mechanism, the model then learns to map a character onto itself whenever the context requires it. One drawback is that sequences are much longer, which increases long-range dependencies and may result in a performance decrease. As a result, character-based models have mostly been learned for data-to-text generation where the input is not too long, such as, for instance, in the E2E challenge where 5 out of 62 submissions operate on the character-level. On this data set, character-based models have been shown to perform on a par with or slightly better than token-based approaches. On WebNLG data however, word-based models were found to perform better [Jagfeld et al., 2018].

4.3 COVERAGE

As illustrated in Figure 4.6, neural text generators tend to repeat (blue fragment) information from the input. Because they lack a mechanism to indicate which part of the source has been covered, they may fail to take into account part of the input and, conversely, they may repeatedly attend to the same part of the input.

Tu et al. [2016] and See et al. [2017] use a coverage mechanism to tackle these issues. At each decoding step, a coverage vector is computed to measure what part of the input has been attended to so far. This coverage vector is then used both to inform the attention mechanism and to modify the loss.

The coverage vector $\mathbf{c}_t$ is defined as the sum of all attention distributions so far.[5]

$$\mathbf{c}_t = \sum_{t'=0}^{t-1} \alpha_{t'}.$$

In other words, the coverage of a particular source word is equal to the amount of attention it has received so far. The coverage vector is used as extra input to the attention mechanism, changing Eq. (4.1) to:

$$e_{t,j} = a(\mathbf{s}_{t-1}, \mathbf{h}_j, \mathbf{c}_t). \tag{4.11}$$

In this way, the attention mechanism is informed by a summary of its previous decisions and repetitions become less likely.

In addition, the loss is modified to integrate an additional loss term (Eq. (4.11)) designed to penalise the overlap between the coverage vector and the attention distribution. This discourages the network from attending to what has already been covered.

$$\text{covloss}_t = \sum_i \min(a_i^t, c_i^t) \tag{4.12}$$

$$\text{loss}_t = -\log P(w_t^*) + \lambda \, \text{covloss}_t. \tag{4.13}$$

The copy mechanism is often paired with coverage. Copy and coverage were used for instance for neural machine translation [Tu et al., 2016] and for summarisation [See et al., 2017]. Figure 4.7 illustrates the impact of coverage on repetitions in the summarisation task considered by See et al. [2017]. It shows that the proportion of duplicate n-grams decreases when using the coverage mechanism (blue bars) and that it is, in fact, similar in the reference summaries and in the summaries produced by the model with coverage.

Semantically Conditioned LSTM (SC-LSTM)

Previous to the coverage mechanism used in summarisation, Wen et al. [2015] proposed another way to deal with repetitions which extends the LSTM architecture and which he dubbed semantically conditioned LSTM (SC-LSTM). The approach is used in the context of a dialogue system to generate dialogue turns from dialogue acts. To control coverage, a control vector (DA vector, $\mathbf{d}_t$) is added which is a one hot representation of the input dialogue act. In addition to the input, output, and forget LSTM gates, a reading gate r_t is introduced which controls how much of the input DA should be retained for future time steps (Eq. (4.19)). The new cell and, therefore, the new hidden state, is computed taking into account the updated DA vector

---

[5]$\mathbf{c}_0$ is a zero vector since on the first timestep none of the input has been covered.

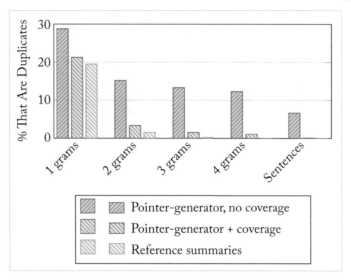

Figure 4.7: The impact of coverage on repetition (source: See et al. [2017]).

(Eq. (4.20)). In this way, predictions are made sensitive to how much of the input dialogue act has already been covered.

$$
\begin{array}{rll}
\text{LSTM Gates} & i_t = \sigma(\mathbf{W}_{wi}\mathbf{w}_t + \mathbf{W}_{hi}\mathbf{h}_{t-1}) & (4.14) \\
& f_t = \sigma(\mathbf{W}_{wf}\mathbf{w}_t + \mathbf{W}_{hf}\mathbf{h}_{t-1}) & (4.15) \\
& o_t = \sigma(\mathbf{W}_{wo}\mathbf{w}_t + \mathbf{W}_{ho}\mathbf{h}_{t-1}) & (4.16) \\
\text{Reading Gate} & r_t = \sigma(\mathbf{W}_{wr}\mathbf{w}_t + \mathbf{W}_{hr}\mathbf{h}_{t-1}) & (4.17) \\
\text{Candidate Cell} & \hat{\mathbf{c}}_t = \tanh(\mathbf{W}_{wc}\mathbf{w}_t + \mathbf{W}_{hc}\mathbf{h}_{t-1}) & (4.18) \\
\text{DA Vector} & \mathbf{d}_t = r_t \odot \mathbf{d}_{t-1} & (4.19) \\
\text{New Cell} & \mathbf{c}_t = i_t \odot \hat{\mathbf{c}}_t + f_t \odot \mathbf{c}_{t-1} + \tanh(\mathbf{W}_{dc}\mathbf{d}_t) & (4.20) \\
\text{New Hidden State} & \mathbf{h}_t = o_t \odot \tanh(\mathbf{c}_t). & (4.21)
\end{array}
$$

Figure 4.8 illustrates the impact of the SC-LSTM on feature activation: when the words and phrases describing a particular slot-value pair have been generated, the corresponding DA feature-value decreases.

4.4   SUMMARY

While neural models tend to produce fluent text, simple encoder-decoder approaches to text production often generate text that contains repetitions that fail to include all relevant information and/or that express information not present in the input. In this chapter, we saw how attention, copy, and coverage could help address these issues. We also briefly discussed alternative

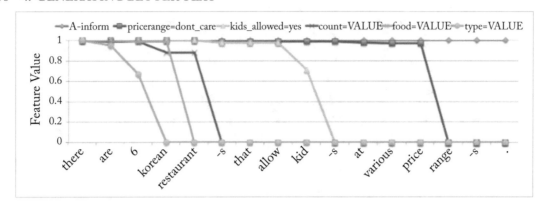

Figure 4.8: Evolution of the DA vector as generation progresses (source: [Wen et al., 2015]).

methods such as delexicalisation, character-based models, and Wen et al. [2015]'s semantically-conditioned LSTM.

One commonality of attention, copy, and coverage is that they modify the decoding part of the model. Attention helps the decoder focusing on the relevant part of the input; copy permits decoding either from the background vocabulary or from the input; and coverage informs the decoder of what has already been attended to.

In the following chapters, we will examine various ways of improving the basic encoder-decoder model, focusing first on the encoder and, second, on learning. Chapter 5 introduces neural architectures whose encoders are designed to better model the structure of the input, and Chapter 6 presents different ways in which key features of the generation tasks can be integrated in the learning process.

CHAPTER 5

Building Better Input Representations

In Chapter 4, we saw how to improve neural networks so that they can produce better quality text which is more consistent with the input and does not omit or repeat information. This was mainly done by modifying the decoding part of the encoder-decoder framework for text production. The *attention* mechanism [Bahdanau et al., 2014] helps improve precision, and the *coverage* mechanism [See et al., 2017] helps ensure that the produced text covers the input. We also saw how the *copy* mechanism [Gu et al., 2016, See et al., 2017] could be used both to handle rare or unknown words and to facilitate output text to be copied from the input. In short, so far we have focused on how to improve the generation process to improve the quality of the output text. This chapter focuses on how to best model the input to text production.

The standard encoder-decoder framework models input as a sequence of tokens. This makes it a natural fit for these text-to-text production tasks, such as sentence simplification and compression, where the input is a single sentence. Surprisingly, these models have also shown promising results for text-production tasks which consider more complex inputs such as long documents (summarisation) and graph- or tree-structured inputs (e.g., data- and MR-to-text generation). For example, in the case of document summarisation, the standard encoder-decoder framework was used to model the document as a long sequence of words [Nallapati et al., 2016, Paulus et al., 2018, See et al., 2017]. Similarly, Konstas et al. [2017] adopted a sequence-to-sequence model to generate from Abstract Meaning Representation (AMR) graphs [Banarescu et al., 2013, May and Priyadarshi, 2017] by simply linearising AMR graphs into a sequence of tokens.

Several studies challenge the notion of modelling input as a sequence of tokens while ignoring the structure of the input. Many researchers have argued that the modelling of the input structure could lead to better representation learning and benefit the task at hand. In this chapter we discuss some of these approaches that try to learn input representations that facilitate input understanding and are better suited for task-specific communication goals.

We will mainly focus on encoding inputs consisting of long text or graph-structured data. We will first look at some solutions which have been proposed to better encode text structure. These were mainly developed for the summarisation task. We will then look at how to better encode input data used in data-to-text generation; here the main focus is how to better encode graphs or trees.

5.1 PITFALLS OF MODELLING INPUT AS A SEQUENCE OF TOKENS

Let us first review a few examples of how sequential models are used to model structured input and discuss their limitations.

5.1.1 MODELLING LONG TEXT AS A SEQUENCE OF TOKENS

As its name indicates, a sequential model processes an input text as a sequence (see Section 3.2.1). It learns a representation of the input by sequentially going through the input text one token at a time. In recent years, this has been a very pervasive approach, used for all types of text-production tasks. It has been used, for instance, in sentence simplification [Zhang and Lapata, 2017], paraphrase generation [Mallinson et al., 2017], sentence compression [Filippova et al., 2015], and conversational systems [Li et al., 2016b]. It has also been used for longer text, i.e., for summarisation [Nallapati et al., 2016, Paulus et al., 2018, See et al., 2017].

One of the most common approaches in this trend is to use bidirectional RNNs to encode a document as a sequence of words. Bidirectional RNNs process the input document one word at a time, both from left to right and from right to left (see Section 3.2.1); they build word representations which take into account information from the whole input document, not just the preceding words. Figure 5.1 shows the pointer-generator document summarisation model from See et al. [2017], encoding an input document with a bidirectional RNN. There have been several follow-up studies on document summarisation which build on this Pointer-Generator model [Gehrmann et al., 2018, Pasunuru and Bansal, 2018, Paulus et al., 2018].

5.1.2 MODELLING GRAPHS OR TREES AS A SEQUENCE OF TOKENS

Sequential encoders have been applied to model graph or tree-structured input data to text production. First, the input is pre-processed and linearised into a sequence of tokens. Then, a bidirectional RNN is applied to encode this sequence.

Linearising AMR Graphs. Abstract Meaning Representations (AMRs) are a semantic formalism which encode the meaning of natural language text using a directed graph while abstracting away from the surface forms in the input text [Banarescu et al., 2013, May and Priyadarshi, 2017]. As illustrated in Figure 5.2, an AMR encodes semantic dependencies between entities mentioned in the sentence, such as "New York" being the "location" of the verb "hold".

Konstas et al. [2017], Castro Ferreira et al. [2017], and Cao and Clark [2018] have adapted sequence-to-sequence models to generate text from AMR graphs by first linearising AMR graphs into a sequence of tokens and then using a sequential decoder to generate text. Figure 5.2 presents an example of the intermediate representations produced by the pre-processing procedure used to linearise an AMR graph through a depth first traversal. It basically involves simplifying the AMR graphs, anonymising named entities and dates, grouping entity categories, and encoding nesting information to mark scope. This pre-processing aims to overcome the data

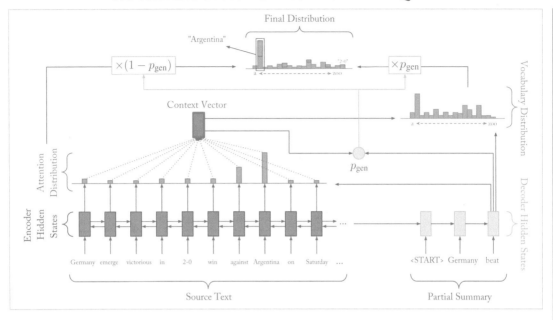

Figure 5.1: Pointer-generator summarisation model with a bidirectional RNN modelling document as a sequence of tokens (source: See et al. [2017]).

sparsity and also to reduce the complexity of the AMR graphs to make it suitable for sequence-to-sequence models.

Linearising RDF Triples.   Gardent et al. [2017b] introduced the WebNLG data set, a benchmark for the generation of short texts from RDF (Resource Description Frameworks) tree-structured data. Figure 5.3 presents an example input/output pair from their data set. It also highlights the tree structure of the input RDF data along with its linearisation.

While the WebNLG input data is tree structured, most neural systems that participated in the WebNLG shared task in fact used a sequence-to-sequence approach to model the generation process.

Linearising Dialogue Moves and Wikipedia Infoboxes.   Another type of meaning representation stems from dialogue. Given a user input, a dialogue system first generates an abstract representation of the system response called a dialogue move. Generation is then used to generate the system answer from this dialogue move. Typically, a dialogue move consists of a dialogue act (inform, query, instruct, etc.) and a set of key value pairs.

Generation from dialogue moves was explored, for instance, in Mairesse and Young [2014] and Wen et al. [2015]. More recently, the E2E challenge [Novikova et al., 2017b] provided a training corpus for generation from meaning representations that are simplified versions

```
(h / hold-04                                  (a)          US officials held an expert group meeting in January 2002 in New York.
                                                    hold
  :ARG0 (p2 / person                                  :ARG0 person :ARG0-of have-org-role :ARG1 country :name name :op1
                                                    United :op2 States :ARG2 official
   :ARG0-of (h2 / have-org-role-91                   :ARG1 meet :ARG0 person :ARG1-of expert :ARG2-of group
                                                     :time date-entity :year 2002 :month 1
      :ARG1 (c2 / country                            :location city :name name :op1 New :op2 York
                                              (b)          country_0 officials held an expert group meeting in month_0 year_0 in city_1.
       :name (n3 / name                              hold
                                                     :ARG0 person :ARG0-of have-org-role :ARG1 country_0 :ARG2 official
         :op1 "United" op2: "States"))               :ARG1 meet :ARG0 person :ARG1-of expert :ARG2-of group
                                                     :time date-entity year_0 month_0
      :ARG2 (o / official)))                         :location city_1
                                              (c)          loc_0 officials held an expert group meeting in month_0 year_0 in loc_1.
  :ARG1 (m / meet-03                                  hold
                                                     :ARG0 person :ARG0-of have-org-role :ARG1 loc_0 :ARG2 official
   :ARG0 (p / person                                 :ARG1 meet :ARG0 person :ARG1-of expert :ARG2-of group
                                                     :time date-entity year_0 month_0
      :ARG1-of (e / expert-01)                       :location loc_1
                                              (d)          loc_0 officials held an expert group meeting in month_0 year_0 in loc_1.
        :ARG2-of (g / group-01)))                    hold
                                                     :ARG0 ( person :ARG0-of ( have-org-role :ARG1 loc_0 :ARG2 official ) )
  :time (d2 / date-entity :year 2002 :month 1)       :ARG1 ( meet :ARG0 ( person :ARG1-of expert :ARG2-of group ) )
                                                     :time ( date-entity year_0 month_0 )
  :location (c / city                                :location loc_1

   :name (n / name :op1 "New" :op2 "York")))
```

Input: *hold   :ARG0   (person   :ARG0-of   (have-org-role   :ARG1   loc_0 :ARG2   official   )   )   :ARG1   (meet   :ARG0   (person   :ARG1-of   expert :ARG2-of   group   )   )   :time   (date-entity   year_0   month_0   )   :location   loc_1*

Output: *US officials held an expert group meeting in January 2002 in New York.*

Figure 5.2: Linearising AMR (top left column) for text production: input-output pairs (bottom blocks) after AMR linearisation using (a) graph simplification, (b) named entity anonymisation, (c) named entity clustering, and (d) insertion of scope markers (source: Konstas et al. [2017]).

of dialogue moves in that, since the dialogue act always is to recommend a restaurant to a user, the "recommend" dialogue act is left implicit and the input is reduced to a set of key-value pairs (rather than a dialogue act combined with a set of key-value pairs). Figure 5.4 illustrates an example from this data set. Dušek et al. [2018] reported that many of the neural systems that participated in the E2E challenge used sequence-to-sequence models and took as input a linearised version of the input meaning representations.

Perez-Beltrachini and Lapata [2018] focus on generating text from noisy or loosely aligned data. In particular, they generate text from Wikipedia infoboxes using comparable rather than parallel data. Figure 5.5 illustrates an example from their paper. In their paper, they also linearise Wikipedia infoboxes to use an attention-based sequence-to-sequence models for text production.

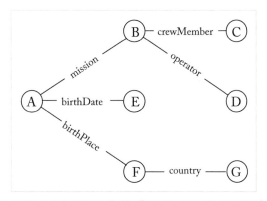

Input: *A (birthPlace F (country G)) (birthDate E) (mission B (operator D) (crewMember C))*

Output: *A who was born on E in F, G, participated in mission B with a crew member C. The mission was operated by D.*

Figure 5.3: Linearising RDF (top block) to prepare input-output pairs (bottom blocks) for text production. Note, name entities are already anonymised in the RDF.

```
name[The Eagle],

eatType[coffee shop],

food[French],

priceRange[moderate],

customerRating[3/5],

area[riverside],

kidsFriendly[yes],

near[Burger King];
```

Output: *The three star coffee shop, The Eagle, gives families a mid-priced dining experience featuring a variety of wines and cheeses. Find The Eagle near Burger King.*

Figure 5.4: Linearising dialogue moves for response generation.

Born	Robert Joseph Flaherty
	February 16, 1884
	Iron Mountain, Michigan, U.S.
Died	July 23, 1951 (aged 67)
	Dummerston, Vermont, U.S.
Cause of death	Cerebral thrombosis
Occupation	Filmmaker
Spouse(s)	Frances Johnson Hubbard

Output: *Robert Joseph Flaherty, (February 16, 1884 July 23, 1951) was an American film-maker. Flaherty was married to Frances H. Flaherty until his death in 1951.*

Figure 5.5: Linearising Wikipedia descriptions for the generation from loosely aligned data.

5.1.3   LIMITATIONS OF SEQUENTIAL REPRESENTATION LEARNING

While sequential encoders have proved remarkably effective for text production, they are intuitively unsatisfactory for following reasons:

Ignoring the Apparent Structure in the Input.   The sequential encoders do not capture the structure in the input. On the contrary, they often dilute the structure that is evident in the input. This is particularly striking for document summarisation where the input is a longer text, and for data-to-text generation where the input is often a graph or a tree.

For summarisation, a document can be seen as a sequence of paragraphs where each paragraph consists of a sequence of sentences and each sentence consists of a sequence of words. This hierarchical structure of the document is interleaved with an underlying discourse structure. Modelling a document as a flat sequence of words is counterintuitive, especially when pre-neural approaches to summarisation have (already) shown that exploiting the document structure could be beneficial for summarisation [Durrett et al., 2016].

For generation from graph-structured data, linearising the graph breaks local dependencies turning them into long-range dependencies. This is illustrated in Figure 5.3. While in the input graph, B, E, and F are all directly related to A, in the linearisation, only F retains this local dependency. More generally, by linearising the input graph, we strain the model, requiring it to learn dependencies that were already given in the input.

Limited Ability to Learn Long-Range Dependencies.   A second, related issue that arises from the sequential encoding of the input is that the long-range dependencies that are induced by this sequencing negatively impact performance. Although LSTMs were shown to handle long-range dependencies much better than RNNs, the power of LSTMs to handle these dependencies remains limited.

There has been increasing interest in understanding the capabilities of LSTMs to handle long-range dependencies [Gulordava et al., 2018, Marvin and Linzen, 2018]. However, most of these studies have focused on sentence-level syntactic evaluations (e.g., subject-verb agreement and reflexive anaphora agreement) of sequential encoders used in language models. Learning long-range dependencies from flattened long documents or complex graphs is undoubtedly a problem. Eventually, the poor representation of the input affects the model's ability to produce good-quality text.

5.2   MODELLING TEXT STRUCTURES

In this section, we discuss how we can improve representation learning by taking text structure into consideration. We will mainly focus on the task of document summarisation, which requires modelling a long text.

For text structure, two main types of architecture have been recently proposed. The first approach focuses on modelling a document as a sequence of sentences. Here, we describe two types of hierarchical document encoders: one which uses LSTMs to encode sentences [Tan et al., 2017] and another which uses CNNs [Narayan et al., 2018c]. In both cases, a document is then encoded as a sequence of sentences using an LSTM. The second approach focuses on modelling a document as a sequence of paragraphs [Celikyilmaz et al., 2018].

5.2.1   MODELLING DOCUMENTS WITH HIERARCHICAL LSTMS

A first, somewhat obvious approach to document structure is to model a document as a sequence of sentences rather than as a sequence of tokens. This was first proposed by Li et al. [2015], and further exploited by several researchers working on summarisation. The approach is often referred to as hierarchical simply because it uses separate encoders at the sentence and at the text level. A word encoder is used to generate representations for each input sentence, modelling it as a sequence of words. These representations are then input to another LSTM, the sentence encoder, which will produce a representation of the whole text using the representations produced by the word encoder for each of the input sentences.

Figure 5.6 sketches the hierarchical representation of the document from Tan et al. [2017]. First, sentences are modelled as sequences of words, and then the document is modelled as a sequence of sentences. A learned document representation c is passed to the decoder. One advantage of this approach is that the standard mechanisms we saw were used for standard LSTMs that can also be used here. In particular, the attention mechanism can be used with this architecture, i.e., while generating an output, the model finds which relevant part of the input to focus on.

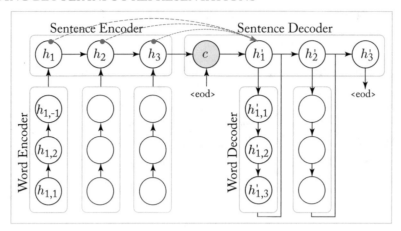

Figure 5.6: Hierarchical document representation from Tan et al. [2017] for abstractive document summarisation. First, sentences are modelled as sequences of words, and then the document is modelled as a sequence of sentences (source: Tan et al. [2017]).

We could easily integrate this architecture with a standard sequential decoder to generate output text as a sequence of tokens. However, Tan et al. [2017] propose a hierarchical decoder which takes into account the hierarchical structure of more-than-one-sentence-long summaries, i.e., it first predicts a sequence of sentences, then for each sentence, it predicts a sequence of words. More formally, the decoding is hierarchical whereby each output sentence is decoded separately and the encoded representation of the previously generated sentence h'_{t-1} is used as input to the next sentence decoding step. That is, the encoded representation of the previously generated sentence provides the initial state for the first decoding step of the next sentence.

Training a hierarchical encoder with a hierarchical decoder can be difficult. Tan et al. [2017] use a coarse attention mechanism which learns which input sentence to focus on rather than which word. This makes it hard to integrate the copy mechanism described in Section 4.2. As a result, Tan et al.'s model underperforms on out-of-vocabulary words and is outperformed by See et al. [2017].[1]

---

[1]Tan et al. [2017] proposed a graph-based attention mechanism to enhance the learning of hierarchical document summariser modifying the attention scores to identify salient sentences. The proposed method is inspired from traditional graph-based sentence extraction algorithms such as TextRank [Mihalcea and Tarau, 2004] and LexRank [Erkan and Radev, 2004] to assist the attention mechanism to only focus on salient sentences in the document. We will discuss their graph-based attention mechanism in Chapter 6.

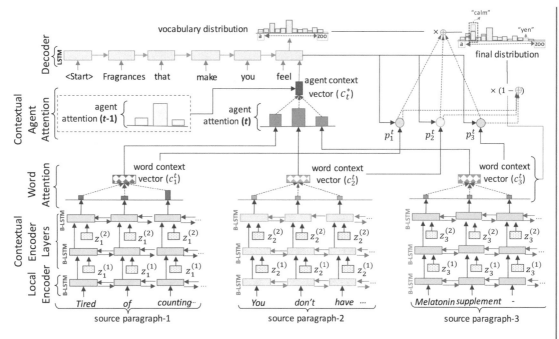

Figure 5.7: Hierarchical document representation from Celikyilmaz et al. [2018] for abstractive document summarisation (source: Celikyilmaz et al. [2018]).

5.2.2   MODELLING DOCUMENT WITH ENSEMBLE ENCODERS

While Tan et al. [2017] used independent word encoders to model sentences in a document, Celikyilmaz et al. [2018] proposed a hierarchical document encoder which uses collaborating encoder to encode different paragraphs of the document. Paragraph encoders are referred to as agents. Figure 5.7 sketches this hierarchical encoding. At each layer, an agent (paragraph encoder) encodes its assigned paragraph independently, and broadcasts its encoding to other agents. This way, agents share global context information with one another about different sections of the document and learn globally informed paragraph representations. After repeating this process across multiple layers, generating new messages at each layer, each agent passes its final paragraph representation to a sequential decoder which generates a summary predicting one word at a time. In addition, the decoder uses a contextual agent attention to integrate information from multiple agents smoothly at each decoding step. The network is trained end-to-end using reinforcement learning [Ranzato et al., 2015, Rennie et al., 2016, Williams, 1992] to generate focused and coherent summaries.

Multi-Agent Encoder Message Passing.   Each agent encodes a paragraph as a sequence of words using multilayer bidirectional LSTMs. At each layer, agents communicate with each other to modify their representations of paragraphs, sharing the global context from different sections

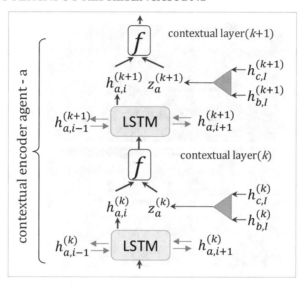

Figure 5.8: Communication among multiple encoders or agents, each encoding a paragraph. Here, we describe how agent a updates its state with messages from agents b and c (source: Celikyilmaz et al. [2018]).

of the text. The message passing captures the fact that paragraphs in a document are not independent of each other, but collectively form the document.

Figure 5.8 describes the message passing between agents and how it influences the paragraph representation more formally. For agent a at layer $(k + 1)$, the Bi-LSTM at step i takes input from previous layer ($\mathbf{h}_{a,i}^{(k)}$), left and right encoders ($\overrightarrow{\mathbf{h}}_{a,i-1}^{(k+1)}$ and $\overleftarrow{\mathbf{h}}_{a,i+1}^{(k+1)}$), and from other agents ($\mathbf{z}_a^{(k)}$):

$$\overrightarrow{\mathbf{h}}_{a,i}^{(k+1)}, \overleftarrow{\mathbf{h}}_{a,i}^{(k+1)} = \text{BiLSTM}(f(\mathbf{h}_{a,i}^{(k)}, \mathbf{z}_a^{(k)}), \overrightarrow{\mathbf{h}}_{a,i-1}^{(k+1)}, \overleftarrow{\mathbf{h}}_{a,i+1}^{(k+1)}) \tag{5.1}$$

$$\mathbf{h}_{a,i}^{(k+1)} = \mathbf{W}_1[\overrightarrow{h}_{a,i}^{(k+1)}, \overleftarrow{h}_{a,i}^{(k+1)}] \tag{5.2}$$

$\mathbf{z}_a^{(k)}$ is estimated as an average of all other encoders except present encoder a from previous layer k:

$$\mathbf{z}_a^{(k)} = \frac{1}{M-1} \sum_{m \neq a} \mathbf{h}_{m,I}^{(k)} \tag{5.3}$$

where $\mathbf{h}_{m,I}^{(k)}$ is the last hidden state output from the k-th contextual layer of each agent when it is not a; M is the total number of agents. The function $f(\mathbf{h}_{a,i}^{(k)}, \mathbf{z}_a^{(k)}) = \mathbf{v}_1^T \tanh(\mathbf{W}_2 \mathbf{h}_{a,i}^{(k)} + \mathbf{W}_3 \mathbf{z}_a^{(k)})$ filters the context of the current token from this paragraph with the information sent by other agents; $\mathbf{v}_1$, $\mathbf{W}_1$, $\mathbf{W}_2$ and $\mathbf{W}_3$ are model parameters shared by all agents. Figure 5.8 depicts a scenario with three agents a, b, and c. To update the representation for agent a, it takes input from agents b and c. This process is repeated at each layer, generating new messages at each layer.

Decoding with Hierarchical Agent Attention.   Once agents complete encoding, they deliver their information to the decoder with a novel hierarchical agent attention (see Figure 5.7). The hierarchical agent attention implements an attention mechanism attending to both agents and words in a selected paragraph. Consequently, it enables the decoder to integrate information from multiple agents smoothly at each decoding step.

First, a word attention distribution ℓ_a^t for each paragraph is computed over every token $\mathbf{h}_{a,i}^{(K)}$ for each agent a:

$$\ell_a^t = \mathrm{softmax}(\mathbf{v}_2^T \tanh(\mathbf{W}_4 \mathbf{h}_a^{(K)} + \mathbf{W}_5 \mathbf{s}_t + b_1)) \tag{5.4}$$

where $\mathbf{h}_a^K$ is the representation learned from agent a at the top layer K, $\mathbf{s}_t$ is the decoder state at step t, and others are model parameters. $\ell_a^t \in [0, 1]^I$ is the soft attention over all tokens in the paragraph read by the agent a. Each word context distribution represents the information extracted by the agent from the paragraph it has read. Now the decoder has to decide on which agent is more relevant to the current decoding step. This is done by estimating the document global agent attention distribution $\mathbf{g}^t$:

$$c_a^t = \sum_i \ell_{a,i}^t \mathbf{h}_{a,i}^{(K)} \tag{5.5}$$

$$\mathbf{g}^t = \mathrm{softmax}(\mathbf{v}_3^T \tanh(\mathbf{W}_6 \mathbf{c}^t + \mathbf{W}_7 \mathbf{s}_t + b_2)) \tag{5.6}$$

where $\mathbf{g}^t \in [0, 1]^M$ is a soft selection over M agents. Then, we compute the agent context vector $\mathbf{c}_t^*$:

$$\mathbf{c}_t^* = \sum_a \mathbf{g}_a^t \mathbf{c}_a^t. \tag{5.7}$$

The agent context $\mathbf{c}_t^*$ is a fixed-length vector encoding salient information from the entire document provided by the agents. It is then concatenated with the decoder state $\mathbf{s}_t$ and fed through a multi-layer perceptron to produce a vocabulary distribution (over all vocabulary words) at time t as:

$$p(w_t|s_t, w_{t-1}) = \mathrm{softmax}(\mathrm{MLP}([\mathbf{s}_t, \mathbf{c}_t^*])). \tag{5.8}$$

This way, the decoder at each time step t first attends to agents and then to their words to estimate the target vocabulary distribution.

Multi-Agent Pointer Network.   To our knowledge, Celikyilmaz et al. [2018] were the first to show how hierarchical document encoders could be coupled with sequential decoders integrating a copy mechanism. Like See et al. [2017], their model permits copying words from different paragraphs of the document. At each timestep t, a generation probability p_a^t is computed for each agent a as:

$$p_a^t = \sigma(\mathbf{v}_4^T \mathbf{c}_a^t + \mathbf{v}_5^T \mathbf{s}_t + \mathbf{v}_6^T \mathbf{y}^t + b) \tag{5.9}$$

using the context vector $\mathbf{c}_a^t$, decoder state $\mathbf{s}_t$, and decoder input $\mathbf{y}_t$ and where b is a bias term. For each agent a, this generation probability is then used to estimate an extended vocabulary distribution over the union of the output vocabulary and the OOV (out-of-vocabulary) words present in the input document:

$$p^a(w_t|s_t, w_{t-1}) = p_a^t p(w_t|s_t, w_{t-1}) + (1 - p_a^t)\mathbf{u}_{a,w}^t \tag{5.10}$$

where $\mathbf{u}_{a,w}^t$ is the sum of all attention for all instances of $w = w_t$ in the paragraph encoded by a. The generation probability determines whether to generate a word from the vocabulary by sampling from $p(w|\Delta)$, or copying a word from the corresponding agent's input paragraph by sampling from its attention distribution. The final distribution p^f over the extended vocabulary is obtained by weighting each agent by their corresponding agent attention values $\mathbf{g}_a^t$:

$$p^f(w_t|s_t, w_{t-1}) = \sum_a \mathbf{g}_a^t p^a(w_t|s_t, w_{t-1}). \tag{5.11}$$

The hierarchical document encoders of Celikyilmaz et al. [2018] coupled with its sequential decoder integrating a copy mechanism achieves state-of-the-art performance, outperforming both abstractive summarisation systems of See et al. [2017] and Tan et al. [2017].

5.2.3   MODELLING DOCUMENT WITH CONVOLUTIONAL SENTENCE ENCODERS

Another alternative approach to LSTMs as a means to encode text is to use CNNs (LeCun et al., 1990). As mentioned in Section 3.1.1, CNNs have been shown to be very effective in computer vision [Krizhevsky et al., 2012], and in recent years they have also proven useful for various NLP tasks [Cheng and Lapata, 2016, Collobert et al., 2011, Kalchbrenner et al., 2014, Kim, 2014, Kim et al., 2016, Lei et al., 2015, Zhang et al., 2015]. In particular, they have been shown to be very efficient at identifying properties from the input that correlate well with the output. For example, for the task of image caption generation, CNNs can learn to align objects in the images to words in their captions [Xu et al., 2015a]. In this section, we will describe a case of an extractive document summariser [Cheng and Lapata, 2016, Narayan et al., 2018c] where a CNN is used to encode sentences and an RNN is used to encode the document as a sequence of sentences. This hierarchical modelling of the document, using CNNs to encode sentences, seeks to better capture salient named entities and events which correlate well with the gold summary.

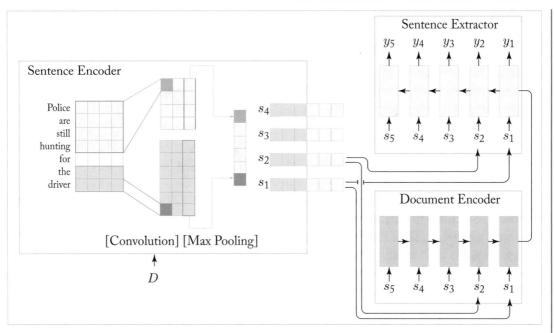

Figure 5.9: Extractive summarisation with a hierarchical encoder-decoder model (source: Narayan et al. [2018c]).

Convolutional Sentence Encoder.   Figure 5.9 (left block) sketches a convolutional sentence encoder from Cheng and Lapata [2016] and Narayan et al. [2017, 2018a,c]. Intuitively, slide (convolve) one or more filters across the input sentence, followed by a non-linearity and max-pooling operation to encode the sentence into a continuous representation.

More formally, a sentence s of length k in D can be represented as a dense matrix $\mathbf{W} = [\mathbf{w}_1 \oplus \mathbf{w}_2 \oplus \ldots \oplus \mathbf{w}_k] \in R^{k \times d}$ where $\mathbf{w}_i \in R^d$ is the word embedding of the i-th word in s and $\oplus$ is the concatenation operator. A kernel filter $\mathbf{K} \in R^{h \times d}$ of width h is then applied to a window of h words in s to produce a new feature. This filter is applied to each possible h-size window of words in s to produce a feature map $\mathbf{f} = [f_1, f_2, \ldots, f_{k-h+1}] \in R^{k-h+1}$ where f_i is defined as:

$$f_i = \text{ReLU}(\mathbf{K} \circ \mathbf{W}_{i:i+h-1} + b) \tag{5.12}$$

where $\circ$ is the Hadamard product followed by a sum over all elements, ReLU is a rectified linear activation, and $b \in R$ is a bias term. In order to accelerate the convergence of stochastic gradient descent, the ReLU activation function is used rather than the sigmoid or the tanh function [Krizhevsky et al., 2012]. Max pooling over time [Collobert et al., 2011] is then applied over the feature map $\mathbf{f}$ to yield $f_{\max} = \max(\mathbf{f})$, the feature corresponding to this particular filter $\mathbf{K}$. Max pooling is followed by local response normalisation for better generalisation [Krizhevsky et al., 2012]. Multiple kernels $\mathbf{K}_h$ of width h are used to compute a list of features $\mathbf{f}^{K_h}$. In addition, kernels of varying widths are used so as to learn a set of feature lists ($\mathbf{f}^{K_{h1}}, \mathbf{f}^{K_{h2}}, \ldots$). The final sentence representation is obtained by concatenating all feature lists.

The left part of Figure 5.9 sketches the workings of this convolutional sentence encoder. Kernels of sizes 2 (shown in red) and 4 (shown in blue) are applied three times each. The max pooling over time operation leads to two feature lists $\mathbf{f}^{K_2}$ and $\mathbf{f}^{K_4} \in R^3$. The final sentence embeddings have six dimensions.

Document Modelling for Extractive Document Summarisation.   Narayan et al. [2018c] proposed a hierarchical encoder-decoder architecture assembled by RNNs and CNNs for extractive summarisation. The main components of their model are a CNN sentence encoder, an RNN document encoder, and an attention-based RNN sentence extractor (see Figure 5.9). Like the model described in Section 5.2.1, this model also exploits the compositionality of the document. It captures the fact that a document is built of a meaningful sequence of sentences and each sentence is built of a meaningful sequence of words. Convolution sentence encoders are first used to learn sentence representations, then an RNN is used to compose a sequence of sentences into a document embedding. Finally, extractive summarisation is designed as a sequence labelling problem using a standard encoder-decoder architecture.

Formally, given a document D consisting of a sequence of sentences $(s_1, s_2, \ldots, s_n)$, an extractive summariser aims to produce a summary S by selecting m sentences from D (where $m < n$). For each sentence $s_i \in D$, we predict a label $y_i \in \{0, 1\}$ (where 1 means that s_i should be included in the summary) and assign a score $p(y_i|s_i, D, \theta)$ quantifying s_i's relevance to the summary. The model learns to assign $p(1|s_i, D, \theta) > p(1|s_j, D, \theta)$ when sentence s_i is more relevant than s_j. Model parameters are denoted by θ. We estimate $p(y_i|s_i, D, \theta)$ using a neural network model and assemble a summary S by selecting m sentences with top $p(1|s_i, D, \theta)$ scores.

Following Filippova et al. [2015], Li et al. [2015], Narayan et al. [2017], Sutskever et al. [2014], given a document D consisting of a sequence of sentences $(s_1, s_2, \ldots, s_n)$, Narayan et al. [2018c] feed sentences to an RNN in reverse order to ensure that the network also considers the top sentences of the document which are particularly important for summarisation [Nallapati et al., 2016, Rush et al., 2015]. Finally, the sentence extractor sequentially labels each sentence in a document with 1 (relevant for the summary) or 0 (otherwise). It is implemented with another RNN with LSTM cells and a softmax layer. At time t_i, it reads sentence s_i and makes a binary prediction, conditioned on the document representation (obtained from the document encoder) and the previously labelled sentences. This way, the sentence extractor is able to identify locally and globally important sentences within the document. The sentences in a document D are then ranked using the confidence scores, $p(y_i = 1|s_i, D, \theta)$, assigned by the softmax layer of the sentence extractor.

In addition, CNNs can be trained effectively as the computations involved in CNNs (linear computation of the convolutional layer followed by a nonlinearity) are much lighter than the cell computation involved in LSTMs (which includes three gates with non-linear layers plus two non-linear layers to compute the candidate cell and the output hidden state, respectively, cf. Section 3.1.3). There are no temporal dependencies between filters, so they can be applied concurrently, and they can also capture long-range dependencies by hierarchically increasing the receptive field. Narayan et al. [2018c] demonstrate that hierarchical document modelling with CNNs is effective in identifying salient sentences in the document, achieving state-of-the-art performance for extractive document summarisation.

5.3   MODELLING GRAPH STRUCTURE

In the previous section, we saw how to improve encoders to handle long text structures for tasks like document summarisation. Several text productions (e.g., meaning representations and data-to-text productions, Section 5.1.2) rely on more complex forms of inputs such as graphs, trees, or tables. For example, the AMR-to-text generation [May and Priyadarshi, 2017] focuses on generation from abstract meaning representation graphs, and the RDF-to-text generation [Gardent et al., 2017a,b] focuses on generation from the DBPedia knowledge base. The standard sequential encoders used to model graph- or tree-structured data input as a sequence of tokens (see Section 5.1) fail to capture rich dependencies apparent in the input structure. This section discusses how we can improve representation learning by taking various input structures into consideration.

We will focus on three popular directions encoding graph structures: a graph-to-sequence model [Song et al., 2018], a graph-based triple encoder model [Trisedya et al., 2018], and graph convolutional networks [Marcheggiani and Perez-Beltrachini, 2018]. The first one has been applied for AMR-to-text generation, and the last two have been applied for RDF-to-text generation. However, none of these architectures are task-specific and all can be applied to any graph structure.

5.3.1   GRAPH-TO-SEQUENCE MODEL FOR AMR GENERATION

Song et al. [2018] introduced a graph-to-sequence model for AMR-to-text generation which, instead of linearising AMR to a sequence of tokens, encode AMR structures directly. They proposed a graph-state LSTM which directly operates on the input AMR. Figure 5.10 sketches this graph-to-sequence encoder operating on an AMR shown at the top. As can be seen, at each time step, the encoder operates directly on the graph structure of the input, updating node representations within a graph state using their parents and dependents in the graph. Multiple recurrent transition steps are taken so that information can propagate non-locally, and LSTM [Hochreiter and Schmidhuber, 1997] is used to avoid gradient diminishing and bursting in the recurrent process.

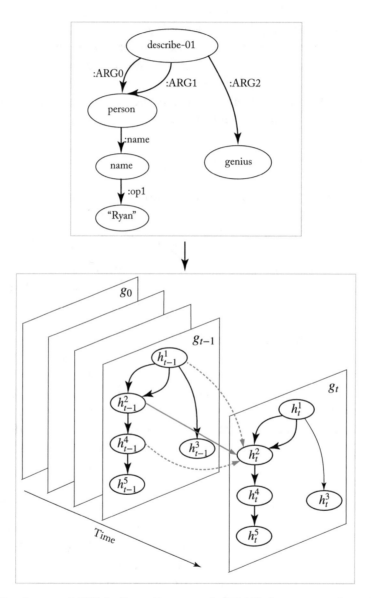

Figure 5.10: Graph-state LSTMs from Song et al. [2018] for text production from AMR graphs.

More formally, given a graph $G = (V, E)$, where V and E denote the sets of nodes and edges, respectively, we denote the hidden node representations by $\mathbf{h}^j$ for each node $v_j \in V$. At each time step t, the graph state maintains a state $\mathbf{g}_t = \{\mathbf{h}_t^j\}|_{v_j \in V}$. The initial state $\mathbf{g}_0$ consists of a set of initial node states $\mathbf{h}_0^j = \mathbf{h}_0$, where $\mathbf{h}_0$ is a hyperparameter of the model. At each state transition step t, we update the graph state from $\mathbf{g}_{t-1}$ to $\mathbf{g}_t$, allowing direct communication between a node and all nodes that are directly connected to the node using an LSTM recurrent cell.

The inputs to each LSTM cell include representations of edges that are connected to v_j. We define each edge as a triple (i, j, l), where i and j are indices of the source and target nodes, respectively, and l is the edge label. $\mathbf{x}_{i,j}^l$ is the representation of edge (i, j, l). Let $E_{in}(j)$ and $E_{out}(j)$ denote the sets of incoming and outgoing edges of v_j, respectively; we define incoming and outgoing input edge representations for the node v_j as:

$$\mathbf{x}_j^{in} = \sum_{(i,j,l) \in E_{in}(j)} \mathbf{x}_{i,j}^l \tag{5.13}$$

$$\mathbf{x}_j^{out} = \sum_{(j,k,l) \in E_{out}(j)} \mathbf{x}_{j,k}^l. \tag{5.14}$$

The edge representation $\mathbf{x}_{i,j}^l$ for each edge (i, j, l) is estimated as $\mathbf{x}_{i,j}^l = \mathbf{W}([\mathbf{e}_l; \mathbf{e}_i]) + b$, where $\mathbf{e}_l$ and $\mathbf{e}_i$ are the embeddings of edge label l and source node v_i, and $\mathbf{W}$ and b are trainable parameters. In addition to the edge representations, LSTM cells also take hidden states of their incoming nodes and outgoing nodes as input during a state transition. For node v_j, we define incoming and outgoing hidden state representations as:

$$\mathbf{h}_j^{in} = \sum_{(i,j,l) \in E_{in}(j)} \mathbf{h}_{t-1}^i \tag{5.15}$$

$$\mathbf{h}_j^{out} = \sum_{(j,k,l) \in E_{out}(j)} \mathbf{h}_{t-1}^k. \tag{5.16}$$

Using these inputs, the state transition from $\mathbf{g}_{t-1}$ to $\mathbf{g}_t$ is achieved as:

$$\mathbf{i}_t^j = \sigma(\mathbf{W}_i \mathbf{x}_j^{in} + \hat{\mathbf{W}}_i \mathbf{x}_j^{out} + \mathbf{U}_i h_j^{in} + \hat{\mathbf{U}}_i h_j^{out} + \mathbf{b}_i) \tag{5.17}$$

$$\mathbf{o}_t^j = \sigma(\mathbf{W}_o \mathbf{x}_j^{in} + \hat{\mathbf{W}}_o \mathbf{x}_j^{out} + \mathbf{U}_o h_j^{in} + \hat{\mathbf{U}}_o h_j^{out} + \mathbf{b}_o) \tag{5.18}$$

$$\mathbf{f}_t^j = \sigma(\mathbf{W}_f \mathbf{x}_j^{in} + \hat{\mathbf{W}}_f \mathbf{x}_j^{out} + \mathbf{U}_f h_j^{in} + \hat{\mathbf{U}}_f h_j^{out} + \mathbf{b}_f) \tag{5.19}$$

$$\mathbf{u}_t^j = \sigma(\mathbf{W}_u \mathbf{x}_j^{in} + \hat{\mathbf{W}}_u \mathbf{x}_j^{out} + \mathbf{U}_u h_j^{in} + \hat{\mathbf{U}}_u h_j^{out} + \mathbf{b}_u) \tag{5.20}$$

$$\mathbf{c}_t^j = \mathbf{f}_t^j \odot \mathbf{c}_{t-1}^j + \mathbf{i}_t^j \odot \mathbf{u}_t^j \tag{5.21}$$

$$\mathbf{h}_t^j = \mathbf{o}_t^j \odot \tanh(\mathbf{c}_t^j) \tag{5.22}$$

where $\mathbf{i}_t^j$, $\mathbf{o}_t^j$ and $\mathbf{f}_t^j$ are the input, output, and forget gates, similar to the LSTM gates in Section 3.1.3; all $\mathbf{W}$, $\hat{\mathbf{W}}$, $\mathbf{U}$ and $\hat{\mathbf{U}}$ are model parameters.

At each transition, each node representation accumulates information from all incoming and outgoing nodes and edges. At time $t = 0$, the graph state $\mathbf{g}_0$ will represent each node itself; at $t = 1$, each node representation in $\mathbf{g}_1$ will be aware of its immediate parents and children; and at $t = d$, where d is the longest path in the graph, each node representation in $\mathbf{g}_d$ will be informed of the whole graph. This way the graph encoder allows node representations to gather non-local information guided by the structure of the input. In addition, the forget gate allows it to be selective of what information needs to be propagated to other nodes, avoiding vanishing and exploding gradients.

Song et al. [2018] used a standard attention-based sequential decoder with a copy mechanism [Gu et al., 2016, Gulcehre et al., 2016, See et al., 2017] with the final graph state $\mathbf{g}_f$ learned from the graph encoder. The decoder is initiated with the average of node representations $\mathbf{h}_f^j$ in $\mathbf{g}_f$. The graph-to-sequence model achieved state-of-the-art performance, outperforming the sequence-to-sequence model of Konstas et al. [2017] for AMR generation.

5.3.2 GRAPH-BASED TRIPLE ENCODER FOR RDF GENERATION

Another graph encoder using RNNs for RDF generation has been proposed by Trisedya et al. [2018]. Instead of maintaining a whole graph state at each time step, as with the graph encoder of Song et al. [2018], this encoder takes the input triples in the form of a graph and builds a dynamic recurrent structure traversing the graph one node at a time and introducing adjacent nodes, preserving the original structure of the triples.

Figure 5.11 shows the RDF input (in its graph form) at the bottom and corresponding recurrent encoder at the top. Since the input graph can contain cycles, a combination of topological sort and breadth-first traversal algorithms is used to traverse the graph and to create an order of nodes in which they are fed into the recurrent encoder to compute or update their representations. First, topological sort establishes an order of the nodes until no further nodes have a zero in-degree. The breadth-first traversal is then used to establish an order among the remaining strongly connected nodes. For example, in Figure 5.11, we start with a node with zero in-degree. As the graph is fully connected, there are no nodes with zero in-degree. We randomly select a node ("John" in this case) as a starting point. We compute the node representation $\mathbf{h}_{john}$ for "John" using $\mathbf{h}_0$ as the initial state, where $\mathbf{h}_0$ is a hyperparameter of the model. Using the breadth-first traversal, we visit "John" and compute node representations $\mathbf{h}_{mary}$ and $\mathbf{h}_{london}$ for "Mary" and "London", respectively, using $\mathbf{h}_{john}$ as the previous hidden state. Next, we visit "Mary" but we do not compute or update any node, as it does not have any adjacent nodes. Next, we visit "London" and compute $\mathbf{h}_{england}$ for "England" using $\mathbf{h}_{london}$ as the previous hidden state. Finally, we visit "England" and update $\mathbf{h}_{john}$.

Formally speaking, given a directed graph $G = (V, E)$ as input, where V is a set of nodes that represent RDF entities and E is a set of directed edges that represent RDF predicates, the recurrent unit receives two inputs, i.e., the entity and the predicates, and compute the hidden state of each unit using modified LSTMs:

$$i_t = \sigma\left(\sum_e (\mathbf{U}^{ie}\mathbf{x}_{te} + \mathbf{W}^{ie}\mathbf{h}_{t-1})\right) \tag{5.23}$$

$$f_{te} = \sigma(\mathbf{U}^f\mathbf{x}_{te} + \mathbf{W}^f\mathbf{h}_{t-1}) \tag{5.24}$$

$$o_t = \sigma\left(\sum_e (\mathbf{U}^{oe}\mathbf{x}_{te} + \mathbf{W}^{oe}\mathbf{h}_{t-1})\right) \tag{5.25}$$

$$\mathbf{g}_t = \tanh\left(\sum_e (\mathbf{U}^{ge}\mathbf{x}_{te} + \mathbf{W}^{ge}\mathbf{h}_{t-1})\right) \tag{5.26}$$

$$\mathbf{c}_t = \left(\mathbf{c}_{t-1} * \sum_e f_{te}\right) + (\mathbf{g}_t * i_t) \tag{5.27}$$

$$\mathbf{h}_t = \tanh(\mathbf{c}_t) * o_t \tag{5.28}$$

$\mathbf{U}$ and $\mathbf{W}$ are model parameters, t stands for the current time step, and e an entity or a predicate. $\mathbf{x}_{te}$ is the input embedding at the current time step t with the input entity or predicate e. Note that it uses a separate forget gate for each input e that allows the LSTM unit to incorporate information from each input selectively, like in Tree LSTMs [Tai et al., 2015] and Graph LSTMs [Liang et al., 2016]. The graph-based triple encoder of Trisedya et al. [2018] encodes not only the elements of the triples but also the relationships both within a triple and between the triples. Unlike Tree LSTM [Tai et al., 2015], it allows cycles by first using a combination of topological sort and breadth-first traversal over a graph, and, unlike Graph LSTM [Liang et al., 2016], it allows any input property by treating the property as part of the input for hidden state computations.

Trisedya et al. [2018] plug their graph-based triple encoder into a standard sequential decoder to generate text. However, they use an attention model [Luong et al., 2015] to capture the global information of the knowledge graph. In the absence of the copy mechanism, they propose to use "Entity masking" to better generalise their model to unseen entities. Entity masking replaces entity mentions with entity IDs and entity types in both the input triples and the target sentences. They are retrieved later as a post-processing step. The graph-based triple encoder holds current state-of-the-art performance for RDF generation on the WebNLG dataset [Gardent et al., 2017a,b].

5.3.3   GRAPH CONVOLUTIONAL NETWORKS AS GRAPH ENCODERS

Graph convolutional networks (GCNs; Kipf and Welling, 2017) have been used to encode dependency syntax and predicate-argument structures in neural machine translation [Bastings et al., 2017, Marcheggiani et al., 2018] and semantic role labelling [Marcheggiani and Titov, 2017]. Recently, Marcheggiani and Perez-Beltrachini [2018] used GCNs as graph encoders to explicitly encode RDFs [Gardent et al., 2017a,b], and dependency graphs [Belz et al., 2011, 2012] to generate texts from them.

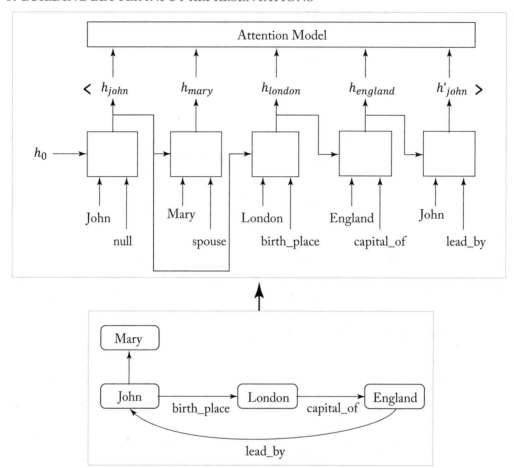

Figure 5.11: Graph-triple encoder from Trisedya et al. [2018] for text production from RDF triple sets.

GCNs provide a simple yet effective way of modelling graphs. Figure 5.12 sketches the modelling of an underlying syntactic structure for the sentence "Lane disputed those estimates." using a GCN. Like graph-to-sequence models (see Section 5.3.1) and graph triple encoders (see Section 5.3.2), GNCs aim to calculate the representation of each node in a graph considering the graph structure explicitly modelling edge labels and directions.

More formally, given an input directed graph $G = (V, E)$, where V is a set of nodes and E is a set of edges, in the graph, we update the node representation $\mathbf{h}_v^{(k)}$ for node $v \in V$ at layer k as:

$$\mathbf{h}_v^{(k+1)} = \text{ReLU}\Big(\sum_{u \in N(v)} \mathbf{W}_{e^l_{(u,v)}, e^d_{(u,v)}}^{(k)} \mathbf{h}_v^{(k)} + b_{e^l_{(u,v)}, e^d_{(u,v)}}^{(k)} \Big) \tag{5.29}$$

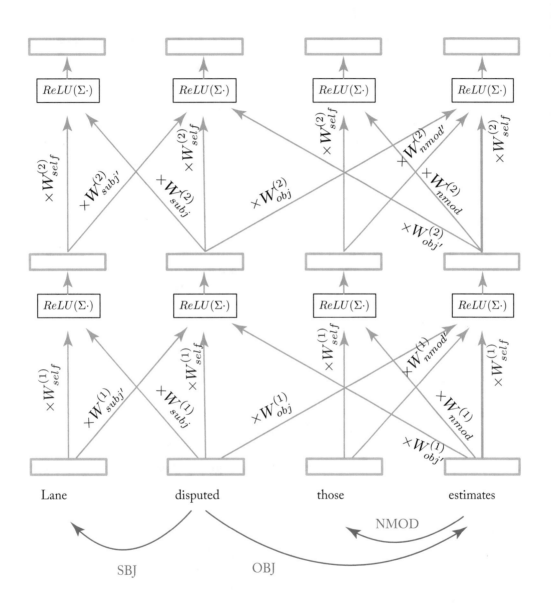

Figure 5.12: Graph convolutional networks for encoding the underlying syntactic structure for the sentence "Lane disputed those estimates" (source: Diego Marcheggiani).

where $N(v)$ is the set of neighbouring edges to v including itself, $e_{(u,v)}^l$ and $e_{(u,v)}^d$ are edge label and direction, respectively, for the edge e between nodes u and v, and $\mathbf{W}_{e_{(u,v)}^l, e_{(u,v)}^d}^{(k)}$ and $b_{e_{(u,v)}^l, e_{(u,v)}^d}^{(k)}$ are model parameters at layer k, with the edge label $e_{(u,v)}^l$ and the edge direction $e_{(u,v)}^d$. Note, in Figure 5.12, GCNs do not differentiate between incoming and outgoing edges; as such $\mathbf{W}$ and b are independent of edge directions. ReLU is the rectified linear activation function. As with standard CNNs [LeCun et al., 1990], GCN layers can be stacked to consider non-local neighbours. At the layer $k = 1$, we initialise $\mathbf{h}_v^{(1)} = \mathbf{x}_v$ where $\mathbf{x}_v \in R^d$ is a feature vector for a node $v \in V$. This way, the node representations $\mathbf{h}_v^{(2)}$ at layer $k = 2$ will accumulate information from its immediate neighbours; similarly $\mathbf{h}_v^{(3)}$ at layer $k = 3$ will accumulate information from its immediate parents and children as well as grandparents and children, and so on. Marcheggiani and Perez-Beltrachini [2018] use residual [He et al., 2016] and dense [Huang et al., 2017] connections between GCN layers to allow the gradient flow to be more efficient through stacked hidden layers.

Bastings et al. [2017] and Marcheggiani et al. [2018] integrate LSTMs with GCNs to encode sentences for machine translation; first a GCN is used to get better representations of words in a sentence considering the underlying syntactic structure of the sentence, then an LSTM is used to encode a sentence using those word representations. In contrast, Marcheggiani and Perez-Beltrachini [2018] solely rely on a GCN to get node representations for an input graph. The latter is also fast to train compared to LSTMs; there are no temporal dependencies between filters, so they can be applied concurrently.

Like the graph-to-sequence encoders (Section 5.3.1), Marcheggiani and Perez-Beltrachini [2018] use the learned graph representation with a standard attention-based encoder-decoder architecture [Bahdanau et al., 2014, Luong et al., 2015] to generate a natural language text verbalising the content expressed in the graph. They show that the generators with the GCN encoders on two graph-to-sequence tasks, e.g., RDF generation (WebNLG task; Gardent et al., 2017b, 2017a) and deep dependency graph realisation (Surface Realisation Challenge; Belz et al. 2011) outperform standard LSTM-based sequential encoders.

5.4   SUMMARY

In this chapter, we discussed advance encoders which explicitly tries to model apparent structure in the input. The hierarchical document encoders are modelling document as a meaningful sequence of sentences or paragraphs, whereas the graph encoders explicitly model the input graph. When evaluated, these models advance state-of-the-art document summarisation, AMR-to-text generation, and RDF-to-text generation tasks.

There is another trend which focuses on improving input understanding by implicitly capturing relevant structure present in the input. The Transformer model [Vaswani et al., 2017], based solely on attention mechanisms, and the convolutional sequence-to-sequence model [Gehring et al., 2017, Narayan et al., 2018b], based solely on convolutional network, avoid modelling long text using complex recurrent networks and better capture long-range dependencies. The contextualised word embeddings [Devlin et al., 2019, Peters et al., 2018, Radford et al., 2018, 2019] show that they accout for long-range dependencies much better than their traditional counterpart Word2Vec [Mikolov et al., 2013] and GloVe [Pennington et al., 2014] representations. However, it has not yet been explored if these representations could be useful with the structural encoders.

CHAPTER 6

Modelling Task-Specific Communication Goals

In Chapter 1, we saw that two main factors impact text production: the input type (data, text, or meaning representations) and the communication goal (e.g., summarising a text, simplifying a text, or generating a user-specific response for dialogue generation). In this chapter, we focus on the second factor: communication goals. Models discussed in earlier chapters are agnostic to the communication goal. They are often trained in a supervised setting using a maximum likelihood objective; they solely rely on the training data for signals implicitly capturing communicative goals. In this chapter, we will discuss how communication goal-oriented generators can be useful for text production. In particular, we will focus on generators that are specifically trained for summarisation, simplification, to profile user for dialogue-response generation, or to generate from loosely aligned data.

We will focus on two categories of communication goal-oriented generators. The first category focuses on augmenting the neural architecture to better accommodate the task-specific requirements such as *content selection* for document summarisation and generation from loosely aligned data, and *user profiling* for dialogue-response generation. The second category focuses on augmenting the training objective to either encourage *content selection* using *multi-tasking* or optimise task-specific evaluation measures using *reinforcement learning*.

6.1 TASK-SPECIFIC KNOWLEDGE FOR CONTENT SELECTION

Communication goals from different text-production tasks often focus on very different aspects. For example, paraphrase generation [Madnani and Dorr, 2010] aims at generating text that verbalises the exact content expressed by the input text but differently; an output text from paraphrase generation often has a one-to-one semantic correspondence with the input text. However, this is not the case with document summarisation [Mani, 1999, Nenkova and McKeown, 2011, Spärck Jones, 2007]. The summaries generated in document summarisation must distil the content of the document into a few important facts. This is very challenging as the compression ratio is extremely high, and pertinent content can easily be missed.

Similar issues arise when dealing with generation from data (e.g., RDF triples Gardent et al., 2017a) or meaning representations (e.g., AMRs May and Priyadarshi, 2017, and dependency

Input Sentence	Output Sentence
The Sri Lankan government on Wednesday announced the closure of government schools with immediate effect as a military campaign against Tamil separatists escalated in the north of the country.	Sri Lanka closed schools as war escalates.

Figure 6.1: An example of abstractive sentence summarisation from Zhou et al. [2017]. A summariser should be able to distil the salient information (highlighted in blue) from the rest to generate a good summary sentence.

trees Mille et al., 2018) compared to generation from loosely aligned data (e.g., summarising Wikipedia infoboxes Lebret et al., 2016 or NBA basketball game data records; Wiseman et al., 2017). When the goal is to verbalise RDF triples or AMR graphs, the output text aims at capturing the exact content expressed by the input representation. However, in the case of text production from loosely aligned data, the information present in the input may not be expressed in the output text.

Modelling both types of text-production tasks, one where there is a one-to-one semantic correspondence between the input representation and the output text, and another, where this is not the case, with a communication-goal agnostic architecture may not be optimal. In the first case, the model must learn to verbalise all the input and only the input content, whereas in the second case, it must both learn to select relevant content and to verbalise it.

In recent years, several approaches have been proposed which particularly aim at improving content selection for text production by proposing task-specific architectures or augmenting training objectives. In this section, we discuss some of those; in particular we describe architectures for text summarisation and for generation from loosely aligned data.

6.1.1 SELECTIVE ENCODING TO CAPTURE SALIENT INFORMATION

The standard attention-based sequence-to-sequence model has achieved huge success in tasks like machine translation [Bahdanau et al., 2014] and paraphrase generation [Mallinson et al., 2017]. Its success is partly credited to its ability to dynamically align tokens between all parts of the input and output. However, these models are shown to be inadequate for text summarisation where the compression ratio is extremely high and, consequently, the alignment becomes strenuous [Narayan et al., 2018b, Zhou et al., 2017].

Figure 6.1 shows an example for sentence summarisation or title generation. As can be seen, the main challenge here is not to infer the alignment, but to first select the important content from the input, and then to rephrase or paraphrase to produce an abstractive summary. The standard attention-based encoding-decoding framework implicitly models this, but it suffers from generating inconsistent outputs. Zhou et al. [2017] extend the sequence-to-sequence

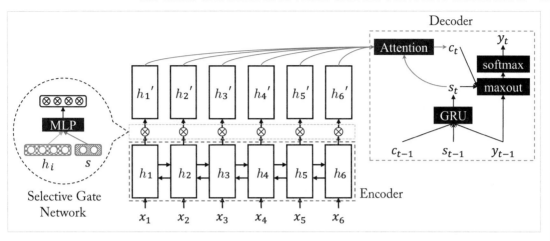

Figure 6.2: Selective encoding proposed by Zhou et al. [2017] for abstractive sentence summarisation.

framework for abstractive sentence summarisation which explicitly models this selection process. Figure 6.2 sketches their model.

Zhou et al. [2017] augments the standard sequence-to-sequence framework to a three-phase process: encoding of an input sentence (encoder), content selection using a selective gate network, and decoding an output summary (decoder) using the selected information. First, the input sentence is read using a bidirectional GRU to get the first-level sentence representation. However, instead of directly passing this representation to the decoder as in the standard sequence-to-sequence framework, the selective gate network controls the information flow from encoder to decoder by applying a gate network to construct the second-level sentence representation. A standard attention-based decoder works with the second-level sentence representation and produces the output summary using the selected information.

Formally, the first-level sentence representation $\mathbf{s} = [\overleftarrow{\mathbf{h}}_1; \overrightarrow{\mathbf{h}}_n]$ is learned by concatenating forward and backward hidden states of the bidirectional GRU encoder. The selective gate network builds a second level of sentence representation identifying the importance of each input word before decoding. At each time step i, the selective gate takes two inputs, the sentence representation $\mathbf{s}$ and the word representation $\mathbf{h}_i$ for the word w_i from the encoder layer, to compute the gate vector sGate_i:

$$\text{sGate}_i = \sigma(\mathbf{W}\mathbf{h}_i + \mathbf{U}\mathbf{s} + b) \tag{6.1}$$

where, $\mathbf{W}$, $\mathbf{U}$, and b are model parameters. Finally, the second-level word representations $\mathbf{h}'_i$ for word w_i are learned as:

$$\mathbf{h}'_i = \mathbf{h}_i \odot \text{sGate}_i. \tag{6.2}$$

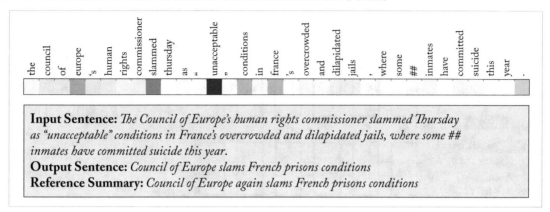

Input Sentence: *The Council of Europe's human rights commissioner slammed Thursday as "unacceptable" conditions in France's overcrowded and dilapidated jails, where some ## inmates have committed suicide this year.*
Output Sentence: *Council of Europe slams French prisons conditions*
Reference Summary: *Council of Europe again slams French prisons conditions*

Figure 6.3: Heat map shown in Zhou et al. [2017] learned with the selective gate mechanism. The important words relevant for the output are selected in the input sentence, such as "Europe", "slammed", and "unacceptable".

The final word representations $(\mathbf{h}'_1, \mathbf{h}'_2, \ldots, \mathbf{h}'_n)$ from the selective gate network are passed to the attention-based sequential decoder to generate the summary. This way the selective gate modifies the representation of each word with its salience before it passes them to the attentive decoder.

Figure 6.3 shows an example input sentence, the corresponding system-generated summary, reference summary, and attention heat map of the output with respect to the selective gate. As is shown, the selective gate assists sequence-to-sequence models to do better content selection and successfully identifies salient words, e.g., "Europe", "slammed", and "unacceptable" in the input sentence. Zhou et al. [2017] evaluate their selective gating mechanism on sentence summarisation [Graff et al., 2003] and sentence compression [Toutanova et al., 2016] and show that their model outperforms standard attention-based sequence-to-sequence models.

6.1.2   BOTTOM-UP COPY ATTENTION FOR CONTENT SELECTION

Zhou et al. [2017] use the selective gate to identify the importance of each word in the input sentence. The selective encoding mechanism is shown to be effective for sentence summarisation; however, modelling content selection effectively for a long input sequence (e.g., in document summarisation) can be troublesome. Gehrmann et al. [2018] took a different approach for content selection for abstractive document summarisation. They proposed a simple two-step process for addressing this issue: first, use a separate data-efficient content selection module to determine phrases in a source document that could be relevant for the summary, and second, augment the attentional neural decoder with the copy mechanism [See et al., 2017] to copy only from the masked relevant phrases. Figure 6.4 describes this two-step process for content selection followed by summary generation.

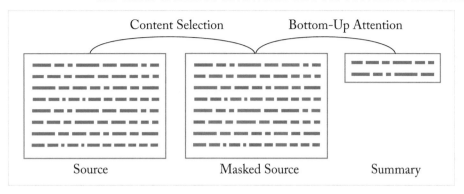

Figure 6.4: The two-step process for content selection and summary generation proposed by Gehrmann et al. [2018].

Content Selection.   The process of identifying relevant phrases in the source document can be defined as a word-level extractive summarisation task [Cheng and Lapata, 2016]. Given a document D as a sequence of tokens $\{w_1, w_2, \ldots, w_n\}$, it generates a sequence of binary tags $\{t_1, t_2, \ldots, t_n\}$ labelling each token in the document; $t_i = 1$ if the token is relevant for the summary and $t_i = 0$, otherwise. Gehrmann et al. [2018] models this sequence labelling task with a standard bidirectional LSTM model with deep contextualised word embeddings (ELMo; Peters et al., 2018) trained with maximum likelihood for the sequence labelling problem. Let $\mathbf{h}_i$ be the estimated representation from Bi-LSTM for a word w_i; the probability p_i that the word is relevant is computed as $p_i = \sigma(\mathbf{W}\mathbf{h}_i + b)$, where $\mathbf{W}$ and b are model parameters. We set $t_i = 1$ if $p_i > \epsilon$ and $t_i = 0$, otherwise; ϵ is a hyperparameter.

Bottom-up Attention.   Next, an attention mask is applied to constrain copying words to the selected parts ($t_i = 1$) of the source text to produce a fluent summary with relevant words from the source text. Gehrmann et al. [2018] only use this during the inference time. First, a standard pointer-generator model of See et al. [2017] is trained on the full data set. During the inference time, we modify the attention a_j^i at the decoding step j to the word w_i in the source document to $\tilde{a}_j^i = a_j^i$, if $t_i = 1$, or $\tilde{a}_j^i = 0$, otherwise. The resulting attention distribution is normalised and then passed as the new copy probabilities to the pointer-generator decoder.

Summarisation data sets often do not come with gold word-level extractive labels to train the content selector. However, these supervised training data are often easily extrapolated by aligning the summaries to the document in the extractive approaches [Cheng and Lapata, 2016, Nallapati et al., 2017, Narayan et al., 2018c]. One obvious advantage of the two-step alternative to content selection is that it does not require large amounts of training data and can be adapted to new domains and to long input sequences.

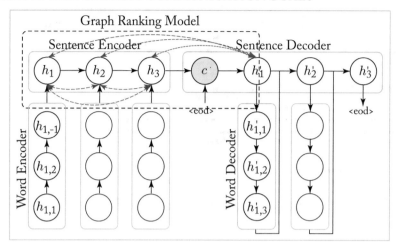

Figure 6.5: Graph-based attention mechanism [Tan et al., 2017] to select salient sentences for abstractive document summarisation.

6.1.3   GRAPH-BASED ATTENTION FOR SALIENT SENTENCE DETECTION

In the previous two sections, we discussed two approaches that focus on selecting salient words in the source text. Few other approaches [Chen and Bansal, 2018, Hsu et al., 2018, Tan et al., 2017] have focused on content selection at the sentence level. In this section, we describe a graph-based attention mechanism of Tan et al. [2017] that blends ideas from pre-neural graph-based extractive approaches with the standard attention mechanism [Bahdanau et al., 2014] in the encoder-decoder framework to identify salient sentences in the input document.

Tan et al. [2017] proposed a hierarchical encoder-decoder architecture for abstractive document summarisation (we have discussed this model in Section 5.2.1 for their hierarchical representation of the document; for better input understanding, see Figure 5.6). The hierarchical encoder first models sentences as sequences of words, and then the document is modelled as a sequence of sentences. The summary decoder is also hierarchical; it first predicts a sequence of sentences, then for each sentence, predicts a sequence of words. The decoder uses a graph-based attention mechanism (see Figure 6.5) to find sentence s_i in the source document to attend while generating sentence s'_j with the decoding state $\mathbf{h}'_j$. The proposed graph-based attention mechanism improves over the standard attention mechanism [Bahdanau et al., 2014] in (i) identifying s_i that are relevant to current decoding state $\mathbf{h}'_j$ (by aligning input and output sentences) and (ii) identifying s_i that are globally important in the input document.

Graph-Based Attention Mechanism.   The graph-based attention is inspired by the idea that "a sentence is important in a document if it is heavily linked with many important sentences" from graph-based sentence extraction algorithms such as TextRank [Mihalcea and Tarau, 2004] and LexRank [Erkan and Radev, 2004], which are based on the PageRank [Page et al., 1998] algorithm.

More formally, the global salience score of sentence s_i in traditional graph-based extractive summarisation is estimated by comparing its similarity to all other sentences in the document. A graph $G = (V, E)$ is constructed where V is the set of n sentences in the document and E denotes the set of edges between sentences capturing similarity among them. The saliency scores of the sentences are determined as:

$$\mathbf{f} = (1 - \lambda)(1 - \lambda \mathbf{W} \mathbf{D}^{-1})^{-1} \mathbf{y} \qquad (6.3)$$

where, $\mathbf{f} \in R^n$ denotes the salience scores of the n sentences. $\mathbf{W} \in R^{n \times n}$ is the adjacent matrix with $\mathbf{W}(i, j) = \mathbf{h}_i^T \mathbf{M} \mathbf{h}_j$ where h_i and h_j are sentence representations for s_i and s_j, respectively, $\mathbf{M}$ is a model parameter. $\mathbf{D}$ is a diagonal matrix with $\mathbf{D}(i, i) = \sum_j \mathbf{W}(i, j)$. λ is a damping factor and $\mathbf{y} \in R^n$, with all elements equal to $1/n$.

In addition to estimating the global saliency of each sentence s_i in the document, we would like to compare the similarity of s_i to the currently generated sentence s'_j. This is modelled as a query-focused graph-based extractive summarisation problem [Wan et al., 2007] using the topic-sensitive PageRank algorithm [Haveliwala, 2002]. In particular, we treat the current decoding state $\mathbf{h}'_j$ as the topic and construct a new graph G^j by adding it into G as the 0-th pseudo sentence. We modify $\mathbf{y}$ as $\mathbf{y}^j \in R^{n+1}$, a one hot vector with $y(0) = 1$ indicating that the 0-th sentence s'_j is the query. Finally, the importance score $\mathbf{f}^j$ for all the input sentences when generating sentence s'_j is estimated as:

$$\mathbf{f}^j = (1 - \lambda)(1 - \lambda \mathbf{W}^j \mathbf{D}^{j^{-1}})^{-1} \mathbf{y}^j, \qquad (6.4)$$

$\mathbf{W}^j$ is the new adjacent matrix for graph G^j with $\mathbf{h}'_j$ and $\mathbf{D}^j$ is the new diagonal matrix corresponding to $\mathbf{W}^j$. This way the attention score $a_i^j = f^j(i)$ for sentence s_i in the document when decoding s'_j finds sentences which are both globally important and relevant to current decoding state $\mathbf{h}'_j$.[1] Equation (6.4) for the graph-based attention is differentiable; it can be trained jointly within the encoder-decoder framework using traditional gradient-based methods.

Tan et al.'s graph-based attention is limited to identifying salient sentences in the document. The sequences of words in s'_j are generated starting with the decoding state $\mathbf{h}'_j$ without any word-level attention. Consequently, Tan et al. report inferior performance to the pointer-generator model of See et al. [2017]. Hsu et al. [2018] took a different approach and model content selection both at a sentence and word levels. They modulate the word-level attention from the pointer-generator model with the sentence-level attention from the extractive model of Nallapati et al. [2017] such that words in less attended sentences are less likely to be generated.

---

[1]Tan et al. [2017] also use a distraction mechanism [Chen et al., 2016] to compute the final attention value as an alternative to the coverage mechanism [See et al., 2017]. We refer the reader to Tan et al. [2017] for more details.

Born	Robert Joseph Flaherty February 16, 1884
Died	July 23, 1951, U.S.
Occupation	Filmmaker
Spouse(s)	Frances Johnson Hubbard

Robert Joseph Flaherty (February 16, 1884 July 23, 1951) was an **American film-maker**. Flaherty was married to **Frances H. Flaherty** until his death in 1951.

Figure 6.6: Generating biography for "Robert Flaherty" from its Wikipedia infobox. The infobox consists of a set of property-value pairs (source: Laura Perez-Beltrachini).

6.1.4   MULTI-INSTANCE AND MULTI-TASK LEARNING FOR CONTENT SELECTION

So far we have mainly discussed text-to-text generation (in particular, text summarisation) where content selection is of significant interest. Here, we present a case of text generation from loosely aligned data-text resources. Figure 6.6 shows an example of generating biographies from Wikipedia data [Lebret et al., 2016, Perez-Beltrachini and Lapata, 2018]. As can be seen, multiple property-value pairs in the input Wikipedia data (shown on the left) are not expressed in its biography (shown on the right). It is essential for a model to recognise property-value pairs that are important from those that are not in order to do better in this task. The standard attention-based encoder-decoder architecture [Bahdanau et al., 2014, Luong et al., 2015] does this implicitly but is not optimal; the soft attention mechanism will distribute the attention weights over the whole set of property-value pairs in the input.

Perez-Beltrachini and Lapata [2018] proposed a two-step process: first, a specific content selector is trained using the multi-instance learning [Keeler et al., 1991] to discover alignments between data and text pairs, and then, the alignments are used to guide the generation process to focus on salient property-value pairs. The latter is achieved by incorporating the alignment information in the training objective using multi-task learning [Caruana, 1997] and reinforcement learning [Williams, 1992]. Here, we will mainly focus on their best performing model using the multi-task learning based objective. We will shed some light on the reinforcement learning objective in Section 6.2.

Multi-Instance Learning for Data and Text Pair Alignment.   Given a loosely coupled data and text pair $(\mathcal{P}, \mathcal{T})$, where $\mathcal{P}$ is a set of property values $\{p_1 : v_1, \ldots, p_{|\mathcal{P}|} : v_{|\mathcal{P}|}\}$ and the related text $\mathcal{T}$ is a sequence of sentences $\{s_1, \ldots, s_{|\mathcal{T}|}\}$, we aim to learn a fine-grained alignment set

Words	Properties
married	*spouse : Frances Johnson Hubbard*
to	*spouse : Frances Johnson Hubbard*
Frances	*spouse : Frances Johnson Hubbard*
Flaherty	*spouse : Frances Johnson Hubbard*
death	*died : July 23, 1951*
in	*died : July 23, 1951*
1951	*died : July 23, 1951*

Figure 6.7: Example of word-property alignments for the Wikipedia abstract and facts in Figure 6.6 (source: Laura Perez-Beltrachini).

$\mathcal{A}(\mathcal{P}, \mathcal{T})$ which contains property-value word pairs. We first derive $|\mathcal{T}|$ pairs of the form $(\mathcal{P}, s)$ where $|\mathcal{T}|$ is the number of sentences in $\mathcal{T}$. We encode property sets $\mathcal{P}$ and sentences s into a common multimodal h-dimensional embedding space.

The property-value set $\mathcal{P}$ is encoded as $\{\mathbf{p}_1, \ldots, \mathbf{p}_{|\mathcal{P}|}\}$, where $\mathbf{p}_i$ is the bidirectional LSTM representation of $p_i : v_i$ encoded individually as a sequence $p_i v_i$. Similarly, s is encoded as a sequence of words $\{w_1, \ldots, w_{|s|}\}$ using a bidirectional LSTM into $\{\mathbf{w}_1, \ldots, \mathbf{w}_{|s|}\}$, where $\mathbf{w}_i$ is concatenation of the forward and backward outputs of the networks for word w_i. We define similarity between $\mathcal{P}$ and s as the sum of similarity between each word to the best scoring property value:

$$S_{\mathcal{P}s} = \sum_{j=1}^{|s|} \max_{i \in \{1, \ldots, |\mathcal{P}|\}} \mathbf{p_i} \cdot \mathbf{w_j}. \tag{6.5}$$

Note that the similarity function automatically seeks to align each word to the best scoring property value. We use a multi-instance learning objective [Keeler et al., 1991] to maximise the similarity between related pairs $(\mathcal{P}, s)$ while minimising it for unrelated pairs $(\mathcal{P}', s)$ or $(\mathcal{P}, s')$:

$$L_{MIL} = max(0, S_{\mathcal{P}s} - S_{\mathcal{P}'s} + 1) + max(0, S_{\mathcal{P}s} - S_{\mathcal{P}s'} + 1). \tag{6.6}$$

Perez-Beltrachini and Lapata [2018] use the trained content aligner to predict fine-grained alignment between property-value pairs to words in $\mathcal{T}$. Figure 6.7 shows an example of word-property alignment for the input shown in Figure 6.6. This alignment is then used to enhance the content signal while training a generator in a multi-task setting.

Multi-Task Objective for Content Selection and Generation.   Perez-Beltrachini and Lapata [2018] use multi-task training [Caruana, 1997] to train a generator which not only learns to output a sequence of words but also to predict alignment labels for each word.

The generator is a standard attention-based sequence-to-sequence [Bahdanau et al., 2014, Luong et al., 2015] model which takes a set of properties $\mathcal{P}$ and generates a text Y as a sequence of words one word at a time. However, instead of encoding $\mathcal{P}$ using a single encoder, we individually encode each property-value pair as done earlier by the content aligner. Hence, $\mathcal{P}$ is encoded as $\{\mathbf{p}_1, \ldots, \mathbf{p}_{|\mathcal{P}|}\}$. The decoder is initialised with the averaged sum of the encoded property-value pair representations, and it generates a word y_t at time step t with a probability:

$$p(y_{t+1}|y_{1:t}, \mathcal{P}) = \text{softmax}(\mathbf{W}_o \tanh(\mathbf{W}_c[\mathbf{h}_t; \mathbf{c}_t])) \tag{6.7}$$

where $\mathbf{h}_t$ is the decoder state, $\mathbf{c}_t$ is the dynamic context vector estimated comparing $\mathbf{h}_t$ and $\{\mathbf{p}_1, \ldots, \mathbf{p}_{|\mathcal{P}|}\}$, and $\mathbf{W}_o$ and $\mathbf{W}_c$ are model parameters. The generator is then trained to optimise negative log-likelihood:

$$L(\boldsymbol{\theta})_{\text{NLL}} = -\sum_{t=1}^{|Y|} \log p(y_t|y_{1:t-1}, \mathcal{P}; \boldsymbol{\theta}). \tag{6.8}$$

In addition to predicting a word at each time step t, the decoder is also trained to predict a binary label a_t indicating whether it aligns with some property in the input set $\mathcal{P}$:

$$p(a_{t+1}|y_{1:t}, \mathcal{P}) = \text{sigmoid}(\mathbf{W}'_o \tanh(\mathbf{W}'_c[\mathbf{h}_t; \mathbf{c}_t])) \tag{6.9}$$

where, $\mathbf{W}'_o$ and $\mathbf{W}'_c$ are model parameters. This leads to another auxiliary objective function:

$$L(\boldsymbol{\theta})_{\text{Align}} = -\sum_{t=1}^{|Y|} \log p(a_t|y_{1:t-1}, \mathcal{P}; \boldsymbol{\theta}). \tag{6.10}$$

The combined multi-task learning objective $L(\boldsymbol{\theta})_{\text{MTL}}$ aims to optimise the weighted sum of the primary word prediction loss and the auxiliary alignment prediction loss:

$$L(\boldsymbol{\theta})_{\text{MTL}} = \lambda L(\boldsymbol{\theta})_{\text{NLL}} + (1 - \lambda)L(\boldsymbol{\theta})_{\text{Align}} \tag{6.11}$$

where, λ is a hyperparameter of the model to guide the update of the gradient caused by each loss.

Instead of using content-specific architectures, Perez-Beltrachini and Lapata [2018] augment the training with the content-specific objectives. The sequential decoder with a negative log-likelihood objective only works as a conditional language model and is prone to generating texts that are very common in the training data but are not consistent with the input. The auxiliary alignment objective will smooth the probabilities of frequent sequences when trying to simultaneously predict alignment labels. Perez-Beltrachini and Lapata [2018] evaluate their model on the task of generating biographies from Wikipedia data [Lebret et al., 2016]. They show that models trained with content-specific objectives improve upon vanilla encoder-decoder architectures which rely solely on the attention mechanism.

In summary, there is surge of interest in developing neural models with dedicated architectures and objectives for selecting content for the text-production task. We only reviewed some of them here. We refer the reader to a few other publications of interest: Li et al. [2018a] extract a set of keywords from the document that is used to guide the summarisation process; Zhou et al. [2017], Li et al. [2018c] use dedicated gates to filter input representation; and Gehrmann et al. [2018] and others modulate the attention based on how likely a word or a sentence is included in a summary [Cohan et al., 2018, Hsu et al., 2018]. Recently, Narayan et al. [2018b] used topic vectors automatically learned using the latent Dirichlet allocation model [Blei et al., 2003] within the convolutional sequence-to-sequence learning framework [Gehring et al., 2017] to foreground salient words in the document for summarisation. Puduppully et al. [2019] learn a content plan to generate summaries for the RotoWire corpus consisting of basketball game data records [Wiseman et al., 2017].

6.2   OPTIMISING TASK-SPECIFIC EVALUATION METRIC WITH REINFORCEMENT LEARNING

Most of the text-production models we have studied so far are typically trained using cross-entropy loss in order to maximise the likelihood of the ground-truth sequence (e.g., abstractive summary generation) or labels (e.g., labels for extreme summarisation). This leads to two main discrepancies between the model and the text-production task in hand. The model is trained to maximise the likelihood of the next correct word or label given the previous words and the input context. However, at test time the model generates the entire output from scratch. This discrepancy leads to a problem called *exposure bias* [Ranzato et al., 2015] in sequential decoders, and it makes the generation brittle. Another discrepancy is an obvious outcome of cross-entropy loss: the model maximises the likelihood of the ground-truth output and not the task-specific evaluation metrics. The latter is specially a matter of concern in the context of text production; it is essential that what we generate is meaningful and consistent with the input.

Recently, several models have addressed these discrepancies by directly optimising the task-specific evaluation metric at test time. One thing that they have in common is the use of reinforcement learning [Sutton and Barto, 1998, Williams, 1992] in their training algorithm. Instead of maximising the likelihood of each prediction at each time step, the model first generates the whole sequence, and a reward (often the evaluation metric at test time) is estimated by comparing the predicted sequence to the ground-truth sequence. The reward is then used to update the model parameters; eventually the model learns to maximise the reward during training.

This section discusses how reinforcement learning can be used to directly optimise the task-specific evaluation metric. In particular, we will discuss a common algorithm called *policy learning* which allows us to maximise a non-differentiable reward efficiently. We will discuss several models for text summarisation and generation from loosely aligned data, where reinforcement learning has been used.

6.2.1   THE PITFALLS OF CROSS-ENTROPY LOSS

Text-production models are typically trained using cross-entropy loss in order to maximise the likelihood of the ground-truth sequence and do not necessarily learn to optimise task-specific objectives. To recap, they optimise the likelihood of a ground-truth sequence y given some input data or text x by maximising $p(y|x, \theta) = \prod_{i=1}^{n} p(y_i|y_{1,i-1}, x, \theta)$, where y could be either a sequence of words (e.g., text-production tasks such as abstractive summarisation [See et al., 2017] or AMR generation [Konstas et al., 2017], or a sequence of binary labels labelling each word or sentence in the input x (e.g., text-production tasks such as extractive summarisation; Cheng and Lapata, 2016), and θ are model parameters. This objective can be achieved by minimising the negative log probability at each decoding step:

$$L(\theta) = -\sum_{i=1}^{n} \log p(y_{1,i-1}, x, \theta). \tag{6.12}$$

The Cross-entropy training leads to two kinds of discrepancies in the model.

Exposure Bias with Cross-Entropy Training.   The first discrepancy comes from the way the cross-entropy objective exposes models to different levels of information during training and test times. During training, a model with the cross-entropy objective is trained to maximise the likelihood of the next correct word or label y_i given the previous ground-truth words $y_{1,i-1}$ and the input context x. However, at test time, the model is supposed to generate the entire output y' from scratch as a sequence $\{y'_1, \ldots, y'_n\}$, i.e., at time step i, the model generates y_i given the input context x and the previously generated sequence $y'_{1,i-1}$ and not the ground truth sequence. Figure 6.8, borrowed from Ranzato et al. [2015], sketches this *exposure bias* problem in cross-entropy trained models.

   The exposure bias in-text production models makes the generation brittle because the models were exposed to ground-truth data distribution during the training time, but during the test time they only have access to their own predictions. As a result, the errors made by the models at various time steps will accumulate and deteriorate the overall quality of an output sequence y'.

Disconnect between Task and Training Objectives.   The second discrepancy results from the disconnect between the text-production task and maximum-likelihood training objectives. Models trained with the maximum-likelihood objective are optimised to learn the likelihood of ground-truth label sequences; they are not necessarily trained to optimise task-specific objectives.

   Automatic task-specific objectives primarily focus on measuring the n-gram overlap between the model-generated text and the reference text. The precision-oriented metric BLEU [Papineni et al., 2002] from machine translation is very common among text-production tasks involving sentence generation, e.g., from AMRs [May and Priyadarshi, 2017] and from RDF [Gardent et al., 2017a], dialogue act generation [Novikova et al., 2017b], sentence com-

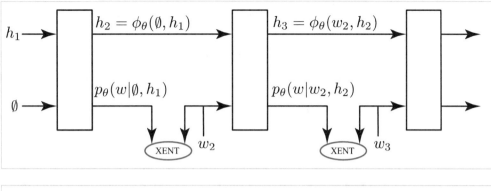

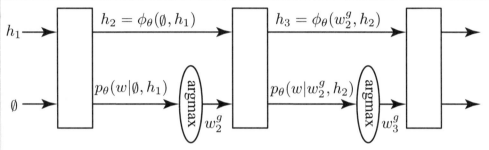

Figure 6.8: The exposure bias in cross-entropy trained models [Ranzato et al., 2015]. The figure sketches the difference in behaviours in RNN-based models during training with the cross-entropy loss (XENT, top) and at test time for generation (bottom). At training time, the model is provided with the reference words at each time step, but at test time, it uses the best predicted word (with argmax) form the previous step.

pression [Filippova et al., 2015], and sentence simplification [Narayan and Gardent, 2014]. Several other metrics have been developed to capture task-specific characteristics: document summarisation models are often evaluated using the recall-oriented metric ROUGE [Lin and Hovy, 2003]; for sentence simplification, SARI [Xu et al., 2016] has been particularly developed to not only capture the similarity of the generated text to the reference text, but also its dissimilarity from the input text; and, SMATCH [Cai and Knight, 2013] used for AMR generation takes the input AMR structure into account.

Automatic task-specific metrics like BLEU or ROUGE are quick ways to evaluate text-production systems, but they are not optimal [Reiter, 2018, Schluter, 2017] and do not always correlate well with humans, given the tasks at hand. Hence, automatic evaluation is often accompanied by human evaluators accessing the generated texts for their general qualities (e.g., correctness, fluency, grammaticality, and discourse coherency), task-specific requirements (e.g., informativeness for summarisation and readability for simplification), and human preference.

While minimising cross-entropy loss is a simple way of training models, it falls short of correctly modelling the communication goals that underly text-production.

A Case of Extractive Summarisation.   We describe a case of extractive summarisation where the issues related to the cross-entropy objective get doubly amplified in the absence of ground-truth labels.

Earlier work for neural extractive summarisation [Cheng and Lapata, 2016, Nallapati et al., 2017] optimises neural models by maximising $p(y|D, \theta) = \prod_{i=1}^{n} p(y_i|s_i, D, \theta)$, the likelihood of the ground-truth labels $y = (y_1, y_2, ..., y_n)$ for sentences $(s_1, s_2, ..., s_n)$, given document D and model parameters θ, by minimising the cross-entropy loss. This way of training suffers from exposure bias and fails to optimise the ROUGE metric used for evaluation. Irrespective of these issues, cross-entropy training is not optimal for extractive summarisation due to its reliance on ground-truth labels.

Document collections for training-summarisation systems do not naturally contain labels indicating which sentences should be extracted. Instead, they are typically accompanied by abstractive summaries from which sentence-level labels are extrapolated.[2] Cheng and Lapata [2016] follow Woodsend and Lapata [2010] in adopting a rule-based method which assigns labels to each sentence in the document *individually* based on its semantic correspondence with the gold summary (see the fourth column in Table 6.1). An alternative method [Cao et al., 2016, Nallapati et al., 2017, Svore et al., 2007] identifies the set of sentences which *collectively* gives the highest ROUGE with respect to the gold summary. Sentences in this set are labelled with 1, otherwise 0. Table 6.1 shows the two types of sentence labelling (individual vs. collective oracle columns) for an example CNN article.

Maximum-likelihood training with either individual or collective labels will fail to generalise to unseen data. Labelling sentences individually often generates too many positive labels, causing the model to overfit the data. For example, the document in Table 6.1 has 12 positively labelled sentences out of 31 in total (only the first 10 are shown). Collective labels present a better alternative since they only pertain to the few sentences deemed most suitable to form the summary. However, a model trained with cross-entropy loss on collective labels will underfit the data as it will only maximise probabilities $p(1|s_i, D, \theta)$ for sentences in this set (e.g., sentences {0, 11, 13} in Table 6.1) and ignore all other sentences. We found that there are many candidate summaries with high ROUGE scores which could be considered during training.

Table 6.1 (last column) shows candidate summaries ranked according to the mean of ROUGE-1, ROUGE-2, and ROUGE-L F_1 scores. Interestingly, multiple top-ranked summaries have reasonably high ROUGE scores. For example, the average ROUGE for the summaries ranked second (0,13), third (11,13), and fourth (0,1,13) is 57.5%, 57.2%, and 57.1%, and all top 16 summaries have ROUGE scores more or equal to 50%. A few sentences are indicative of important content and appear frequently in the summaries: sentence 13 occurs in all sum-

---

[2]This is often true for other extractive text-production tasks such as sentence compression [Filippova et al., 2015]. Binary word labels are extrapolated by comparing the input sentence to the reference sentence.

Table 6.1: An abridged CNN article (only first 15 out of 31 sentences are shown) and its "story highlights". The latter are typically written by journalists to allow readers to quickly gather information on stories. Highlights are often used as gold-standard abstractive summaries in the summarisation literature. (*Continues.*)

Sent. Pos.	CNN Article Sentences	Sent-Level ROUGE	Individual Oracle	Collective Oracle	Multiple Collective Oracle
0	A debilitating, mosquito-borne virus called Chikungunya has made its way to North Carolina, health officials say.	21.2	1	1	(0, 11, 13) : 59.3 (0,13) : 57.5
1	It's the state's first reported case of the virus.	18.1	1	0	(11,13) : 57.2
2	The patient was likely infected in the Caribbean, according to the Forsyth County Department of Public Health.	11.2	1	0	(0,1,13) : 57.1 (1,13) : 56.6
3	Chikungunya is primarily found in Africa, East Asia and the Caribbean islands, but the Centers for Disease Control and Prevention has been watching the virus,+ for fear that it could take hold in the U.S.—much like West Nile did more than a decade ago.	35.6	1	0	(3,11,13) : 55.0 (13) : 54.5 (0,3,13) : 54.2 (3,13) : 53.4
4	The virus, which can cause joint pain and arthritis-like symptoms, has been on the U.S. public health radar for some time.	16.7	1	0	(1,3,13) : 52.9 (1,11,13) : 52.0
5	About 25–28 infected travelers bring it to the U.S. each year, said Roger Nasci, chief of the CDC's Arboviral Disease Branch in the Division of Vector-Borne Diseases.	9.7	0	0	(0,9,13) : 51.3 (0,7,13) : 51.3 (0,12,13) : 51.0
6	"We haven't had any locally transmitted cases in the U.S. thus far," Nasci said.	7.4	0	0	(9,11,13) : 50.4 (1,9,13) : 50.1
7	But a major outbreak in the Caribbean this year—with more than 100,000 cases reported—has health officials concerned.	16.4	1	0	(12,13) : 49.3 (7,11,13) : 47.8
8	Experts say American tourists are bringing Chikungunya back home, and it's just a matter of time before it starts to spread within the U.S.	10.6	0	0	(0,10,13) : 47.8 (11,12,13):47.7 (7,13) : 47.6
9	After all, the Caribbean is a popular one with American tourists, and summer is fast approaching.	13.9	1	0	(9,13) : 47.5 (1,7,13) : 46.9

Table 6.1: (*Continued*.) An abridged CNN article (only first 15 out of 31 sentences are shown) and its "story highlights". The latter are typically written by journalists to allow readers to quickly gather information on stories. Highlights are often used as gold-standard abstractive summaries in the summarisation literature.

10	"So far this year we've recorded 8 travel-associated cases, and 7 of them have come from countries in the Caribbean where we know the virus is being transmitted," Nasci said.	18.4	1	0	(3,7,13) : 46.0 (3,12,13) : 46.0 (3,9,13) : 45.9
11	Other states have also reported cases of Chikungunya.	13.4	0	1	(10,13) : 45.5
12	The Tennessee Department of Health said the state has had multiple cases of the virus in people who have travelled to the Caribbean.	15.6	1	0	(4,11,13) : 45.3 (1,12,13) : 45.2
13	The virus is not deadly, but it can be painful, with symptoms lasting for weeks.	54.5	1	1	(0,4,13) : 45.2 (10,11,13):45.2
14	Those with weak immune systems, such as the elderly, are more likely to suffer from the virus' side effects than those who are healthier.	5.5	0	0	(9,12,13) : 43.5 ...

Story Highlights

• North Carolina reports first case of mosquito-borne virus called Chikungunya • Chikungunya is primarily found in Africa, East Asia and the Caribbean islands • Virus is not deadly, but it can be painful, with symptoms lasting for weeks

maries except one, and sentence 0 appears in several summaries, too. Also note that summaries (11,13) and (1,13) yield better ROUGE scores compared to longer summaries, and may be as informative, yet more concise, alternatives.

These discrepancies render the model less efficient at ranking sentences for the summarisation task. Instead of maximising the likelihood of the ground-truth labels, we could train the model to predict the individual ROUGE score for each sentence in the document and then select the top m sentences with the highest scores. But sentences with individual ROUGE scores do not necessarily lead to a high-scoring summary, e.g., they may convey overlapping content and form verbose and redundant summaries. For example, sentence 3, despite having a high individual ROUGE score (35.6%), does not occur in any of the top five summaries.

6.2.2   TEXT PRODUCTION AS A REINFORCEMENT LEARNING PROBLEM

We next explain how we address these issues by framing text-production in the reinforcement-learning paradigm [Sutton and Barto, 1998] to directly optimise the task-specific metric used

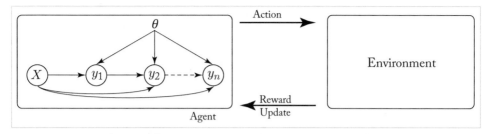

Figure 6.9: Text production as a reinforcement learning problem.

at test time. Figure 6.9 sketches a standard sequential decoder in the reinforcement learning paradigm.

In a standard setting, we view a text-production model as an *agent* which interacts with an *environment* with an access to reference texts. Each input data or text represents a *state*, and each *action* is an output text generated by the agent. At first, the agent is initialised randomly. It reads an input x and predicts an output sequence y' using *policy* $p(y'|x, \theta)$ where θ are model parameters. For abstractive cases, y' is the final output text, but for extractive cases, y' is the output sequence of labels; these labels are then used to extract words or sentences to assemble the final output text. After each action, the agent receives an immediate *reward r* commensurate with how well the final output text resembles the reference text. The transition between states is trivial because the inputs are interdependent. We learn to optimise the policy such that the agent can take an optimal action optimising its reward given a state.

We use reinforcement learning to optimise task-specific objectives; the reward function plays a crucial role here. We define the reward function such that it captures the key aspects of the target output with respect to the task. For example, it is common to use ROUGE [Lin and Hovy, 2003] as a reward function when building text summarisation systems [Celikyilmaz et al., 2018, Narayan et al., 2018c, Pasunuru and Bansal, 2018, Paulus et al., 2018]. Others encode more specific reward functions: Perez-Beltrachini and Lapata [2018] use content-selection-based rewards to generate from loosely aligned data; and Zhang and Lapata [2017] use SARI [Xu et al., 2016], relevance, and fluency as a joint reward for sentence simplification. We describe some of these works in a following section.

The REINFORCE Algorithm.   The reward functions or task-specific objectives are typically evaluated using discrete metrics and are not differentiable. We describe a commonly used policy gradient method which provides a workaround to optimise non-differentiable rewards. In particular, we describe the REINFORCE algorithm [Ranzato et al., 2015, Williams, 1992] to update the agent to minimise the negative expected reward:

$$L(\theta) = -\mathbb{E}_{\hat{y} \sim p_\theta}[r(\hat{y})] \tag{6.13}$$

$$= -\sum_{\hat{y} \sim p_\theta} r(\hat{y}) p(\hat{y}|x, \theta) \tag{6.14}$$

where, p_θ stands for $p(y|x, \theta)$. REINFORCE is based on the observation that the expected gradient of a non-differentiable reward function $r(\cdot)$ can be computed using the likelihood ratio trick as follows:

$$\nabla L(\theta) = -\sum_{\hat{y} \sim p_\theta} r(\hat{y}) \nabla p(\hat{y}|x, \theta) \tag{6.15}$$

$$= -\sum_{\hat{y} \sim p_\theta} r(\hat{y}) \frac{p(\hat{y}|x, \theta)}{p(\hat{y}|x, \theta)} \nabla p(\hat{y}|x, \theta) \tag{6.16}$$

$$= -\sum_{\hat{y} \sim p_\theta} (r(\hat{y}) \nabla \log p(\hat{y}|x, \theta)) p(\hat{y}|x, \theta) \tag{6.17}$$

$$= -\mathbb{E}_{\hat{y} \sim p_\theta}[r(\hat{y}) \nabla \log p_\theta(\hat{y}|x, \theta)]. \tag{6.18}$$

Computing the expectation term in Eq. (6.18) is prohibitively expensive, since there is a large number of possible output texts. In practice, we approximate the expected gradient using a single sample $\hat{y}$ from p_θ for each training example:

$$\nabla L(\theta) \approx -r(\hat{y}) \nabla \log p(\hat{y}|x, \theta) \tag{6.19}$$

$$\approx -r(\hat{y}) \sum_{i=1}^{n} \nabla \log p(\hat{y}_i|\hat{y}_{1,i-1}, x, \theta). \tag{6.20}$$

Hence, the REINFORCE algorithm defines an objective function that combines the maximum-likelihood cross-entropy loss with rewards from policy gradient reinforcement learning to globally optimise the evaluation metric relevant for the task. Presented in its original form, the algorithm starts learning with a random policy which can make model training challenging for complex tasks, like text production, where there is a very large number of candidate output texts. Often a baseline strategy is employed to decrease the learning variance [Ranzato et al., 2015, Zaremba and Sutskever, 2015]. An addition neural model is learned to estimate a baseline reward b given the input text x and the generated output text $\hat{y}$. The final gradient is then estimated as:

$$\nabla L(\theta) \approx -\sum_{i=1}^{n} \nabla \log p(\hat{y}_i|\hat{y}_{1,i-1}, x, \theta)][r(\hat{y}) - b]. \tag{6.21}$$

We refer the reader to Williams [1992] for the full derivation of the gradients. Equation (6.21) encourages the prediction of $\hat{y}$ if $r(\hat{y}) > b$, or discourages it if $r(\hat{y}) < b$. Consequently, b decreases the variance of the gradient shown in Eq. (6.21) compared to Eq. (6.20) where it is not used. Analogously, Narayan et al. [2018c] take a different approach to reduce the variance in Eq. (6.20) for extractive summarisation. Instead of sampling a random sample $\hat{y}$ from p_θ, they sample $\hat{y}$ from largest probability samples $\hat{\mathcal{Y}}$, to estimate the gradient. Narayan et al. [2018c] approximate $\hat{\mathcal{Y}}$ by k top scoring extracts against the reference summary. Table 6.1 (last column) shows candidate extracts ranked according to the mean of ROUGE-1, ROUGE-2, and ROUGE-L F_1 scores.

The latter approach of sampling $\hat{y}$ from the largest probability samples $\hat{\mathcal{Y}}$ to reduce the variance in Eq. (6.20) relies on the fact that $\hat{\mathcal{Y}}$ can be easily approximated.

For extractive summarisation, Narayan et al. [2018c] approximate $\hat{\mathcal{Y}}$ by the k extracts which receive highest ROUGE scores. More concretely, they assemble candidate summaries efficiently by first selecting p sentences from the document which on their own have high ROUGE scores. They then generate all possible combinations of p sentences subject to maximum length m and evaluate them against the gold summary. Summaries are ranked according to F_1 scores by taking the mean of ROUGE-1, ROUGE-2, and ROUGE-L. $\hat{\mathcal{Y}}$ contains these top k candidate summaries. During training, $\hat{y}$ is sampled from $\hat{\mathcal{Y}}$ instead of $p(\hat{y}|x, \theta)$.

The estimation of $\hat{\mathcal{Y}}$ for abstractive text-production tasks is unattainable. For example, for abstractive summarisation, writing k different top-ranking abstracts against the gold summary for each document in the training data is implausible. In such cases, the gradient estimator in Eq. (6.21) or the curriculum learning (see the next paragraph) are more reasonable solutions.

The Curriculum Learning Algorithm.   Ideally, REINFORCE algorithm starts with a random policy and gradually trains the model to converge toward the optimal policy; this could be expensive due to a large search space of text production. The curriculum learning strategy [Bengio et al., 2009, Ranzato et al., 2015] modifies the REINFORCE algorithm to effectively deal with the large search space of text production. It starts with a sub-optimal policy and then gradually teaches the model to converge toward the optimal policy exploring its own predictions. Algorithm 6.2 presents the pseudo-code for the curriculum learning algorithm.

The model $\mathcal{M}$ is first trained to a sub-optimal policy using the cross-entropy training for N^{CL} epochs. Then, we continue training the model for N^{CL+RL} epochs with the cross-entropy loss for the first $T - L$ tokens and the reinforcement algorithm for the remaining L tokens; we gradually increase the value of L to T and repeat training for another N^{CL+RL} epochs. This way the model learns to gradually introduce its own predictions during training, reducing its dependence on oracle label sequences and increasing its confidence in its predictions. By the end of training, the model learns to produce stable sequences at test time. Figure 6.10 sketches the curriculum learning strategy from Ranzato et al. [2015].

Algorithm 6.2 Curriculum Learning.

Input : Training data with (x, y) pairs, where x is the input data or text, y is the associated text or labels, and a text-production model $\mathcal{M}$ to optimise

Output : $\mathcal{M}$ optimised for generation

1: Initialise $\mathcal{M}$ with random parameters, set N^{CL}, N^{CL+RL} and δ
2: **for** $L \in \{0, \delta, 2\delta, \ldots, T\}$ **do**
3:    $S = T - L$
4:    **if** $S == T$ **then**
5:       Train $\mathcal{M}$ for N^{CL} epochs using the cross-entropy loss only
6:    **else**
7:       Train $\mathcal{M}$ for N^{CL+RL} epochs, use the cross-entropy loss for first S steps and the RE-INFORCE algorithm for the rest L steps
8:    **end if**
9: **end for**

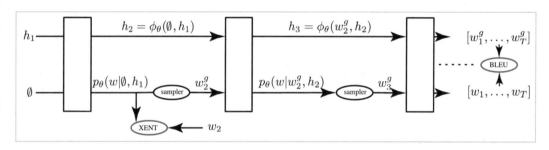

Figure 6.10: The curriculum learning in application [Ranzato et al., 2015]. The algorithm uses the cross-entropy loss for the first S steps (XENT block) and the REINFORCE algorithm for the rest L steps (sampler block). Finally, a reward (e.g., BLEU) is computed once the end of a sentence is reached. REINFORCE is then used to back propagate the gradients through the network updating model parameters.

To recap this section, models trained with reinforcement learning directly optimise the evaluation metric instead of maximising the likelihood of the ground-truth text or labels. In addition, reinforcement learning allows models to explore the space of possible outcomes, making models more robust to unseen data. As a result, models trained with reinforcement learning are better at discriminating among possible outcomes.

Q-learning [Mnih et al., 2013] can be used as an alternative to the policy gradient methods such as the REINFORCE algorithm to maximise the expected future reward. However, a

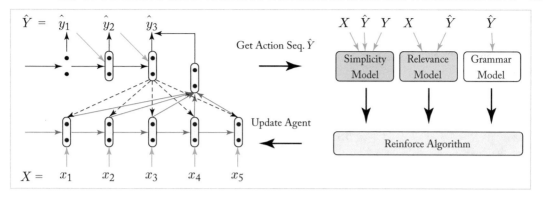

Figure 6.11: Deep reinforcement learning for sentence simplification from Zhang and Lapata [2017]. X is the complex sentence, Y the reference (simple) sentence and $\hat{Y}$ the predicted sentence produced by the encoder-decoder model.

policy gradient is more appropriate for text-production models; it easily allows the model to be initialised with the cross-entropy loss training before tuning it further toward a policy that maximises a long-term reward. This way the policy gradient methods avoid cold start problems, reducing the large variance of text production. Q-learning, on the other hand, directly estimates the future expected reward of each action. As such it is not able to use the cross-entropy loss for initialisation and is prone to falling into cold start problems.

Lastly, several other approaches have been proposed to optimise a policy toward a long-term reward, but they often require a large number of samples to work well [Auli and Gao, 2014, Shen et al., 2016]. The REINFORCE algorithm uses a single sample from its distribution to estimate the policy gradient and is comparatively faster.

6.2.3   REINFORCEMENT LEARNING APPLICATIONS

The REINFORCE algorithm [Williams, 1992] has been widely used in text-production models in recent years to directly optimise a non-differentiable task-specific objective [Li et al., 2016c, Paulus et al., 2018, Ranzato et al., 2015], to inject task-specific constraints [Nogueira and Cho, 2017, Perez-Beltrachini and Lapata, 2018, Zhang and Lapata, 2017], or to train a sentence ranker in the context of extractive summarisation [Narayan et al., 2018c]. We describe some of these models with their reward functions.

Sentence Simplification.   Zhang and Lapata [2017] use the REINFORCE algorithm to optimise their sequence-to-sequence sentence simplifier to optimise simplification-specific objectives (see Figure 6.11). Given an input sentence X, the model first generates the whole sentence

$\hat{Y}$ and receives an immediate reward comparing $\hat{Y}$ to the associated reference sentence Y. The reward function $r(X, Y, \hat{Y})$ aims at capturing key aspects of the target output, namely simplicity r^S, relevance r^R, and fluency r^F:

$$r(X, Y, \hat{Y}) = \lambda^S r^S + \lambda^R r^R + \lambda^F r^F \tag{6.22}$$

$$r^S = \beta \text{SARI}(X, \hat{Y}, Y) + (1 - \beta)\text{SARI}(X, Y, \hat{Y}) \tag{6.23}$$

$$r^R = \cos(\mathbf{q}_x, \mathbf{q}_{\hat{Y}}) = \frac{\mathbf{q}_x \cdot \mathbf{q}_{\hat{Y}}}{||\mathbf{q}_x||||\mathbf{q}_{\hat{Y}}||} \tag{6.24}$$

$$r^F = \exp\left(\frac{1}{|\hat{Y}|} \sum_{i=1}^{|\hat{Y}|} \log p_{\text{lm}}(\hat{y}_i | \hat{y}_{1:i-1})\right) \tag{6.25}$$

where λ^S, λ^R, λ^F, $\beta \in [0, 1]$ are model hyperparameters; $\lambda^S + \lambda^R + \lambda^F = 1$; and r^S, r^R and r^F stand for $r^S(X, Y, \hat{Y})$, $r^R(X, \hat{Y})$ and $r^F(\hat{Y})$, respectively.

The simplicity reward r^S uses $\text{SARI}(X, \hat{Y}, Y)$ [Xu et al., 2016] to compare system output $\hat{Y}$ against reference Y and against the input sentence X, focusing on three rewrite operations (addition, copying, and deletion) to simplify the input. It also uses reverse $\text{SARI}(X, Y, \hat{Y})$ where the system output and the reference are swapped to estimate how good a reference is with respect to the system output.

The relevance reward r^R encourages outputs that are meaning preserving to their sources. It is estimated as a cosine product between input sentence representation $\mathbf{q}_x$ and output sentence representation $\mathbf{q}_{\hat{Y}}$; both are obtained using an LSTM sentence encoder.

The fluency reward r^F encourages well-formed and fluent output sentences; it is estimated as the normalised sentence probability assigned by an LSTM language model p_{lm} trained on simple sentences. Jointly, these three rewards enforce the model to generate outputs that are simple, meaning preserving and fluent.

Finally, Zhang and Lapata [2017] use the curriculum learning and a baseline reward estimator (Eq. (6.21)) to effectively address large variance issue in sentence simplification.

Dialogue Generation. Li et al. [2016c] use the REINFORCE algorithm to optimise their sequence-to-sequence dialogue simulator consisting of two agents. A dialogue is represented as an alternating sequence of sentences generated by the two agents: $p_1, q_1, p_2, q_2, \ldots, p_i, q_i$, where p and q denote sentences generated from the first agent and the second agent, respectively. A state is denoted by the previous two dialogue turns $[p_i, q_i]$ and encoded as a sequence $p_i q_i$ using an LSTM encoder. Action a is the dialogue utterance to generate using an LSTM decoder. The reward r received after an action a aims to contribute to the success of a dialogue in terms of ease of answering r^E, information flow r^I, and semantic coherence r^S:

$$r(a, [p_i, q_i]) = \lambda^E r^E + \lambda^I r^I + \lambda^S r^S \tag{6.26}$$

$$r^E = -\frac{1}{N_S} \sum_{s \in S} \frac{1}{N_s} \log p_{\text{Seq2Seq}}(s|a) \tag{6.27}$$

$$r^I = -\log \cos(\mathbf{h}_{p_i}, \mathbf{h}_{p_{i+1}}) = -\log \cos \frac{\mathbf{h}_{p_i} \cdot \mathbf{h}_{p_{i+1}}}{||\mathbf{h}_{p_i}|| ||\mathbf{h}_{p_{i+1}}||} \tag{6.28}$$

$$r^S = \frac{1}{N_a} \log p_{\text{Seq2Seq}}(a|q_i, p_i) + \frac{1}{N_{q_i}} \log p_{\text{Seq2Seq}}^{\text{backward}}(q_i|a) \tag{6.29}$$

where $\lambda^E, \lambda^I, \lambda^S \in [0, 1]$ are model hyperparameters, $\lambda^E + \lambda^I + \lambda^S = 1$.

The ease of answering reward r^E estimates the negative log likelihood of responding to an action a with a dull response $s \in S$; S is a manually defined set of dull responses such as "I don't know what you are talking about", "I have no idea", etc., N_S is the size of S and N_s is the length of the response s.

The information flow reward r^I measures new information contributed at each turn by an agent. It is estimated as the negative log of cosine similarity between h_{p_i} and $h_{p_{i+1}}$, the encoder representations of two consecutive turns p_i and p_{i+1} by an agent.

The semantic coherence reward r^S encourages the adequacy of responses. It is estimated as the mutual information between the action a and previous turns $[p_i, q_i]$ to ensure the generated responses are coherent and appropriate. $p_{\text{Seq2Seq}}(a|q_i, p_i)$ is the probability of generating a given $[p_i, q_i]$ and $p_{\text{Seq2Seq}}^{\text{backward}}(q_i|a)$, the backward probability of generating the previous utterance q_i based on response a. $p_{\text{Seq2Seq}}^{\text{backward}}$ is trained in the same fashion as in p_{Seq2Seq}; however, sources and targets are swapped.

The action space a is infinite since arbitrary-length sequences can be generated. Li et al. [2016c] also use the curriculum learning and a baseline reward-estimator strategy to decrease the learning variance.

Extractive Document Summarisation.   The REINFORCE algorithm is used in Narayan et al. [2018c] to optimise their hierarchical encoder-decoder model for extractive document summarisation (see Figure 6.12). See Section 5.2.3 for more details on the model. In short, given a document D consisting of a sequence of sentences $(s_1, s_2, \ldots, s_n)$, the document encoder reads sentences in a reverse order and, finally, the sentence extractor sequentially labels each sentence in a document with 1 (relevant for the summary) or 0 (otherwise). A summary is then assembled by concatenating all sentences that were labelled 1, and an immediate reward r is received comparing the output summary to the reference summary.

The reward function commensurates with how well the extract resembles the gold-standard summary in terms of fluency and informativeness. Specifically, as reward function Narayan et al. [2018c] use mean F_1 of ROUGE-1, ROUGE-2, and ROUGE-L. Unigram and bigram overlap (ROUGE-1 and ROUGE-2) are meant to assess informativeness, whereas the longest common subsequence (ROUGE-L) is meant to assess fluency. Narayan et

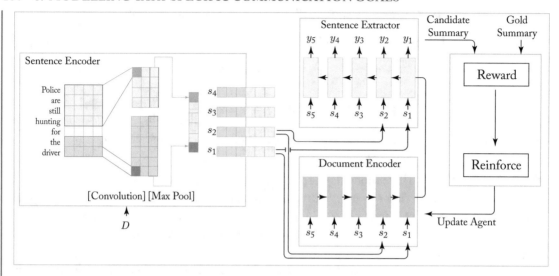

Figure 6.12: Extractive summarisation model with reinforcement learning: a hierarchical encoder-decoder model ranks sentences for their extract-worthiness and a candidate summary is assembled from the top-ranked sentences; the REWARD generator compares the candidate against the gold summary to give a reward which is used in the REINFORCE algorithm [Williams, 1992] to update the model.

al. [2018c] does not use the curriculum learning or the baseline reward-estimator strategy to decrease the learning variance; instead they sample from a set of high-probability extracts to estimate their gradient effectively.

Abstractive Document Summarisation.   Most of the state-of-the-art models for abstractive document summarisation on the CNN/DailyMail and New York Times data sets [Hermann et al., 2015, Sandhaus, 2008] use the REINFORCE training objective to optimise the ROUGE metric [Celikyilmaz et al., 2018, Pasunuru and Bansal, 2018, Paulus et al., 2018]. Given a document D as a sequence of tokens, a full sequence $\hat{Y}$ is generated and is compared against the ground truth sequence Y to generate an immediate reward r. They argue that optimising just a specific metric like ROUGE does not guarantee an increase in quality and readability of the output; they propose a mixed training objective which optimises other relevant criteria along with ROUGE.

Paulus et al. [2018] use a mixed learning objective maximising ROUGE and maximum-likelihood of the output text:

$$L_{\mathrm{mixed}} = \gamma L_{\mathrm{rl}} + (1 - \gamma)L_{\mathrm{ml}}, \tag{6.30}$$

L_{rl} is the reinforcement learning objective optimising ROUGE (Eq. (6.21)); L_{ml} is the maximum-likelihood objective; and γ is the a scaling factor accounting for the difference in magnitude between L_{rl} and L_{ml}. ROUGE measures the n-gram overlap between the generated summary and a reference sequence, the language modelling objective measures readability.

Celikyilmaz et al. [2018] also use the mixed learning objective of Paulus et al. [2018] to jointly maximise the reinforcement objective with the maximum-likelihood objective. In addition, they also use a modified version of Eq. (6.30):

$$L_{\text{mixed-sem}} = \gamma L_{\text{rl}} + (1 - \gamma) L_{\text{ml-sem}} \tag{6.31}$$

where λ is a model hyperparameter and $L_{\text{ml-sem}} = L_{\text{ml}} + \lambda L_{\text{sem}}$. L_{sem} is the semantic cohesion reward encouraging sentences in the summary to be informative without repetition:

$$L_{\text{sem}} = \sum_{i=2}^{n} \cos(\mathbf{h}_{s_i}, \mathbf{h}_{s_{i-1}}), \tag{6.32}$$

L_{sem} essentially computes the cosine similarity between two consecutively generated sentences s_{i-1} and s_i in the summary; $\mathbf{h}_{s_{i-1}}$ and $\mathbf{h}_{s_i}$ are their hidden state representations, respectively.

Pasunuru and Bansal [2018] also use the mixed learning objective of Paulus et al. [2018]. However, they use the reinforcement objective to not only optimise ROUGE but multiple other relevant objectives. They use ROUGE-L to assess fluency with respect to a reference summary. In addition, they introduce two new reward functions: saliency and entailment rewards. The saliency reward modifies ROUGE to give higher weight to the important, salient words/phrases. The saliency weights are predicted using a saliency predictor trained on the popular SQuAD reading comprehension data set [Rajpurkar et al., 2016], where answer spans for important questions (which are used as representative salient information) are marked in the document. Lastly, the entailment reward ensures that the summary is entailed by the given source document. An entailment classifier [Parikh et al., 2016] trained on the Stanford Natural Language Inference [Bowman et al., 2015] and Multi-Genre Natural Language Inference [Williams et al., 2018] data sets is used to calculate the entailment probability between the reference summary and each sentence of the generated summary, the average of which is used as the entailment reward. To optimise these three rewards, Pasunuru and Bansal [2018] proposed a multi-reward optimisation approach inspired from multi-task learning, where each reward is treated as a different task. Specifically, three loss functions L_{rl}^r, L_{rl}^s and L_{rl}^e are defined for the ROUGE, saliency, and entailment rewards, respectively. During training, all three rewards are optimised by using one of these loss functions in Eq. (6.30) in subsequent mini-batches. This is in contrast to earlier approaches [Li et al., 2016c, Zhang and Lapata, 2017] where a final reward has been estimated as a weighted combination of rewards focusing on different aspects.

For the baseline estimator, all models [Celikyilmaz et al., 2018, Pasunuru and Bansal, 2018, Paulus et al., 2018] learn using a self-critical training approach [Rennie et al., 2016], which learns by exploring new sequences and comparing them to the best greedily decoded sequence.

Generating from Loosely Aligned Data.   Perez-Beltrachini and Lapata [2018] use the reinforcement learning objective to optimise the content selection for the task of generation from loosely aligned data (see Section 6.1.4 for more details). Given an input data X, the system generates an output sequence $\hat{Y}$ verbalising X and receives a reward $r(\hat{Y}) = \gamma r^{\mathrm{pr}}(\hat{Y})$, where γ adjusts the reward value $r^{\mathrm{pr}}(\hat{Y})$, which is the unigram precision of the predicted sequence $\hat{Y}$ and the set of words in the reference sequence Y that were aligned to some property-value pairs in X.

6.3   USER MODELLING IN NEURAL CONVERSATIONAL MODEL

Earlier sections focused on dedicated architectures to better accommodate task-specific requirements such as content selection and on augmenting the training objective to optimise task-specific evaluation measures using reinforcement learning. In this section, we look at how to build neural generators with personality.[3]

There has been a growing interest in modelling personality traits in neural agents, especially for applications such as personal assistants, call center agents, or avatars in video games [Ficler and Goldberg, 2017, Ghazvininejad et al., 2018, Li et al., 2016a, Ram et al., 2017, Ritter et al., 2011, Sordoni et al., 2015, Vinyals and Le, 2015] to simulate human-like behaviour. Very often a standard sequence-to-sequence model is trained on large volumes of human-to-human interactions. The underlying conditional language model learns to optimise the likelihood of the generated response and ends up frequently generating inconsistent or repetitive responses [Li et al., 2016b]. Figure 6.13 shows several examples of inconsistent responses generated by a sequence-to-sequence model trained on Twitter conversation data. These behaviours could be unflattering to users on the addressee end.

In the spirit of better input understanding, one could frame this as a dialogue understanding problem where the generator first needs to understand the full context of the response from the previous conversations and not simply output the response conditioned on the last query [Wu et al., 2018]. Techniques from content-selection approaches could be useful in identifying appropriate context, given the query. Reinforcement learning could also be used to directly optimise the dialogue-based rewards to improve the model. Li et al. [2016b] use an interesting alternative and propose persona-based models for handling the issue of consistent response generation in conversational systems. In particular, the model learns to adapt to the user profile (background facts, language behaviour, and interaction style) to generate a consistent response.

Li et al. [2016b] propose a simple approach to incorporate user personality as embeddings. In particular, they propose two models, a single-speaker model and a speaker-addressee model, within a sequence-to-sequence framework [Sutskever et al., 2014]. We describe them below.

---

[3]Should an AI agent have a personality? It is debatable [Reeves and Nass, 1996]. Nevertheless, we describe a neural model which dynamically adapts a personality to get better at response generation.

message	Where do you live now?
response	I live in Los Angeles.
message	In which city do you live now?
response	I live in Madrid.
message	In which country do you live now?
response	England, you?
message	Where were you born?
response	I was born in Canada.
message	Where are you from?
response	England, you?
message	Where did you grow up?
response	I grew up in Texas.
message	How old are you?
response	16 and you?
message	What's your age?
response	18.
message	What is your major?
response	I'm majoring in psychology.
message	What did you study in college?
response	English lit.

Figure 6.13: Inconsistent responses generated by a sequence-to-sequence model trained on Twitter conversation data (source: Li et al. [2016b]).

Single-Speaker Model.   The single-speaker model models the respondent, i.e., it integrates a speaker-level representation into the decoder part of the sequence-to-sequence model. Figure 6.14 sketches the single-speaker model. First the encoder encodes the speaker's question using an RNN, then at each step of the decoding the response generator uses the embeddings of the previously generated word and the speaker embedding to generate a response that is better suited to the speaker. Interestingly, the speaker representation is not obtained manually, but they are learned automatically with the response-generator training. Authors show that the learned-speaker representation were able to classify speakers into meaningful clusters of personality traits (e.g., age and country of residence).

Speaker-Addressee Model.   The speaker model learns an addressee that responds to different speakers differently. It does not model the personality traits of the addressee itself. The speaker-addressee model takes into consideration both users participating in the communication. In particular, it learns an interactive style representation of user i toward user j, using their representations v_i and v_j, respectively, as $V_{ij} = tanh(W_1 \cdot v_i + W_2 \cdot v_j)$. The speaker-addressee model incorporates V_{ij} in the same fashion the speaker model incorporates the speaker repre-

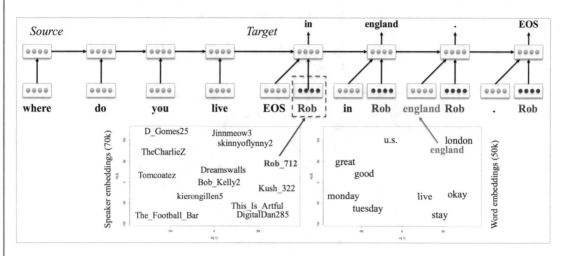

Figure 6.14: Single-speaker model from Li et al. [2016b]. The model learns to represent speakers in an embedding space such that they respond in the same manner if they appear closer in the embedding space. These speaker embeddings are learned jointly with word embeddings and all other parameters of the model.

User1		User2	
message	Where is your hometown?	*message*	Where is your hometown?
response	I'm from England.	*response*	I'm from Indonesia.
message	Where are you from?	*message*	Where are you from?
response	I'm from England.	*response*	England, you?
message	In which city do you live now?	*message*	In which city do you live now?
response	I live in London.	*response*	I live in Jakarta.
message	In which country do you live now?	*message*	In which country do you live now?
response	I live in England.	*response*	I live in Indonesia.
message	What is your major?	*message*	What is your major?
response	Business. You?	*response*	Business. You?
message	What did you study in college?	*message*	What did you study in college?
response	I did business studies.	*response*	Psychology, you?
message	How old are you?	*message*	How old are you?
response	I'm 18.	*response*	I'm 18.
message	What's your age?	*message*	What's your age?
response	I'm 18.	*response*	I'm 16.

Figure 6.15: Examples of speaker consistency and inconsistency generated by the speaker model (source: Li et al. [2016b]).

message	Do you love me?
baseline	Of course, I love you.
response	*addressee: Emily, speaker: Sheldon* Of course, I love you, Emily.
response	*addressee: Emily, speaker: Penny* Of course, I love you, Emily.
response	*addressee: Leonard, speaker: Penny* Of course, I love you, Leonard.
response	*addressee: Monica, speaker: Chandler* Of course, I love you. I want to marry you.
response	*addressee: Rachel, speaker: Chandler* Of course, I love you.
response	*addressee: Ross, speaker: Chandler* Of course, I love you.
response	*addressee: Rachel, speaker: Rachel* Of course, I love you. (Kisses him)
response	*addressee: Emily, speaker: Rachel* Of course, I love you.

Figure 6.16: Responses to "Do you love me?" from the speaker-addressee model using different addressees and speakers. We notice that the model modelling different addressee and speaker pairs responds to the same message differently (source: Li et al. [2016b]).

sentation. At each step of the decoding, the speaker-addressee model uses the embeddings of the previously generated word and V_{ij} to generate a response that varies with the speaker and the addressee.

Figure 6.15 shows that the persona-modelling in the speaker model improves its consistency during the conversation. As can be seen, the speaker model is able to generate a diverse set of responses adapting different user persona. Figure 6.16 shows some examples for the speaker-addressee model and how it generates different responses for the same query depending on both the speaker and the addressee.

6.4   SUMMARY

In this chapter, we have discussed two ways of developing communication goal-oriented generators. The first type focused on developing dedicated architectures for content selection and user modelling. The second type focused on augmenting the training objective to encourage task-specific communication goals, either using multi-task objectives or reinforcement learning. We focused on document summarisation systems, conversational systems, and generators generating from loosely aligned data.

PART III

Data Sets and Conclusion

CHAPTER 7

Data Sets and Challenges

In this chapter, we describe some of the most prominent shared tasks and data sets used in neural approaches to text production.

7.1 DATA SETS FOR DATA-TO-TEXT GENERATION

Several data sets were recently created to support the training of neural data-to-text production models. They vary in terms of output lengths, generation tasks, and domain specificity. Chisholm et al. [2017], Lebret et al. [2016] introduce data sets which are restricted to the generation of one-sentence biographical descriptions, whereas Gardent et al. [2017b], Wiseman et al. [2017] supports the generation of multi-sentence text describing entities of different types. Sometimes, the generation task is restricted to microplanning [Gardent et al., 2017b]. Other times, it additionally involves content selection [Chisholm et al., 2017, Lebret et al., 2016, Wiseman et al., 2017]. The data set may cover a single domain [Chisholm et al., 2017, Lebret et al., 2016, Wiseman et al., 2017] or several [Gardent et al., 2017b].

7.1.1 GENERATING BIOGRAPHIES FROM STRUCTURED DATA

The WikiBio data set created by Lebret et al. [2016] consists of 728,321 data-text biography pairs. The text is the first sentence of a Wikipedia biography article and the data is the corresponding infobox (a fact table). The data set comprises all biography articles in the Biography WikiProject which have an infobox. Data and text are not necessarily aligned so that information present in the input may not be expressed in the text and vice versa. The output text is a single sentence.

Perez-Beltrachini and Lapata [2018] modify the WikiBio data set to multi-sentence output text by using the entire Wikipedia abstract rather than the first sentence. They also eliminate all examples with less than 6 property-value pairs, 2 sentences, or 23 words. The resulting data set includes 213,885 data-text pairs, with an average number of sentences per document varying between 3.22 (test) and 3.51 (train). As text and data are not aligned, the generation task includes content selection and focuses on learning which part of the input data should be verbalised.

Chisholm et al. [2017] use Wikidata and Wikipedia to create a data set of 501,789 data-text pairs. The input data is a set of (at least 6) slot-value pairs describing a person, while the output text is the first sentence of the corresponding Wikipedia page. Only the 15 most frequent slots are considered.

Data	TITLE: Frederick Parker-Rhodes BORN 21 November 1914 DIED 2 March 1987 (aged 72) RESIDENCE UK NATIONALITY British FIELDS Mycology, Plant Pathology, Mathematics, Linguistics, Computer Science KNOWN FOR Contributions to computational linguistics, combinatorial physics, Mycology, Plant Pathology AUTHOR ABBREV. Park.-Rhodes
Text	*Frederick Parker-Rhodes (21 March 1914 — 21 November 1987) was an English linguist, plant pathologist, computer scientist, mathematician, mystic, and mycologist.*

Figure 7.1: Infobox/text example from the WikiBio data set.

Born	Robert Joseph Flaherty February 16, 1884 Iron Mountain, Michigan, U.S.	**Robert Joseph Flaherty. (February 16, 1884 July 23, 1951)** was an **American film-maker**. Flaherty was married to **Frances H. Flaherty** until his death in 1951.
Died	July 23, 1951 (aged 67) Dummerston, Vermont, U.S.	
Cause of death	Cerebral thrombosis	
Occupation	Filmmaker	
Spouse(s)	Frances Johnson Hubbard	

Figure 7.2: Example data-document pair from the extended WikiBio data set (source: Perez-Beltrachini and Lapata [2018]).

7.1.2   GENERATING ENTITY DESCRIPTIONS FROM SETS OF RDF TRIPLES

The WebNLG data set consists of data-text pairs where the data is a set of RDF triples extracted from DBPedia. The data was automatically extracted from DBPedia using a content-selection method designed to extract varied, relevant, and coherent data units [Gardent et al., 2017b]. The text, written by humans, verbalises the content of the input triples. Crowdsourcing was used both

Data	COUNTRY OF CITIZENSHIP United States of America DATE OF BIRTH 16/04/1927 DATE OF DEATH 19/05/1959 OCCUPATION Formula one driver PLACE OF BIRTH Redlands PLACE OF DEATH Indianapolis SEX OR GENDER male TITLE Bob Cortner
Text	*Robert Charles Cortner (April 16, 1927—May 19, 1959) was an* *American automobile racing driver from Redlands, California.*

Figure 7.3: Wikidata/text example from Chisholm et al. [2017].

to collect the text and to verify the quality (fluency, semantic adequacy, and grammaticality) of the text entered by the crowdworkers.

The data set includes 37,975 pairs, 14,237 distinct inputs, and covers 15 domains (Astronaut, University, Monument, Building, ComicsCharacter, Food, Airport, SportsTeam, WrittenWork, Athlete, Artist, City, MeanOfTransportation, CelestialBody, Politician).

Part of this data set (25,298 data-text pairs) was used for the WebNLG'17 Challenge [Gardent et al., 2017a, Shimorina et al., 2017]. The test data was divided into two parts of roughly equal size: a test set containing inputs created for entities belonging to DBpedia categories that were seen in the training data, and a test set containing inputs extracted for entities belonging to five unseen categories.

7.1.3   GENERATING SUMMARIES OF SPORTS GAMES FROM BOX-SCORE DATA

Wiseman et al. [2017] introduce a large-scale corpus of basketball-game summaries paired with their corresponding box and line scores. Two sources are used: RotoWire, where the articles are written by professionals, and SBNation, where summaries are written by fans. This data set is much more challenging as the language is informal and the summaries do not always align well with the data. There are 4,853 distinct RotoWire summaries and 10,903 distinct SBNation summaries. Some games have multiple summaries. As illustrated in Figure 7.4, the task includes both content selection and microplanning.

	WIN	LOSS	PTS	FG_PCT	RB	AS ...
TEAM						
Hawks	11	12	103	49	47	27
Heat	7	15	95	43	33	20

	AS	RB	PT	FG	FGA	CITY...
Player						
Tyler Johnson	5	2	27	8	16	Miami
Dwight Howard	4	17	23	9	11	Atlanta
Paul Millsap	2	9	21	8	12	Atlanta
Goran Dragic	4	2	21	8	17	Miami
Wayne Ellington	2	3	19	7	15	Miami
Dennis Schroder	7	4	17	8	15	Atlanta
Rodney McGruder	5	5	11	3	8	Miami
Thabo Sefolosha	5	5	10	5	11	Atlanta
Kyle Dorver	5	3	9	3	9	Atlanta
...						

The Atlanta Hawks defeated the Miami Heat , 103 - 95 , at Philips Arena on Wednesday . Atlanta was in desperate need of a win and they were able to take care of a shorthanded Miami team here . Defense was key for the Hawks , as they held the Heat to 42 percent shooting and forced them to commit 16 turnovers . Atlanta also dominated in the paint , winning the rebounding battle , 47 - 34 , and outscoring them in the paint 58 - 26.The Hawks shot 49 percent from the field and assisted on 27 of their 43 made baskets . This was a near wire - to - wire win for the Hawks , as Miami held just one lead in the first five minutes . Miami (7 - 15) are as beat - up as anyone right now and it 's taking a toll on the heavily used starters . Hassan Whiteside really struggled in this game , as he amassed eight points , 12 rebounds and one blocks on 4 - of - 12 shooting ...

Figure 7.4: Example data-document pair from the RotoWire data set. The figure shows a subset of the game's records (there are 628 in total), and a selection from the gold document (source: Wiseman et al. [2017]).

7.2   DATA SETS FOR MEANING REPRESENTATIONS TO TEXT GENERATION

Data sets have been developed for three main types of meaning representations: AMRs, deep and shallow dependency trees, and dialogue moves. These representations have different levels of abstraction and offer different challenges for the generation task. The shallow-dependency trees of the Surface Realisation shared task include all lemmas of the sentence to be generated so that, for these meaning representations, generation reduces to ordering and inflecting the lemmas decorating these trees. In contrast, AMRs and the deep-dependency trees of the Surface Realisation shared task are much more abstract and encode semantic rather than syntactic concepts. For these inputs, the generation task is more complex involving, for instance, lexicalisation (mapping concepts to words) and the mapping of semantic relations to syntactic ones. Finally, dialogue moves are very underspecified, closer, in a sense, to knowledge-base representations. Generation for these inputs involves the full microplanning task.

AMR

```
(a / and
  :op1 (r / remain-01
    :ARG1 (c / country :wiki "Bosnia_and_Herzegovina"
      :name (n / name :op1 "Bosnia"))
    :ARG3 (d / divide-02
      :ARG1 c
      :topic (e / ethnic)))
  :op2 (v / violence
    :time (m / match-03
      :mod (f2 / football)
      :ARG1-of (m2 / major-02))
    :location (h / here)
    :frequency (o / occasional))
  :time (f / follow-01
    :ARG2 (w / war-01
      :time (d2 / date-interval
        :op1 (d3 / date-entity :year 1992)
        :op2 (d4 / date-entity :year 1995)))))
```

Text

Following the 1992-1995 war Bosnia remains ethnically divided and violence during major football matches occasionally occurs here.

Figure 7.5: Example input and output from the SemEval AMR-to-Text Generation Task (source: May and Priyadarshi [2017], pp. 536–545).

7.2.1 GENERATING FROM ABSTRACT MEANING REPRESENTATIONS

The 2017 AMR SemEval shared task on generation [May and Priyadarshi, 2017] requires generating a sentence from an Abstract Meaning Representation (AMR; Banarescu et al., 2013). The data set used for this task includes 39,260 AMR sentences instances where the sentences are taken from news and forums. An additional 1,293 sentences are used for evaluation. As shown in Figure 7.5, AMRs provide a detailed semantic representation of the output sentence. Formally, an AMR is a rooted directed acylical graph whose nodes are labelled with sense-identified verbs, nouns, or AMR specific concepts, for example "remain.01", "Bosnia", and "date-interval" in Figure 7.5. The graph edges are labeled with PropBank-style semantic roles for verbs or other relations introduced for AMR, for example, "arg0" or "op1." The generation task then consists of converting this semantic structure into a well-formed sentence which involves mainly lexicalisation and surface realisation. Four teams participated in this generation task.

```
1    the         _    DET    DT    Definite=Def|PronType=Art        _        2       det       _      _
2    third       _    ADJ    JJ    Degree=Pos             _         3        nsubj_pass        _      _
3    run         _    VERB   VBN   Tense=Past|VerbForm=Part         _        0       ROOT      _      _
4    be          _    AUX    VBD   Tense=Past|Mood=Ind|VerbForm=Fin|Person=3 _                3      aux
5    be          _    AUX    VBG   VerbForm=Ger           _         3        aux_pass          _      _
6    head        _    NOUN   NN    Number=Sing            _         3        obl       _      _
7    .           _    PUNCT  .            _               3         punct    _       _
8    by          _    ADP    IN           _               6         case     _       _
9    the         _    DET    DT    Definite=Def|PronType=Art        _        6       det       _      _
10   firm        _    NOUN   NN    Number=Sing            _         6        nmod      _      _
11   a           _    DET    DT    Definite=Ind|PronType=Art        _        10      det       _      _
12   investment  _           NOUN  NN       Number=Sing            _         10      compound          _      _
13   of          _    ADP    IN           _               10        case     _       _
```

Figure 7.6: Example shallow input from the SR'18 data set for the sentence "*The third was being run by the head of an investment firm*" (source: Mille et al. [2018]).

7.2.2   GENERATING SENTENCES FROM DEPENDENCY TREES

Mille et al. [2018] derived multilingual MR-to-text data sets from 10 UD (universal dependencies) treebanks[1] creating 2 types of input: shallow and deep.

In the shallow input, the nodes of the UD dependency tree are scrambled to remove word-order information and words are replaced by their lemmas. The generation task then consists of ordering and inflecting the lemmas decorating the input tree.

The deep input abstracts away from the surface form by removing additional information from the UD tree. Edge labels are generalised to ProbBank/NomBank labels. Function words, fine-grained morpho-syntactic labels, and relative pronouns are removed. Determiners, auxiliaries, and modals are converted into attribute/value pairs and so on. The generation task is correspondingly more complex and involves inserting missing words, correctly inflecting lemmas based on incomplete information, and determining word order based on underspecified semantic relations.

The data set includes data for Arabic, Czech, Dutch, English, Finnish, French, Italian, Portuguese, Russian, and Spanish with training data size varying between 6,016 (Arabic) and 66,485 (Czech) instances.

Eight teams participated to the SR'18 shared task based on this data. All teams submitted outputs for at least the English shallow track; three teams submitted outputs for all 10 languages of the shallow track and only one team participated in the deep track.

7.2.3   GENERATING FROM DIALOGUE MOVES

Novikova et al. [2017b] introduce a new crowdsourced data set of 50k instances in the restaurant domain, 6K distinct inputs, and an average of 8.27 reference texts per input. The inputs are dialogue moves consisting of three to eight attributes, such as "name", "food", or "area", and their values. On average, output texts consists of 20 words and 1.5 sentences.

---

[1]http://universaldependencies.org

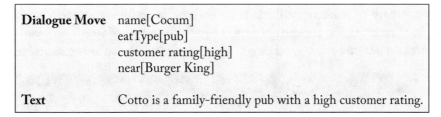

Dialogue Move	name[Cocum]
	eatType[pub]
	customer rating[high]
	near[Burger King]
Text	Cotto is a family-friendly pub with a high customer rating.

Figure 7.7: Example instance from the E2E data set [Dušek et al., 2018].

The data set was used for the E2E'17 challenge and attracted a total of 62 submitted systems by 17 institutions (about 1/3 from industry) [Dušek et al., 2018].

7.3 DATA SETS FOR TEXT-TO-TEXT GENERATION

In this section, we describe data sets for text-to-text generation focusing on four text-to-text generation tasks: summarisation, simplification, compression, and paraphrasing.

7.3.1 SUMMARISATION

Several data sets are commonly used to train and test summarisation systems which differ in terms of size, abstractiveness, diversity, and summarisation tasks. The Document Understanding Conference (DUC) data sets [Harman and Over, 2004] support single-document, multi-document and query-driven summarisation. However, because of their small size (a few hundred document-summary pairs), these are mainly used for testing. The CNN/DailyMail data set (300K pairs, Hermann et al. [2015]) uses bullet-point descriptions as multi-sentence summaries whereas the New York Times (650K pairs, Sandhaus [2008]) contains summaries written by library scientists which are more varied but also shorter than the CNN/DailyMail summaries. Because it is extracted from 38 distinct news sources, NewsRoom (1,3M pairs) provides summaries with greater style diversity and various degrees of abstractiveness. Finally, the Extreme Summarisation (XSUM) data set (227K pairs) targets the generation of more abstractive summaries using British Broadcasting Corporation (BBC) articles and their introductory sentence as summary.

DUC 2001 to 2005. From 2001 to 2005, the DUC[2] organised a series of shared tasks for summarisation of English newspaper and newswire data [Dang, 2006, Harman and Over, 2004]. The DUC data sets gather newswire articles paired with human summaries written specifically for DUC. One distinctive feature of the DUC data sets is the availability of multiple reference summaries for each article. The challenge involved several summarisation tasks including both single-document summaries and summaries of multiple documents.

[2]http://duc.nist.gov/

Table 7.1: Summary of publicly available large corpora for summarisation. We show the average document (source) and summary (target) length (in terms of words and sentences), and vocabulary size on both on source and target. For the vocabulary, we lowercase tokens.

Data Set	# Docs (train/dev/text)	Average Document Length		Average Summary Length		Vocabulary Size	
		Words	Sentences	Words	Sentences	Doc.	Summary
CNN	90,266/ 1,220/1,093	760.50	33.98	45.70	3.59	343,516	89,051
DailyMail	196,961/ 12,148/10,387	653.33	29.33	54.65	3.86	563,663	179,966
NY Times	589,284/ 32,736/32,739	800.04	35.55	45.54	2.44	1,399,358	294,011
News-Room	992,966/ 108,591/108,650	770.09	34.73	30.36	1.43	2,646,681	360,290
XSum	204,045/ 11,322/11,324	431.07	19.77	23.26	1.00	399,147	81,092

For DUC-2001, 60 sets of approximately 10 documents each were provided as input and the task was to create (i) a 100-word summary for each document, and (ii) a summary of the entire set, one summary at each of 4 target lengths (approximately 400, 200, 100, and 50 words). The sets of documents were manually selected and a 100-word summary was manually written for each document, as well as summaries of 400, 200, 100, and 50 words for the entire document set. Sixty additional document sets and their summaries were created for DUC-2002. The 400-word summary was excluded and a headline-length summary added. DUC-2003 included 4 different tasks for summarisation, 1 very short "headline" task for single documents (300 single documents in the test set), and 3 different multi-document summary tasks (each task had 30 document sets used in testing). Finally, for DUC-2005, the task was to synthesise from a set of 25–50 documents a brief answer to a query which could not be answered using a single entity. Fifty topics were used for test data.

Because of their small size, the DUC data sets are usually used for testing rather than training.

CNN/DailyMail. The CNN/DailyMail summarisation data set is adapted from the Deep-Mind question-answering data set developed by Hermann et al. [2015]. In this data set, the input is a news story collected from the CNN and Daily Mail websites, and the summary consists of the bullet points preceding the story. The corpus has around 286K training pairs, 13K

theguardian.com   Coverage: 0.7   Density: 1.77   Compression: 28:1

SUMMARY: **_Orhan Pamuk_**: Monumental state **_treasure-houses_** such as the Louvre or the **Met ignore** the stories of the individual. **Exhibitions** should become ever more **intimate** and **local**

ARTICLE: I love museums and I am not alone in finding that they make me happier with each passing day. I take museums very seriously, and that sometimes leads me to angry, forceful thoughts. But I do not have it in me to speak about museums with anger. In my childhood, there were very few museums in Istanbul. Most of them were simply preserved historical monuments or - quite rare outside the western world - they were places with an air of the government office about them. Later, the small museums in [...]

Read Full Article

Figure 7.8: Example summary from the NewsRoom data set (source: `https://summari.es/explore/`).

validation pairs and 11K test pairs.[3] The input is a long document (781 tokens on average), and the output summary includes multiple sentences (3.75 sentences or 56 tokens on average).

NYT. The New York Times (NYT) data set [Sandhaus, 2008] is a large collection of news articles paired with summaries written by library scientists.[4] While CNN/Daily Mail summaries have a similar wording to their corresponding articles, NYT abstracts are more varied and can use a higher level of abstraction and paraphrasing. The NYT summaries are also shorter, with on average 40 tokens and 1.9 bullet points. The data set includes 589,284 training, 32,736 validation, and 32,739 testing instances.

NewsRoom. The NewsRoom data set [Grusky et al., 2018] differs from the preceding news summarisation corpora in that it is extracted not from a single source but from 38 distinct news sources.[5] As a result, it exhibits greater diversity in terms of summarisation styles, and the summaries copy words and phrases from their input document at varying rates. The summaries were extracted from the metadata available in the HTML pages of articles and were often written by newsroom editors and journalists to appear in socia-media distribution and search results. The resulting data set consists of 1,321,995 article-summary pairs and covers different topic domains, written by many authors, over the span of more than two decades.

---

[3]`https://github.com/abisee/cnn-dailymail`
[4]Available at Linguistic Data Consortium, Philadelphia, 6(12):e26752.
[5]`https://summari.es/`

> **Summary:** A man and a child have been killed after a light aircraft made an emergency landing on a beach in Portugal.
>
> **Document:** Authorities said the incident took place on <u>Sao Joao beach in Caparica</u>, south-west of Lisbon. The National Maritime Authority said <u>a middle-aged man and a young girl died</u> after they were unable to avoid the plane.
> (6 sentences with 139 words are abbreviated from here.)
> Other reports said the victims had been sunbathing when
> <u>the plane made its emergency landing</u>.
> (Another 4 sentences with 67 words are abbreviated from here.)
> Video footage from the scene carried by local broadcasters showed <u>a small recreational plane</u> parked on the sand, apparently intact and surrounded by beachgoers and emergency workers.
> (Last 2 sentences with 19 words are abbreviated.)

Figure 7.9: An abridged example from the XSum data set. The underlined parts in the documents are paraphrased by the summary (source: Narayan et al. [2018b]).

XSum.   Narayan et al. [2018b] introduce the XSum data set for extreme summarisation, a single-document summarisation task which requires abstractive modelling.[6] They create this data set by harvesting online articles from the BBC. Each article starts with an introductory sentence usually written by the author of the article which gathers information from various parts of the document and displays multiple levels of abstraction including paraphrasing, fusion, synthesis, and inference. The data set consists of 226,711 articles, and their one-sentence summary and covers a wide variety of domains (e.g., news, politics, sports, weather, business, technology, science, health, family, education, entertainment and arts). As shown in Table 7.2, the percentage of novel n-grams in the target gold summaries that do not appear in their source documents, and therefore the need for abstraction is much higher in XSum than in the CNN, DailyMail, and NYT data sets.

7.3.2   SIMPLIFICATION

Simplification data sets include PWKP (90K pairs), WikiLarge (300K pairs), and Newsela (56K pairs). The first two data sets are derived from the ordinary and simple English Wikipedia. In contrast, Newsela consists of news-article sentences paired with simplifications written by professional editors for children of four different grade levels.

PWKP.   Zhu et al. [2010] constructed a simplification data set by collecting and aligning sentences from the ordinary and simple English Wikipedias. The test set consists of a hundred

---

[6]https://github.com/shashiongithub/XSum

Table 7.2: The presented data statistics is reported in Narayan et al. [2018b]. We show the proportion of novel *n*-grams in gold summaries. We also report ROUGE scores for the LEAD baseline (selecting top sentences) and EXT-ORACLE, the extractive oracle system (selecting best set of sentences). All results are computed on the test set. All baselines show the abstractiveness of the XSum data set.

Data Set	% of Novel n-grams in Gold Summary				LEAD			EXT-ORACLE		
	Unigrams	Bigrams	Trigrams	4-grams	R1	R2	RL	R1	R2	RL
CNN	16.75	54.33	72.42	80.37	29.15	11.13	25.95	50.38	28.55	46.58
DailyMail	17.03	53.78	72.14	80.28	40.68	18.36	37.25	55.12	30.55	51.24
NY Times	22.64	55.59	71.93	80.16	31.85	15.86	23.75	52.08	31.59	46.72
Newsroom	18.31	46.80	58.06	62.72	33.04	22.35	30.31	57.09	42.94	53.65
XSum	**35.76**	**83.45**	**95.50**	**98.49**	**16.30**	**1.61**	**11.95**	**29.79**	**8.81**	**22.65**

C:	In 1964 Peter Higgs published his second paper in Physical Review Letters describing Higgs mechanism which predicted a new massive spin-zero boson for the first time .
S:	Peter Higgs wrote his paper explaining Higgs mechanism in 1964. Higgs mechanism predicted a new elementary particle.
C:	Being more resistant to cold, bricks enabled the construction of permanent buildings.
S:	S. Bricks were more resistant to cold. Bricks enabled the construction of permanent buildings.
C:	Also contributing to the firmness in copper, the analyst noted, was a report by Chicago purchasing agents, which precedes the full purchasing agents report that is due out today and gives an indication of what the full report might hold.
S:	Also contributing to the firmness in copper, the analyst noted, was a report by Chicago purchasing agents. The Chicago report precedes the full purchasing agents report. The Chicago report gives an indication of what the full report might hold. The full report is due out today.

Figure 7.10: PWKP Complex (**C**) and Simplified (**S**) example pairs from Zhu et al. [2010].

complex/simple sentence pairs. The training set contains 89,042 sentence pairs (after removing duplicates and test sentences). This data set has been extensively used for training and evaluating text-simplification systems [Biran et al., 2011, Narayan and Gardent, 2014, Woodsend and Lapata, 2011, Wubben et al., 2012, Yatskar et al., 2010, Zhu et al., 2010].

C:	Slightly more fourth-graders nationwide are reading proficiently compared with a decade ago, but only a third of them are now reading well, according to a new report.
S1:	Fourth-graders in most states are better readers than they were a decade ago. But only a third of them actually are able to read well, according to a new report.
S2:	Fourth-graders in most states are better readers than they were a decade ago. But only a third of them actually are able to read well, according to a new report.
S3:	Most fourth-graders are better readers than they were 10 years ago. But few of them can actually read well.
S4:	Fourth-graders are better readers than 10 years ago. But few of them read well.

Figure 7.11: Newsela example simplifications from Xu et al. [2015b].

WikiLarge.   Zhang and Lapata [2017] created a larger Wikipedia simplification corpus by combining the PWKP corpus described above with the additional sentence pairs extracted from Wikipedia and Simple Wikipedia by Kauchak [2013][7] and the aligned and revision sentence pairs collected by Woodsend and Lapata [2011]. The development and test sets were constructed by Xu et al. [2016]. They paired complex sentences taken from WikiSmall with crowdsourced simplifications provided by Amazon Mechanical Turk workers.[8] The data set consists of 2,359 sentences with 8 reference simplifications each and is partitioned into 2,000 instances for development and 359 for testing. After removing duplicates and sentences in development and test sets, the WikiLarge training set contains 296,402 sentence pairs.[9]

Newsela.   Xu et al. [2015b] argue that the PWKP data set is suboptimal as it contains automatic sentence-alignment errors, inadequate simplifications, and a uniform writing style which prevents systems from generalising well to other text genres. They construct a new simplification corpus (Newsela)[10] out of 1,130 news articles, each rewritten 4 times by professional editors for children at different grade levels (0 is the most complex level and 4 is simplest). The Newesla corpus contains 56,037 sentences, each of the sentences paired with simplifications of level 1 to 4.

7.3.3   COMPRESSION

For sentence compression, the only publicly available large-scale data set is the Gigaword corpus, which pairs the first sentence of a news article with its headline (4M sentence/compression pairs). Filippova and Altun [2013a] describe an automatic procedure for constructing a parallel corpus of (sentence, compression) pairs and exploit this methods to build a 2M size corpus.

---

[7]http://www.cs.middlebury.edu/~dkauchak/simplification
[8]AMT: https://www.mturk.com/.
[9]https://github.com/XingxingZhang/dress
[10]https://newsela.com/data/

> **D:** brazilian defender pepe is out for the rest of the season with a knee injury , his porto coach jesualdo ferreira said saturday .
> **S:** football : pepe out for season
>
> **D:** colin l. powell said nothing – a silence that spoke volumes to many in the white house on thursday morning .
> **S:** in meeting with former officials bush defends iraq policy
>
> **D:** an international terror suspect who had been under a controversial loose form of house arrest is on the run , british home secretary john reid said tuesday .
> **S:** international terror suspect slips net in britain

Figure 7.12: GigaWord sentence compression or summarisation example from Rush et al. [2015].

They only make available a test set of 10K pairs, however. Moreover the compressions are extractive in that the content words they contain must occur in the input. Drawing on the Manually Annotated Sub-Corpus (MASC), Toutanova et al. [2016] created a multi-reference data set (26,000 pairs) for abstractive-sentence and short-paragraph compression which covers multiple genre and include manual quality judgments. The small manually created corpus of 575 single-reference sentence compression pairs from Cohn and Lapata [2008] has mainly been used for testing.

Gigaword. Using the Gigaword corpus developed by the Linguistic Data Consortium (LDC, [Graff et al., 2003, Napoles et al., 2012]), Rush et al. [2015] created a sentence compression corpus where the input is the first sentence of a news article and the output is its headline. The news articles come from seven newswire sources, including the Associated Press, New York Times Newswire Service, and Washington Post Newswire Service. The corpus is pre-processed to eliminate any pair (i) where input and output have no content words in common, (ii) the output contains a byline or other extraneous editing marks, or (iii) the title has a question mark or colon. The resulting data set consists of roughly 4 million title-article pairs. The complete input-training vocabulary has 119 million word tokens and 110K unique word types with an average sentence size of 31.3 words. The headline vocabulary consists of 31 million tokens and 69K word types, with the average title of length 8.3 words.

Automatic Creation of an Extractive Sentence/Compression Corpus. Filippova and Altun [2013a] describe an automatic procedure for constructing a parallel corpus of (sentence, compression) pairs. The underlying idea is to harvest news articles from the internet, take the first sentence of the article as input, and use the content words of the article headline to recover the

I:	The Ministry of Defense says a British soldier has been killed in a roadside blast in southern Afghanistan.
H:	British soldier killed in Afghanistan
C:	A British soldier killed in a blast in Afghanistan

Figure 7.13: Compression example from Filippova and Altun [2013a]. (I: input sentence, H: headline, C: compression.)

compressed sentence. Specifically, the compressed sentence is built by retrieving from the input parse tree the minimal spanning tree that covers all content words from the title. Figure 7.13 shows an example.

Filippova et al. [2015] use this method to build a corpus of about 2 million parallel sentence-compression instances from the news where every compression is a subsequence of tokens from the input. For testing, they use a publicly released set of 10,000 sentence-compression pairs.[11]

Multi-Reference Corpus for Abstractive Compression. Toutanova et al. [2016] introduce a multi-reference data set for abstractive-sentence and short-paragraph compression. Single sentences and two-sentence paragraphs were collected from several genres in the written text section of the MASC [Ide et al., 2010] of the Open American National Corpus. Non-news genres (academic publications, journal texts, and letters) are better represented in this data set than the Newswire typically used in other compression data sets. Compressions were crowdsourced in two steps: first, the texts were shortened, and then, the compression was evaluated according to its quality.

The resulting data set contains approximately 6,000 source texts with multiple compressions (about 26,000 pairs of source and compressed texts), representing business letters, newswire, journals, and technical documents. Each source/compression pair is annotated with quality judgments. Compressions are provided both for single- and for two-sentences text. A detailed edit history is also provided that allows fine-grained alignment of source and compressed text.

Cohn and Lapata's Corpus. Based on 30 collected newspaper articles from the British National Corpus and the American News Text corpus, Cohn and Lapata [2008] manually created a small corpus of 575 single-reference sentence compression pairs which can be used for testing. In this corpus, the compression are abstractive rather than extractive in that they capture the key information conveyed by the source without necessarily using the same words in the same order.

---

[11]http://storage.googleapis.com/sentencecomp/compressiondata.json

I:	Think of all the ways everyone in your household will benefit from your membership N/A in Audubon.
C1:	Imagine how your household will benefit from your Audubon membership.
C2:	Everyone in your household will benefit from membership in Audubon
I:	Will the administration live up to its environmental promises? Can we save the last of N/A our ancient forests from the chainsaw?
C1:	Can the administration keep its promises? Can we save the last of our forests from loss?
C2:	Will the administration live up to its environmental promises to save our ancient forests?

Figure 7.14: Example of abstractive compression from Toutanova et al. [2016].

I:	Mr Usta was examined by Dr Raymond Crockett, a Harley Street physician specialising in kidney disease.
C:	Dr Raymond Crockett, a Harley Street physician, examined Mr Usta
I:	High winds and snowfalls have, however, grounded at a lower level the powerful US Navy Sea Stallion helicopters used to transport the slabs.
C:	Bad weather, however, has grounded the helicopters transporting the slabs

Figure 7.15: Example of abstractive compression from Cohn and Lapata [2008].

7.3.4 PARAPHRASING

There are two large-scale data sets publicly available for paraphrasing, ParaNMT-80 (50M pairs) and Twitter News URL Corpus (44K pairs). While ParaNMT was artificially constructed using neural machine translation and covers various genres (Web text, Europarl, news), Twitter News URL Corpus is based on manually written tweets sharing a common URL. Similarly the Twitter Paraphrase Corpus (PIT-2015, 19K pairs) was derived from Twitter data, but in that corpus, paraphrase pairs were identified based on shared topics. Smaller data sets include the Microsoft Research Paraphrase (MSRP) Corpus (6K) and Multiple-Translation Chinese (MTC) Corpus. Both data sets were extracted from news texts, but MSRP was created by clustering topically and temporally related articles, whereas MTC results from the manual translation of Chinese news stories into English. MTC associates multiple references (up to 11) to each input sentence and is therefore frequently used for evaluation. We also briefly mentioned Paraphrase Database (PPDB), a large database of lexical and phrasal paraphrases which was automatically built using neural machine translation to identify the (foreign) pivot shared by paraphrases.

Table 7.3: Summary of publicly available large sentential paraphrase corpora

Name	Genre	# Pairs	# Tokens/Sce
MSR Paraphrase Corpus (MSRP)	News	5,801	18.9
Twitter Paraphrase Corpus (PIT-2015)	Twitter	18,762	11.9
Twitter News URL Corpus	Twitter	44,365	14.8
ParaNMT-80	News, Web, Europarl	50M	—

```
S:    so, what's half an hour?
P:    half an hour won't kill you.

S:    well, don't worry. i've taken out tons and tons of guys. lots of guys
P:    don't worry, i've done it to dozens of men

S:    it's gonna be ...... classic.
P:    yeah, sure. it's gonna be great.

S:    but she doesn't have much of a case
P:    but as far as the case goes, she doesn't have much.
```

Figure 7.16: Example paraphrase pairs from ParaNMT-50 [Wieting and Gimpel, 2018].

ParaNMT-50M.   Wieting and Gimpel [2018] introduce a large data set of more than 50 million English-English sentential paraphrase pairs.[12] Following the method outlined in Wieting et al. [2015], they use a Czech-to-English NMT system to translate Czech sentences from parallel English-Czech training data into English. They then pair the translations with the English sources to form English-English paraphrase pairs. The sentences are taken from four sources: Common Crawl, CzEng 1.6, Europarl, and News Commentary.

Twitter News URL Corpus.   Lan et al. [2017] collect sentential paraphrases from tweets that refer to the same URL. Retweets are filtered out to avoid duplicate and enhance rephrasing. The, crowdsourcing is used to label pairs of tweets as paraphrase or non-paraphrase. Crowdworkers are shown an original sentence and asked to select paraphrases from 10 candidate sentences. Each sentence is annotated by six crowdwokers. Paraphrase and non-paraphrase labels are computed using the majority vote. The resulting corpus contains 51,524 sentence pairs, 42,200 tweets (4,272 distinct URLs) annotated in the training set, and 9,324 tweets of 915 distinct URLs in the test set.

---

[12]https://www.cs.cmu.edu/~jwieting

Source	Samsung halts production of its Galaxy Note 7 as battery problems linger.
Paraphrases	#Samsung temporarily suspended production of its Galaxy #Note7 devices following reports.
	News hit that Samsung is temporarily halting production of the #GalaxyNote7.
	Paraphrase Samsung still having problems with their Note 7 battery overheating. Completely halt production.
	SAMSUNG HALTS PRODUCTS OF GALAXY NOTE 7 .
	THE BATTERIES ARE * STILL * EXPLODING .
Non-Paraphrases	in which a phone bonfire in 1995–a real one–is a metaphor for samsung's current note 7 problems
	Non-Paraphrase samsung decides, "if we don't build it, it won't explode." Samsung's Galaxy Note 7 Phones AND replacement phones have been going up in flames due to the defective batteries

Figure 7.17: Examples from the Twitter News URL Corpus [Lan et al., 2017].

S:	Ezekiel Ansah wearing 3D glasses without the lens
P:	Wait, Ezekiel Ansah is wearing 3D movie glasses with the lenses knocked out.
S:	Marriage equality law passed in Rhode Island
P:	Congrats to Rhode Island becoming the 10th state to enact marriage equality.

Figure 7.18: Paraphrase examples from PIT-2015 [Xu et al., 2014].

Twitter Paraphrase Corpus (PIT-2015).   Xu et al. [2014] derived a paraphrase corpus from Twitter data using filtering and crowdsourcing techniques. They crawl Twitter's trending topics and their associated tweets using public application programming interfaces (APIs), then filter the sentences within each topic to select more probable paraphrases for annotation. Crowdworkers are shown a sentence and are asked to pick sentences with the same meaning from 10 candidate sentences. The original and candidate sentences are randomly sampled from the same topic. The Twitter Paraphrase Corpus contains 18,762 sentence pairs and 19,946 unique sentences. The training and development set consists of 17,790 sentence pairs. The test set contains both crowdsourced and expert labels on 972 sentence pairs from 20 randomly sampled Twitter trending topics.

S:	Revenue in the first quarter of the year dropped 15 percent from the same period a year earlier.
P:	With the scandal hanging over Stewart's company, revenue in the first quarter of the year dropped 15 percent from the same period a year earlier.
S:	The Senate Select Committee on Intelligence is preparing a blistering report on prewar intelligence on Iraq.
P:	American intelligence leading up to the war on Iraq will be criticised by a powerful U.S. Congressional committee due to report soon, officials said today.

Figure 7.19: Paraphrase examples from the MSRP corpus [Quirk et al., 2004].

Microsoft Research (MSRP) Paraphrase Corpus.   This corpus contains 5,801 pairs of sentences from news articles, with 4,076 for training and the remaining 1,725 for testing [Quirk et al., 2004]. It was created by extracting from the Web clusters of topically and temporally related articles and using edit distance to identify pairs of sentences within a cluster which are likely paraphrases. Because of the way it was constructed, this corpus contains a large portion of sentence pairs with many ngrams shared in common [Das and Smith, 2009].

Multiple-Translation Chinese (MTC) Corpus.   The MTC corpus [Shudong et al., 2002] contains 105 news stories from three sources of journalistic Mandarin Chinese text translated into English, each with 11 translations.[13] This data set is sometimes used for testing paraphrase models.

PPDB.   Ganitkevitch and Callison-Burch [2014] released a paraphrase database of over a billion paraphrase pairs for 21 languages.[14] This database was created automatically using the bilingual pivoting approach which identifies phrases that share an interpretation because of a shared foreign phrase. The intuition is that if two strings of a given language, "e1" and "e2", translate to the same foreign string "f", then they can be assumed to have the same meaning. In other words, by pivoting over a foreign language phrase "f", we can determine that "e1" is a paraphrase of "e2." Each paraphrase pair in PPDB is associated with a set of scores, including paraphrase probabilities derived from the bitext data and a variety of monolingual distributional similarity scores. PPDB differs from the parallel data sets discussed in this section in that it contains lexical, phrasal, and syntactic paraphrases, rather than pairs of sentential paraphrases.

---

[13]Available by the LDC, Catalog Number LDC2002T01, ISBN 1-58563-217-1.
[14]paraphrase.org

CHAPTER 8

Conclusion

8.1 SUMMARISING

In this book, we aimed to give the reader an overview of the main challenges arising in text production and how they have been addressed by neural approaches. We started by introducing the various kinds of inputs and communication goals considered in text production and briefly surveyed how they were captured in pre-neural approaches. We then went on to show how the basic encoder-decoder model, which is at the heart of early neural approaches to text-production, introduced a shift of paradigm by allowing for all text production tasks to be modeled within a single unifying framework. While powerful, this encoder-decoder model has several shortcomings. We therefore discussed ways of improving its three main components: the decoder, encoder, and learning strategies. We introduced the attention, copy, and coverage mechanisms which are commonly used to improve decoding and produce better quality text. We showed how various encoding techniques (e.g., graph, convolutional, and hierarchical networks) can be used to produce representations which better take into account the structure of the input. And we surveyed various proposals put forward in the literature to improve learning by taking into account the communicative goal specific to the text-production task being considered, using either multi-tasking or reinforcement learning. We also provided a survey of the most prominent data sets and shared tasks used for training and testing neural text-production models.

8.2 OVERVIEW OF COVERED NEURAL GENERATORS

The RNN-based encoder-decoder models and their variants have dominated neural architectures for text production in recent years. They provide a convenient way to encode an input as a sequence of tokens and to produce an output text as a sequence of tokens. With attention, copy, and coverage mechanisms, these models can produce quality texts which are more consistent with the input and do not omit or repeat information (see Chapter 4). It is no surprise that these models have been the go-to approach for all sorts of input representations including text, data, or meaning representations (see Chapters 4, 5, and 6) and are still hard to beat on several text-production tasks.

   The encoding and generation of rare words are known problems in text production; standard neural models with words as units are no exceptions. The copy mechanism (see Chapter 4) is widely used in text-production approaches to address these problems by directly allowing the rare words from the input. Alternatively, text-production models operate on character [Kim,

2014] or subword [Sennrich et al., 2016] units. Taking lessons from these improvements, recent language models, such as OpenAI GPT [Radford et al., 2018] and BERT [Devlin et al., 2019], also employ subword encodings, such as SentencePieces [Kudo and Richardson, 2018] and WordPieces [Wu et al., 2016], respectively.

Longer and complex inputs, e.g., documents or AMRs, have called for linguistically motivated hierarchical encoders for better input representations (see Chapter 5). These models, however, often require careful planning to not sacrifice the attention, copy, and coverage mechanisms of simpler encoder-decoder models. Without them they may perform inferior to the models with sequential encoders. For example, Tan et al. [2017]'s model underperforms on out-of-vocabulary words and is outperformed by See et al. [2017] on document summarisation. A more sophisticated model of Celikyilmaz et al. [2018] with hierarchical encoders and attention, copy, and coverage mechanisms, outperforms See et al. [2017] on the same task. Finally, in Chapter 6 we discussed goal-oriented architectures for text production which allow (i) task-specific requirements such as content selection and (ii) optimisation of task-specific evaluation metrics.

8.3   TWO KEY ISSUES WITH NEURAL NLG

Two key features of neural NLG are (i) powerful language models which take into account a much wider context than the traditional n-gram models, and (ii) the possibility to model NLG as an end-to-end process. While these had a strong impact on the field (in particular, it made NLG accessible to a much larger research community), they also have some drawbacks.

Semantic Adequacy and Evaluation Metrics.   As we saw in Chapter 4, neural generators can produce output with high fluency but low adequacy. This is not a minor issue. As shown in Reiter and Belz [2009], accuracy is generally judged by human raters as more important than readability. Moreover, from an applied perspective, the generation of inaccurate texts is clearly unacceptable. A key challenge for future research in neural generation is therefore how to ensure the semantic adequacy of automatically generated texts. This in turn raises the issue of evaluation: how to best evaluate semantic adequacy and more generally, how to best evaluate generated texts?

Currently available automatic evaluation metrics for machine-generated text are problematic. Because they are computationally efficient, metrics based on n-gram matching are common such as ROUGE, BLEU, METEOR, and CIDER. However, these metrics often fail to appropriately reward correct paraphrases where words of the reference sentence have been reordered or substituted with synonyms. They have also been found to correlate weakly with human judgment [Novikova et al., 2017a, Reiter, 2018]. Recent work on the evaluation of generated text follows three broad directions. One direction is to use or devise tools and scripts to assess diversity and semantic adequacy. For instance, to check for semantic adequacy, Ribeiro et al. [2019] use an entailment recognition model to detect whether the generated text entails and is entailed by the reference (Are the generated text and the reference semantically equivalent?). Similarly, to automatically assess lexical richness and syntactic diversity, Perez-Beltrachini and Gardent [2017] uses Lu [2010]'s system which was originally developed to assess text difficulty in a computer-aided language learning context. These evaluation methods are only as good as the tools they are based on, however, and are never 100% accurate. Thus, they provide an indication of how well the model is performing but cannot be blindly relied upon. A second, frequently used, direction consists of running a human evaluation, often using crowdsourcing and focusing on such aspects as grammaticality, fluency, and semantic adequacy. This in turn is difficult to get right as the criteria being evaluated, such as grammaticality and fluency, are highly subjective and inter-annotator agreement is often low. A third, more recent, direction builds on neural word and sentence embeddings to devise semantic-, rather than word-based method for comparing a generated text with a reference [Alihosseini et al., 2019, Zhang et al., 2019]. Overall though, the question of how to evaluate automatically generated text remains an open issue.

Explainability and Modularity.   While the end-to-end learning supported by the encoder-decoder framework clearly simplifies the design of text-production systems, it also makes it much harder to assess the degree to which the various subtasks discussed in Chapter 2 are appropriately modeled. For instance, the shallow track of the Surface Realisation 2018 Shared Task consists of reordering and inflecting the lemmas present in the input unordered tree. Given an end-to-end process mapping the input tree to the output sentences, it is impossible to know how well the model handles word ordering and how well it handles morphological realisation. More generally, the neural approach to text production raises the issue of transparency and interpretability. How can we assess the degree to which neural text generators handle the various subtasks discussed in Chapter 2? Related issues are how well the subtasks involved in data-to-text generation, simplification, and summarisation can be handled by a single end-to-end process; how to design end-to-end models which explicitly capture these; whether these more detailed models outperforms end-to-end approaches in terms of output quality and robustness to unseen data; and how to integrate linguistic knowledge to guide and constrain these models.

Much recent work in neural text-production in fact departs from the simple encoder-decoder approach to adopt modular approaches which decompose text production into several sub-modules, much as was done in pre-neural approaches.

In the multilingual Surface Realisation shared task, many of the participants decompose surface realisation into two, sometimes three, sub-tasks; word ordering, morphological realisation, and contraction handling [Mille et al., 2018]. Furthermore, Shimorina and Gardent [2019] shows that such a decomposition permits a detailed evaluation of the three sub-tasks, thereby enhancing explainability of the model behaviour.

For data-to-text generation, Moryossef et al. [2019] propose a two-step generation model which, first, structures the input into a document plan (macro-planning) and second, verbalises this plan (micro-planning). Similarly, Castro Ferreira et al. [2019] show that a pipeline architecture which explicitly models intermediate sub-steps of the data-to-text generation process improves the quality of the generated text.

In text-to-text generation, one of the best performing systems on the Gigaword sentence-compression task [Cao et al., 2018a] is a retrieve-and-rewrite approach which, first, retrieves the sentence most similar to the input and, second, uses its compressed form together with the input to generate the compressed version of the input. This two-step approach is reminiscent of template-based approaches such as Kondadadi et al. [2013] where generation proceeds by, first, selecting a template and, second, filling it in using values from the input. For multi-document summarisation and question answering, Fan et al. [2019] shows that introducing an intermediate step to transform the input text into a knowledge graph before applying an end-to-end summarisation model permits scaling to very large input (200K tokens in average).

More generally, much current work on neural NLG is moving away from the early end-to-end models to explore decompositions of the generation tasks, often taking inspiration from pre-neural approaches to provide for more transparent, explainable neural architectures.

8.4   CHALLENGES

Many further challenges remain such as how to process long input or/and output; how to develop generic models that can handle various languages and various domains without requiring large quantities of training data; and how to best integrate linguistic constraints in the neural process.

Long Input/Output.   Recurrent and convolutional networks successfully model sentences, and hierarchical approaches help model the high-level structure of text. However, as the sequential nature of the recurrent networks used for decoding precludes parallelisation, and because RNNs are prone to degenerating into language models that pay little attention to the input, the summarisation of longer documents or the generation of medium-size stories (a few hundred words) continues to raise both efficiency and semantic adequacy issues. Because it eschews recurrence and instead relies on attention to draw global dependencies between input and output, the Transformer architecture [Vaswani et al., 2017] helps address these issues. It was shown to outperform previous results on two machine-translation tasks while requiring significantly less time to train. It also has started to show results in NLG, for instance, for storytelling [Fan et al., 2018]. Thus, neural advances will likely help processing longer documents. We conjecture that additional linguistic knowledge, e.g., about discourse or narrative structure, will further help improve efficiency and semantic adequacy.

Multilingualism, Training Data and Domain Adaptation.   As for many other areas of NLP, most current work on neural NLG focuses on English and is supervised. Training data, e.g., large number of data/text, document/summary, and sentence/simplification pairs, is required for each NLG task. While crowdsourcing, grammar-, and heuristic-based methods have been proposed to facilitate the creation of training data, creating labelled data for generation remains a notoriously difficult task. It is in fact unlikely that these methods will suffice to extend neural

NLG to other languages and to all text-production tasks. To cover multiple languages, multiple tasks, and multiple domains, important directions for further research are zero-shot learning, active learning, transfer learning, and domain adaptation. The recent work by Radford et al. [2019] is an interesting step in that direction as it demonstrates that conditional language models trained on large quantities of Web data perform reasonably well across multiple tasks including reading comprehension, translation, summarisation, and question answering. It remains to be seen to what extent these new language models can help solve the issue of lacking training data on a wider spectrum of text-production tasks, in multiple languages and in various domains while maintaining semantic adequacy.

Deep Learning and Linguistics.   Deep learning alone will not solve the NLG problem. In fact, since the inception of the neural NLG field, much of the work has focused on how best to constrain neural generation using external, often linguistic, knowledge. There are many possible ways.

Reinforcement learning permits enforcing linguistic knowledge through reward. Thus, the SARI and ROUGE metrics have been used to guide simplification and summarisation networks [Narayan et al., 2018c, Zhang and Lapata, 2017].

Large pretrained models such as ELMo [Peters et al., 2018] and BERT [Devlin et al., 2019] help capture the lexical semantics of words. They have also been shown to provide more generic architectures capable of handling multiple NLP tasks.

Additional knowledge derived from the input or extracted from external sources can also be used. For instance, information extraction subject-predicate-object triples and dependency sub-trees have been used in summarisation to improve semantic adequacy [Cao et al., 2018b]. Integration of this knowledge into the neural architecture can be performed in many ways, e.g., using factored models [Elder and Hokamp, 2018] or using multiple encoders and a gating system to weigh the respective contribution of each knowledge source [Zhou et al., 2017]. Alternatively, when training data is available, multi-tasking is another powerful way to include linguistic knowledge into the neural NLG process. Li et al. [2018b] for instance, shows that a multi-task network combining summarisation and entailment recognition significantly improves summarisation on the Gigaword corpus.

8.5   RECENT TRENDS IN NEURAL NLG

As we finish writing this book, early approaches to neural NLG have already evolved. We briefly summarise some of the main novel features which are rapidly revolutionising the field.

Non-Recurrent Networks.   The sequence-to-sequence models predominantly used in early neural NLG are based on complex RNNs which generate a sequence of tokens as a function of the previous hidden state and the current input. This inherently sequential nature of the neural architecture precludes parallelisation within training examples, which impacts computational efficiency. To address this issue, Vaswani et al. [2017] propose a new simple network architecture, the Transformer, which dispenses with recurrence entirely. The Transformer is an encoder-decoder framework where both encoder and decoder are composed of a stack of six layers and where multi-head self attention is used to jointly attend to information from different representation subspaces at different input and output positions.[1]

The Transformer architecture is becoming increasingly popular as it is both efficient (due to its non-recurrent nature) and powerful (through its multi-head self-attention mechanism that is able to capture rich and varied linguistic information over wide context windows and multiple encoding layers). Transformer models have in particular been shown to achieve best results in AMR-to-text generation [Zhu et al., 2019] and generation of abstracts from knowledge graphs [Koncel-Kedziorski et al., 2019].

Pre-Training and Fine-Tuning. Recently, pre-training methods such as ELMo [Peters et al., 2018] OpenAI GPT [Radford et al., 2018], and BERT [Devlin et al., 2019] have substantially advanced the state of the art across a variety of natural language understanding tasks [Baevski et al., 2019, Devlin et al., 2019, Howard and Ruder, 2018, Peters et al., 2018, Radford et al., 2019]. Language models (LMs) learn contextualised word representations by predicting words based on their context using large amounts of text data. In particular, BERT learns deep bidirectional representations by jointly conditioning on both left and right context in all layers of a Transformer model and using the masked language model (MLM) objective function. Some of the input tokens are masked, and the objective is to predict the masked word based only on its context. By building representations which fuse left and right context, the MLM objective permits pre-training a deep bidirectional Transformer for language modelling. Pre-trained BERT representations can then be fine-tuned on task-specific training data such as the GLUE benchmark [Wang et al., 2018] or the SQuAD question-answering training data [Rajpurkar et al., 2016].

Recent work has started investigating how pre-trained language models can be applied to natural language generation.

Dong et al. [2019] introduces a unified pre-training model, Unified Language Model (UniLM), which can be fine tuned for both natural language understanding and natural language generation. UniLM is a multi-layer Transformer network optimised for three types of unsupervised language modelling objectives; unidirectional, bidirectional, and sequence to sequence. For each objective, different contexts are used (all words on the left of the masked word for the unidirectional left-to-right LM, words on both the right and the left context for the bidirectional LM, and all words in the input plus the words on the left of the masked word for the sequence-to-sequence model). This unified pre-training procedure makes the learned text representations more general as they are jointing optimised with respect to different LM objectives and can be used both for NLU and for NLG tasks. Experimental results show that the UniLM model obtains new state-of-the-art results on CNN/DailyMail and Gigaword abstractive summarisation, Stanford Question Answering Data Set question generation, Conver-

---

[1]For a more detailed description of the Transformer, we refer the reader to Vaswani et al. [2017].

sational Question Answering, and Dialogue System Technology Challenge 7 dialogue response generation.

Chan et al. [2019] presents a simple architecture called Kontextuell Encoder Representations Made by Insertion Transformations, or KERMIT, that directly models the joint distribution of input and output sequence and its decompositions (i.e., marginals and conditionals). KERMIT consists of a single Transformer decoder stack. The model is trained to insert the missing tokens into any partially complete sequence and can generate text in an arbitrary order, including bidirectional machine translation and cloze-style infilling. It was shown to match or exceed state-of-the-art performance on three diverse tasks: machine translation, representation learning, and zero-shot cloze question answering.

Song et al. [2019a] propose MAsked Sequence to Sequence pre-training (MASS), a pre-training method for language generation. MASS pre-trains a sequence-to-sequence model by predicting a sentence fragment given the remaining part of the sentence. Its encoder takes a sentence with a randomly masked fragment (several consecutive tokens) as input, and its decoder tries to predict this masked fragment. In this way, MASS can jointly train the encoder and decoder to develop the capability of representation extraction and language modelling. Pre-trained MASS models can be fine tuned on language-generation tasks and were shown to yield significant improvements over the baselines without pre-training, or with other pre-training, methods in neural machine translation, text summarisation, and conversational response generation.

Bidirectional self-attention is a key property of the BERT language model. Unfortunately, the bidirectional nature of the approach makes it difficult to use BERT for sequence generation as it requires the entire sequence to be known beforehand [Wang and Cho, 2019]. Inspired by BERT's MLM objective, Lawrence et al. [2019] propose a model in which placeholder tokens are iteratively replaced by tokens from the output vocabulary to eventually generate the full output sequence. With this novel approach, the self-attention of a Transformer can take both past and future tokens into consideration, allowing for bidirectional sequence generation (BISON). Furthermore, the approach supports a direct integration of the pre-trained language model BERT as well as fine tuning on sequence generation tasks. Evaluated on two conversational data sets, BISON was found to outperform competitive baselines and state of the art neural network approaches in both cases by a significant margin.

Recently, Rothe et al. [2019] propose a Transformer-based sequence-to-sequence model that is compatible with publicly available pre-trained BERT and GPT-2 checkpoints and conduct an extensive empirical study on the utility of initialising Transformer models with these checkpoints. Their models result in new state-of-the-art results on machine translation, summarisation, sentence splitting, and fusion.

Recent trends in neural NLG using pre-training have shifted focus toward pre-training and fine-tuning approaches. Nonetheless, understanding long-form and complex inputs, and integrating complex communicative goals, are keys in making text-production models modular and interpretable; these problems have yet to be explored with these large language models.

Bibliography

Ossama Abdel-Hamid, Abdel rahman Mohamed, Hui Jiang, Li Deng, Gerald Penn, and Dong Yu. Convolutional neural networks for speech recognition. *IEEE/ACM Transactions on Audio, Speech, and Language Processing*, 22(10):1533–1545, 2014. DOI: 10.1109/taslp.2014.2339736 27

Shubham Agarwal and Marc Dymetman. A surprisingly effective out-of-the-box char2char model on the E2E NLG challenge dataset. In *Proc. of the 18th Annual SIGdial Meeting on Discourse and Dialogue*, pp. 158–163, Association for Computational Linguistics, Saarbrücken, Germany, 2017. DOI: 10.18653/v1/w17-5519 53

Danial Alihosseini, Ehsan Montahaei, and Mahdieh Soleymani Baghshah. Jointly measuring diversity and quality in text generation models. In *Proc. of the Workshop on Methods for Optimizing and Evaluating Neural Language Generation*, pp. 90–98, Association for Computational Linguistics, Minneapolis, MN, 2019. DOI: 10.18653/v1/w19-2311 133

Gabor Angeli, Percy Liang, and Dan Klein. A simple domain-independent probabilistic approach to generation. In *Proc. of the Conference on Empirical Methods in Natural Language Processing*, pp. 502–512, Association for Computational Linguistics, Cambridge, MA, 2010. 1, 5, 15

Michael Auli and Jianfeng Gao. Decoder integration and expected BLEU training for recurrent neural network language models. In *Proc. of the 52nd Annual Meeting of the Association for Computational Linguistics*, pp. 136–142, Baltimore, MD, 2014. DOI: 10.3115/v1/p14-2023 101

Jimmy Lei Ba, Jamie Ryan Kiros, and Geoffrey E. Hinton. Layer normalization. *CoRR*, abs/1607.06450, 2016. 39

Alexei Baevski, Sergey Edunov, Yinhan Liu, Luke Zettlemoyer, and Michael Auli. Cloze-driven pretraining of self-attention networks. In *Proc. of the Conference on Empirical Methods in Natural Language Processing and the 9th International Joint Conference on Natural Language Processing*, pp. 5363–5372, Association for Computational Linguistics, Hong Kong, China, 2019. DOI: 10.18653/v1/d19-1539 136

Dzmitry Bahdanau, Kyunghyun Cho, and Yoshua Bengio. Neural machine translation by jointly learning to align and translate. *CoRR*, abs/1409.0473, 2014. 46, 49, 57, 78, 82, 86, 88, 89

Laura Banarescu, Claire Bonial, Shu Cai, Madalina Georgescu, Kira Griffitt, Ulf Hermjakob, Kevin Knight, Philipp Koehn, Martha Palmer, and Nathan Schneider. Abstract meaning representation for sembanking. In *Proc. of the 7th Linguistic Annotation Workshop and Interoperability with Discourse*, pp. 178–186, Association for Computational Linguistics, Sofia, Bulgaria, 2013. 57, 58, 117

Srinivas Bangalore and Aravind K. Joshi. Supertagging: An approach to almost parsing. *Computational Linguistics*, 25(2):237–265, 1999. 16

Srinivas Bangalore and Owen Rambow. Using TAGs, a tree model, and a language model for generation. In *Proc. of the 5th International Workshop on Tree Adjoining Grammar and Related Frameworks*, pp. 33–40, Université Paris 7, France, 2000. 16, 17

Colin Bannard and Chris Callison-Burch. Paraphrasing with bilingual parallel corpora. In *Proc. of the 43rd Annual Meeting of the Association for Computational Linguistics*, pp. 597–604, Ann Arbor, Michigan, 2005. DOI: 10.3115/1219840.1219914 6

Regina Barzilay and Michael Elhadad. Using lexical chains for text summarization. In *Intelligent Scalable Text Summarization*, 1997. 22

Regina Barzilay and Kathleen R. McKeown. Extracting paraphrases from a parallel corpus. In *Proc. of the 39th Annual Meeting of the Association for Computational Linguistics*, pp. 50–57, Toulouse, France, 2001. DOI: 10.3115/1073012.1073020 6

Joost Bastings, Ivan Titov, Wilker Aziz, Diego Marcheggiani, and Khalil Simaan. Graph convolutional encoders for syntax-aware neural machine translation. In *Proc. of the Conference on Empirical Methods in Natural Language Processing*, pp. 1957–1967, Association for Computational Linguistics, Copenhagen, Denmark, 2017. DOI: 10.18653/v1/d17-1209 75, 78

Madeleine Bates. Models of natural language understanding. *Proc. of the National Academy of Sciences of the United States of America*, 92(22):9977–9982, 1995. 1

Anja Belz, Mike White, Dominic Espinosa, Eric Kow, Deirdre Hogan, and Amanda Stent. The first surface realisation shared task: Overview and evaluation results. In *Proc. of the 13th European Workshop on Natural Language Generation*, pp. 217–226, Association for Computational Linguistics, Nancy, France, 2011. 75, 78

Anja Belz, Bernd Bohnet, Simon Mille, Leo Wanner, and Michael White. The surface realisation task: Recent developments and future plans. In *Proc. of the 7th International Natural Language Generation Conference*, pp. 136–140, Association for Computational Linguistics, Utica, IL, 2012. 3, 75

Yoshua Bengio, Patrice Simard, and Paolo Frasconi. Learning long-term dependencies with gradient descent is difficult. *IEEE Transactions on Neural Networks*, 5(2):157–166, 1994. DOI: 10.1109/72.279181 29

Yoshua Bengio, Jérôme Louradour, Ronan Collobert, and Jason Weston. Curriculum learning. In *Proc. of the 26th Annual International Conference on Machine Learning*, pp. 41–48, Montréal, Quebec, Canada, 2009. DOI: 10.1145/1553374.1553380 99

Jonathan Berant and Percy Liang. Semantic parsing via paraphrasing. In *Proc. of the 52nd Annual Meeting of the Association for Computational Linguistics*, pp. 1415–1425, Baltimore, Maryland, 2014. DOI: 10.3115/v1/p14-1133 6

Raffaella Bernardi, Ruket Cakici, Desmond Elliott, Aykut Erdem, Erkut Erdem, Nazli Ikizler-Cinbis, Frank Keller, Adrian Muscat, and Barbara Plank. Automatic description generation from images: A survey of models, datasets, and evaluation measures. *Journal of Artificial Intelligence Research*, 55:409–442, 2016. DOI: 10.24963/ijcai.2017/704 1, 9

Or Biran, Samuel Brody, and Noemie Elhadad. Putting it simply: A context-aware approach to lexical simplification. In *Proc. of the 49th Annual Meeting of the Association for Computational Linguistics: Human Language Technologies*, pp. 496–501, Portland, OR, 2011. 123

David M. Blei, Andrew Y. Ng, and Michael I. Jordan. Latent dirichlet allocation. *Journal of Machine Learning Research*, 3:993–1022, 2003. 91

Bernd Bohnet, Leo Wanner, Simon Mille, and Alicia Burga. Broad coverage multilingual deep sentence generation with a stochastic multi-level realizer. In *Proc. of the 23rd International Conference on Computational Linguistics*, pp. 98–106, Coling Organizing Committee, Beijing, China, 2010. 17

Igor A. Bolshakov and Alexander Gelbukh. Synonymous paraphrasing using WordNet and internet. In Farid Meziane and Elisabeth Métais, Eds., *Natural Language Processing and Information Systems*, pp. 312–323, Springer, Berlin, Heidelberg, 2004. DOI: 10.1007/978-3-540-27779-8_27 20

Kalina Bontcheva and Yorick Wilks. Automatic report generation from ontologies: The miakt approach. In Farid Meziane and Elisabeth Métais, Eds., *Natural Language Processing and Information Systems*, pp. 324–335, Springer, Berlin, Heidelberg, 2004. DOI: 10.1007/978-3-540-27779-8_28 1, 5

Stefan Bott, Horacio Saggion, and Simon Mille. Text simplification tools for Spanish. In *Proc. of the 8th International Conference on Language Resources and Evaluation*, pp. 1665–1671, European Language Resources Association, Istanbul, Turkey, 2012. 18

Samuel R. Bowman, Gabor Angeli, Christopher Potts, and Christopher D. Manning. A large annotated corpus for learning natural language inference. In *Proc. of the Conference on Empirical Methods in Natural Language Processing*, pp. 632–642, Association for Computational Linguistics, Lisbon, Portugal, 2015. DOI: 10.18653/v1/d15-1075 105

Shu Cai and Kevin Knight. Smatch: An evaluation metric for semantic feature structures. In *Proc. of the 51st Annual Meeting of the Association for Computational Linguistics*, pp. 748–752, Sofia, Bulgaria, 2013. 93

Yvonne Margaret Canning. Syntactic simplification of text. Ph.D. thesis, University of Sunderland, 2002. 18

Kris Cao and Stephen Clark. Generating syntactically varied realisations from AMR graphs. *CoRR*, abs/1804.07707, 2018. 58

Ziqiang Cao, Chengyao Chen, Wenjie Li, Sujian Li, Furu Wei, and Ming Zhou. TG-Sum: Build tweet guided multi-document summarization dataset. In *Proc. of the 30th AAAI Conference on Artificial Intelligence*, pp. 2906–2912, Phoenix, AZ, 2016. DOI: 10.1142/9789813223615_0025 94

Ziqiang Cao, Chuwei Luo, Wenjie Li, and Sujian Li. Joint copying and restricted generation for paraphrase. In *Proc. of the 31st AAAI Conference on Artificial Intelligence*, pp. 3152–3158, San Francisco, CA, 2017. 51

Ziqiang Cao, Wenjie Li, Sujian Li, and Furu Wei. Retrieve, rerank and rewrite: Soft template based neural summarization. In *Proc. of the 56th Annual Meeting of the Association for Computational Linguistics*, pp. 152–161, Melbourne, Australia, 2018a. DOI: 10.18653/v1/p18-1015 134

Ziqiang Cao, Furu Wei, Wenjie Li, and Sujian Li. Faithful to the original: Fact aware neural abstractive summarization. In *Proc. of the 32nd AAAI Conference on Artificial Intelligence*, pp. 4784–4791, New Orleans, LA, 2018b. 49, 135

Giuseppe Carenini, Raymond T. Ng, and Xiaodong Zhou. Summarizing email conversations with clue words. In *Proc. of the 16th International Conference on World Wide Web*, pp. 91–100, Association for Computing Machinery, New York, 2007. DOI: 10.1145/1242572.1242586 23

John Carroll and Stephan Oepen. High efficiency realization for a wide-coverage unification grammar. In *Proc. of the 2nd International Joint Conference on Natural Language Processing*, Jeju Island, Korea, 2005. DOI: 10.1007/11562214_15 16

John Carroll, Guido Minnen, Darren Pearce, Yvonne Canning, Siobhan Devlin, and John Tait. Simplifying text for language-impaired readers. In *Proc. of the 9th Conference of the European Chapter of the Association for Computational Linguistics*, Bergen, Norway, 1999. 7

Rich Caruana. Multitask learning. *Machine Learning*, 28(1):41–75, 1997. DOI: 10.1007/978-1-4615-5529-2_5 88, 89

Thiago Castro Ferreira, Iacer Calixto, Sander Wubben, and Emiel Krahmer. Linguistic re-alisation as machine translation: Comparing different MT models for AMR-to-text gener-ation. In *Proc. of the 10th International Conference on Natural Language Generation*, pp. 1–10, Association for Computational Linguistics, Santiago de Compostela, Spain, 2017. DOI: 10.18653/v1/w17-3501 17, 58

Thiago Castro Ferreira, Chris van der Lee, Emiel van Miltenburg, and Emiel Krahmer. Neural data-to-text generation: A comparison between pipeline and end-to-end architectures. In *Proc. of the Conference on Empirical Methods in Natural Language Processing and the 9th Inter-national Joint Conference on Natural Language Processing*, pp. 552–562, Association for Com-putational Linguistics, Hong Kong, China, 2019. DOI: 10.18653/v1/d19-1052 133

Asli Celikyilmaz and Dilek Hakkani-Tur. A hybrid hierarchical model for multi-document summarization. In *Proc. of the 48th Annual Meeting of the Association for Computational Lin-guistics*, pp. 815–824, Uppsala, Sweden, 2010. 21

Asli Celikyilmaz, Antoine Bosselut, Xiaodong He, and Yejin Choi. Deep communicating agents for abstractive summarization. In *Proc. of the Conference of the North American Chapter of the Association for Computational Linguistics: Human Language Technologies*, pp. 1662–1675, New Orleans, LA, 2018. DOI: 10.18653/v1/n18-1150 49, 63, 65, 66, 68, 97, 104, 105, 132

William Chan, Nikita Kitaev, Kelvin Guu, Mitchell Stern, and Jakob Uszkoreit. KERMIT: Generative insertion-based modeling for sequences. *CoRR*, abs/1906.01604, 2019. 137

Raman Chandrasekar and Bangalore Srinivas. Automatic induction of rules for text simplifica-tion. *Knowledge-Based Systems*, 10(3):183–190, 1997. DOI: 10.1016/s0950-7051(97)00029-4 7, 18

Raman Chandrasekar, Christine Doran, and Bangalore Srinivas. Motivations and methods for text simplification. In *Proc. of the 16th International Conference on Computational Linguistics*, pp. 1041–1044, Copenhagen, Denmark, 1996. DOI: 10.3115/993268.993361 7

Mingje Chen, Gerasimos Lampouras, and Andreas Vlachos. Sheffield at E2E: Structured prediction approaches to end-to-end language generation. *Technical Report*, University of Sheffield, 2018. 51

Qian Chen, Xiaodan Zhu, Zhenhua Ling, Si Wei, and Hui Jiang. Distraction-based neural net-works for modeling documents. In *Proc. of the 25th International Joint Conference on Artificial Intelligence*, pp. 2754–2760, New York, 2016. 87

Yen-Chun Chen and Mohit Bansal. Fast abstractive summarization with reinforce—selected sentence rewriting. In *Proc. of the 56th Annual Meeting of the Association for Computational Linguistics*, pp. 675–686, Melbourne, Australia, 2018. DOI: 10.18653/v1/p18-1063 86

Jianpeng Cheng and Mirella Lapata. Neural summarization by extracting sentences and words. In *Proc. of the 54th Annual Meeting of the Association for Computational Linguistics*, pp. 484–494, Berlin, Germany, 2016. DOI: 10.18653/v1/p16-1046 27, 51, 68, 69, 85, 92, 94

Andrew Chisholm, Will Radford, and Ben Hachey. Learning to generate one-sentence biographies from Wikidata. In *Proc. of the 15th Conference of the European Chapter of the Association for Computational Linguistics*, pp. 633–642, Valencia, Spain, 2017. DOI: 10.18653/v1/e17-1060 113, 115

Kyunghyun Cho, Bart van Merrienboer, Caglar Gulcehre, Dzmitry Bahdanau, Fethi Bougares, Holger Schwenk, and Yoshua Bengio. Learning phrase representations using RNN encoder—decoder for statistical machine translation. In *Proc. of the Conference on Empirical Methods in Natural Language Processing*, pp. 1724–1734, Association for Computational Linguistics, Doha, Qatar, 2014. DOI: 10.3115/v1/d14-1179 25, 30, 33

Sumit Chopra, Michael Auli, and Alexander M. Rush. Abstractive sentence summarization with attentive recurrent neural networks. In *Proc. of the Conference of the North American Chapter of the Association for Computational Linguistics: Human Language Technologies*, pp. 93–98, San Diego, CA, 2016. DOI: 10.18653/v1/n16-1012 5, 6

James Clarke and Mirella Lapata. Constraint-based sentence compression: An integer programming approach. In *Proc. of the Joint Conference of the International Committee on Computational Linguistics and the Association for Computational Linguistics*, pp. 144–151, Sydney, Australia, 2006. DOI: 10.3115/1273073.1273092 20

Arman Cohan, Franck Dernoncourt, Doo Soon Kim, Trung Bui, Seokhwan Kim, Walter Chang, and Nazli Goharian. A discourse-aware attention model for abstractive summarization of long documents. In *Proc. of the Conference of the North American Chapter of the Association for Computational Linguistics: Human Language Technologies*, pp. 615–621, New Orleans, LA, 2018. DOI: 10.18653/v1/n18-2097 91

Trevor Cohn and Mirella Lapata. Sentence compression beyond word deletion. In *Proc. of the 22nd International Conference on Computational Linguistics*, pp. 137–144, Coling Organizing Committee, Manchester, UK, 2008. DOI: 10.3115/1599081.1599099 xix, 5, 125, 126, 127

Ronan Collobert, Jason Weston, Léon Bottou, Michael Karlen, Koray Kavukcuoglu, and Pavel Kuksa. Natural language processing (almost) from scratch. *Journal of Machine Learning Research*, 12:2493–2537, 2011. 27, 68, 69

John M. Conroy, Judith D. Schlesinger, and Dianne P. O'Leary. Topic-focused multi-document summarization using an approximate oracle score. In *Proc. of the Joint Conference of the International Committee on Computational Linguistics and the Association for Computational Linguistics*, pp. 152–159, Sydney, Australia, 2006. DOI: 10.3115/1273073.1273093 21

Will Coster and David Kauchak. Learning to simplify sentences using Wikipedia. In *Proc. of the Workshop on Monolingual Text-to-Text Generation*, pp. 1–9, Association for Computational Linguistics, Portland, OR, 2011. 19

Hoa Trang Dang. DUC 2005: Evaluation of question-focused summarization systems. In *Proc. of the Workshop on Task-Focused Summarization and Question Answering*, pp. 48–55, Association for Computational Linguistics, Sydney, Australia, 2006. DOI: 10.3115/1654679.1654689 5, 119

Dipanjan Das and Noah A. Smith. Paraphrase identification as probabilistic quasi-synchronous recognition. In *Proc. of the Joint Conference of the 47th Annual Meeting of the Association for Computational Linguistics and 4th International Joint Conference on Natural Language Processing of the Asian Federation of Natural Language Processing*, pp. 468–476, Suntec, Singapore, 2009. DOI: 10.3115/1687878.1687944 130

Hal Daumé III and Daniel Marcu. Bayesian query-focused summarization. In *Proc. of the 21st International Conference on Computational Linguistics and the 44th Annual Meeting of the Association for Computational Linguistics*, pp. 305–312, Sydney, Australia, 2006. DOI: 10.3115/1220175.1220214 21

Elnaz Davoodi, Charese Smiley, Dezhao Song, and Frank Schilder. The E2E NLG Challenge: Training a sequence-to-sequence approach for meaning representation to natural language sentences. *Technical Report*, Thomson Reuters, 2018. 51

Jan De Belder and Marie-Francine Moens. Text simplification for children. In *Proc. of the SIGIR Workshop on Accessible Search Systems*, Geneva, Switzerland, 2010. 7

Misha Denil, Alban Demiraj, Nal Kalchbrenner, Phil Blunsom, and Nando de Freitas. Modelling, visualising and summarising documents with a single convolutional neural network. *CoRR*, abs/1406.3830, 2014. 27

Jacob Devlin, Ming-Wei Chang, Kenton Lee, and Kristina Toutanova. BERT: Pre-training of deep bidirectional transformers for language understanding. In *Proc. of the Conference of the North American Chapter of the Association for Computational Linguistics: Human Language Technologies*, pp. 4171–4186, Minneapolis, MN, 2019. 32, 79, 132, 135, 136

Li Dong, Nan Yang, Wenhui Wang, Furu Wei, Xiaodong Liu, Yu Wang, Jianfeng Gao, Ming Zhou, and Hsiao-Wuen Hon. Unified language model pre-training for natural language understanding and generation. *CoRR*, abs/1905.03197, 2019. 136

Bonnie Dorr, David Zajic, and Richard Schwartz. Hedge trimmer: A parse-and-trim approach to headline generation. In *Proc. of the Human Language Technologies: The Annual Conference of the North American Chapter of the Association for Computational Linguis-

tics on Text summarization workshop—Volume 5, pp. 1–8, Edmonton, Canada, 2003. DOI: 10.3115/1119467.1119468 19

Mark Dras. Tree adjoining grammar and the reluctant paraphrasing of text. Ph.D. thesis, Macquarie University, Australia, 1999. 6, 19

John Duchi, Elad Hazan, and Yoram Singer. Adaptive subgradient methods for online learning and stochastic optimization. *Journal of Machine Learning Research*, 12:2121–2159, 2011. 39

Susan T. Dumais, George W. Furnas, Thomas K. Landauer, Scott Deerwester, and Richard Harshman. Using latent semantic analysis to improve access to textual information. In *Proc. of the SIGCHI Conference on Human Factors in Computing Systems*, pp. 281–285, Association for Computing Machinery, Washington, D.C., 1988. DOI: 10.1145/57167.57214 21

Greg Durrett, Taylor Berg-Kirkpatrick, and Dan Klein. Learning-based single-document summarization with compression and anaphoricity constraints. In *Proc. of the 54th Annual Meeting of the Association for Computational Linguistics*, pp. 1998–2008, Berlin, Germany, 2016. DOI: 10.18653/v1/p16-1188 5, 6, 62

Ondřej Dušek, Jekaterina Novikova, and Verena Rieser. Findings of the E2E NLG challenge. In *Proc. of the 11th International Conference on Natural Language Generation*, pp. 322–328, Association for Computational Linguistics, Tilburg University, The Netherlands, 2018. DOI: 10.18653/v1/w18-6539 60, 119

Henry Elder and Chris Hokamp. Generating high-quality surface realizations using data augmentation and factored sequence models. In *Proc. of the 1st Workshop on Multilingual Surface Realisation*, pp. 49–53, Association for Computational Linguistics, Melbourne, Australia, 2018. DOI: 10.18653/v1/w18-3606 135

Günes Erkan and Dragomir R. Radev. Lexrank: Graph-based lexical centrality as salience in text summarization. *Journal of Artificial Intelligence Research*, 22:457–479, 2004. DOI: 10.1613/jair.1523 22, 23, 64, 87

Dominic Espinosa, Michael White, and Dennis Mehay. Hypertagging: Supertagging for surface realization with CCG. In *Proc. of the 40th Annual Meeting of the Association of Computational Linguistics: Human Language Technologies*, pp. 183–191, Columbus, Ohio, 2008. 16

Angela Fan, Mike Lewis, and Yann Dauphin. Hierarchical neural story generation. In *Proc. of the 56th Annual Meeting of the Association for Computational Linguistics*, pp. 889–898, Melbourne, Australia, 2018. DOI: 10.18653/v1/p18-1082 134

Angela Fan, Claire Gardent, Chloé Braud, and Antoine Bordes. Using local knowledge graph construction to scale Seq2Seq models to multi-document inputs. In *Proc. of the Conference on Empirical Methods in Natural Language Processing and the 9th International Joint Conference on Natural Language Processing*, pp. 4177–4187, Association for Computational Linguistics, Hong Kong, China, 2019. DOI: 10.18653/v1/d19-1428 134

Jessica Ficler and Yoav Goldberg. Controlling linguistic style aspects in neural language generation. In *Proc. of the Workshop on Stylistic Variation*, pp. 94–104, Association for Computational Linguistics, Copenhagen, Denmark, 2017. DOI: 10.18653/v1/w17-4912 106

Elena Filatova. Multilingual wikipedia, summarization, and information trustworthiness. In *Proc. of the SIGIR Workshop on Information Access in a Multilingual World*, 3, 2009. 5

Katja Filippova. Multi-sentence compression: Finding shortest paths in word graphs. In *Proc. of the 23rd International Conference on Computational Linguistics*, pp. 322–330, Coling Organizing Committee, Beijing, China, 2010. 6

Katja Filippova and Yasemin Altun. Overcoming the lack of parallel data in sentence compression. In *Proc. of the Conference on Empirical Methods in Natural Language Processing*, pp. 1481–1491, Association for Computational Linguistics, Seattle, WA, 2013a. 124, 125, 126

Katja Filippova and Yasemin Altun. Overcoming the lack of parallel data in sentence compression. In *Proc. of the Conference on Empirical Methods in Natural Language Processing*, pp. 1481–1491, Association for Computational Linguistics, Seattle, WA, 2013b. 19

Katja Filippova and Michael Strube. Generating constituent order in German clauses. In *Proc. of the 45th Annual Meeting of the Association of Computational Linguistics*, pp. 320–327, Prague, Czech Republic, 2007. 17

Katja Filippova and Michael Strube. Dependency tree based sentence compression. In *Proc. of the 5th International Natural Language Generation Conference*, pp. 25–32, Association for Computational Linguistics. Salt Fork, OH, 2008. DOI: 10.3115/1708322.1708329 5, 20

Katja Filippova and Michael Strube. Tree linearization in English: Improving language model based approaches. In *Proc. of Human Language Technologies: The Annual Conference of the North American Chapter of the Association for Computational Linguistics*, pp. 225–228, Boulder, CO, 2009. DOI: 10.3115/1620853.1620915 17

Katja Filippova, Enrique Alfonseca, Carlos A. Colmenares, Lukasz Kaiser, and Oriol Vinyals. Sentence compression by deletion with LSTMs. In *Proc. of the Conference on Empirical Methods in Natural Language Processing*, pp. 360–368, Association for Computational Linguistics, Lisbon, Portugal, 2015. DOI: 10.18653/v1/d15-1042 6, 58, 70, 93, 94, 126

Jeffrey Flanigan, Chris Dyer, Noah A. Smith, and Jaime Carbonell. Generation from abstract meaning representation using tree transducers. In *Proc. of the Conference of the North American Chapter of the Association for Computational Linguistics: Human Language Technologies*, pp. 731–739, 2016. DOI: 10.18653/v1/n16-1087 17

Dimitrios Galanis and Ion Androutsopoulos. An extractive supervised two-stage method for sentence compression. In *Proc. of the Human Language Technologies: The Annual Conference of the North American Chapter of the Association for Computational Linguistics*, pp. 885–893, Los Angeles, CA, 2010. 20

Michel Galley and Kathleen McKeown. Improving word sense disambiguation in lexical chaining. In *Proc. of the 18th International Joint Conference on Artificial Intelligence*, pp. 1486–1488, Morgan Kaufmann Publishers Inc., Acapulco, Mexico, 2003. 22

Juri Ganitkevitch and Chris Callison-Burch. The multilingual paraphrase database. In *Proc. of the 9th International Conference on Language Resources and Evaluation*, pp. 4276–4283, European Language Resources Association, Reykjavik, Iceland, 2014. 130

Claire Gardent and Eric Kow. A symbolic approach to near-deterministic surface realisation using tree adjoining grammar. In *Proc. of the 45th Annual Meeting of the Association of Computational Linguistics*, pp. 328–335, Prague, Czech Republic, 2007. 16, 17

Claire Gardent and Laura Perez-Beltrachini. A statistical, grammar-based approach to microplanning. *Computational Linguistics*, 43(1):1–30, 2017. DOI: 10.1162/coli_a_00273 15, 16

Claire Gardent, Anastasia Shimorina, Shashi Narayan, and Laura Perez-Beltrachini. The WebNLG challenge: Generating text from RDF data. In *Proc. of the 10th International Conference on Natural Language Generation*, pp. 124–133, Association for Computational Linguistics, Santiago de Compostela, Spain, 2017a. DOI: 10.18653/v1/w17-3518 45, 71, 75, 78, 81, 92, 115

Claire Gardent, Anastasia Shimorina, Shashi Narayan, and Laura Perez-Beltrachini. Creating training corpora for NLG micro-planners. In *Proc. of the 55th Annual Meeting of the Association for Computational Linguistics*, pp. 179–188, Vancouver, Canada, 2017b. DOI: 10.18653/v1/p17-1017 59, 71, 75, 78, 113, 114

Albert Gatt and Emiel Krahmer. Survey of the state of the art in natural language generation: Core tasks, applications and evaluation. *Journal of Artificial Intelligence Research*, 61:65–170, 2018. DOI: 10.1613/jair.5477 1, 9, 14

Jonas Gehring, Michael Auli, David Grangier, Denis Yarats, and Yann N. Dauphin. Convolutional sequence to sequence learning. In Doina Precup and Yee Whye Teh, Eds., *Proc. of the 34th International Conference on Machine Learning*, volume 70 of *Proc. of Machine Learning Research*, pp. 1243–1252, Sydney, Australia, 2017. 79, 91

Sebastian Gehrmann, Yuntian Deng, and Alexander Rush. Bottom-up abstractive summarization. In *Proc. of the Conference on Empirical Methods in Natural Language Processing*, pp. 4098–4109, Association for Computational Linguistics, Brussels, Belgium, 2018. DOI: 10.18653/v1/d18-1443 58, 84, 85, 91

Marjan Ghazvininejad, Chris Brockett, Ming-Wei Chang, William B. Dolan, Jianfeng Gao, Wen tau Yih, and Michel Galley. A knowledge-grounded neural conversation model. In *Proc. of the 32nd AAAI Conference on Artificial Intelligence*, pp. 5110–5117, New Orleans, LA, 2018. 106

George Giannakopoulos, Elena Lloret, John M. Conroy, Josef Steinberger, Marina Litvak, Peter Rankel, and Benoit Favre. *Proc. of the MultiLing 2017 Workshop on Summarization and Summary Evaluation Across Source Types and Genres*, Valencia, Spain, 2017. Association for Computational Linguistics. 5

Dan Gillick and Benoit Favre. A scalable global model for summarization. In *Proc. of the Workshop on Integer Linear Programming for Natural Langauge Processing*, pp. 10–18, Association for Computational Linguistics, Boulder, CO, 2009. DOI: 10.3115/1611638.1611640 20

Dan Gillick, Korbinian Riedhammer, Benoit Favre, and Dilek Hakkani-Tur. A global optimization framework for meeting summarization. In *Proc. of the IEEE International Conference on Acoustics, Speech and Signal Processing*, pp. 4769–4772, Taipei, Taiwan, 2009. DOI: 10.1109/icassp.2009.4960697 23

Jade Goldstein, Vibhu Mittal, Jaime Carbonell, and Mark Kantrowitz. Multi-document summarisation by sentence extraction. In *Proc. of the NAACL-ANLP Workshop on Automatic summarization*, pp. 40–48, Association for Computational Linguistics, 2000. DOI: 10.3115/1117575.1117580 21

Yihong Gong and Xin Liu. Generic text summarization using relevance measure and latent semantic analysis. In *Proc. of the 24th Annual International ACM SIGIR Conference on Research and Development in Information Retrieval*, pp. 19–25, Association for Computing Machinery, New Orleans, LA, 2001. DOI: 10.1145/383952.383955 21

Ian Goodfellow, Yoshua Bengio, and Aaron Courville. *Deep Learning*. MIT Press, 2016. http://www.deeplearningbook.org 25, 28, 39, 40

Raghav Goyal, Marc Dymetman, and Eric Gaussier. Natural language generation through character-based RNNs with finite-state prior knowledge. In *Proc. of the 26th International Conference on Computational Linguistics*, pp. 1083–1092, The COLING Organizing Committee, Osaka, Japan, 2016. 51, 53

David Graff, Junbo Kong, Ke Chen, and Kazuaki Maeda. English gigaword. *Linguistic Data Consortium*, Philadelphia, 2003. 5, 84, 125

Max Grusky, Mor Naaman, and Yoav Artzi. Newsroom: A dataset of 1.3 million summaries with diverse extractive strategies. In *Proc. of the Conference of the North American Chapter of the Association for Computational Linguistics: Human Language Technologies*, pp. 708–719, New Orleans, LA, 2018. DOI: 10.18653/v1/n18-1065 6, 121

Jiatao Gu, Zhengdong Lu, Hang Li, and Victor O. K. Li. Incorporating copying mechanism in sequence-to-sequence learning. In *Proc. of the 54th Annual Meeting of the Association for Computational Linguistics*, pp. 1631–1640, Berlin, Germany, 2016. DOI: 10.18653/v1/p16-1154 51, 57, 74

Caglar Gulcehre, Sungjin Ahn, Ramesh Nallapati, Bowen Zhou, and Yoshua Bengio. Pointing the unknown words. In *Proc. of the 54th Annual Meeting of the Association for Computational Linguistics*, pp. 140–149, Berlin, Germany, 2016. DOI: 10.18653/v1/p16-1014 74

Kristina Gulordava, Piotr Bojanowski, Edouard Grave, Tal Linzen, and Marco Baroni. Colorless green recurrent networks dream hierarchically. In *Proc. of the Conference of the North American Chapter of the Association for Computational Linguistics: Human Language Technologies*, pp. 1195–1205, New Orleans, LA, 2018. DOI: 10.18653/v1/n18-1108 63

Bikash Gyawali and Claire Gardent. Surface realisation from knowledge-bases. In *Proc. of the 52nd Annual Meeting of the Association for Computational Linguistics*, pp. 424–434, Baltimore, MD, 2014. DOI: 10.3115/v1/p14-1040 16

Ben Hachey. Multi-document summarization using generic relation extraction. In *Proc. of the Conference on Empirical Methods in Natural Language Processing*, pp. 420–429, Association for Computational Linguistics, Singapore, 2009. DOI: 10.3115/1699510.1699565 5

Aria Haghighi and Lucy Vanderwende. Exploring content models for multi-document summarization. In *Proc. of Human Language Technologies: The Annual Conference of the North American Chapter of the Association for Computational Linguistics*, pp. 362–370, University of Colorado, Boulder, 2009. DOI: 10.3115/1620754.1620807 21

Dilek Hakkani-Tur and Gokhan Tur. Statistical sentence extraction for information distillation. In *Proc. of the IEEE International Conference on Acoustics, Speech and Signal Processing*, 4:1–4, Honolulu, HI, 2007. DOI: 10.1109/icassp.2007.367148 22

Donna Harman and Paul Over. The effects of human variation in DUC summarization evaluation. In *Text Summarization Branches Out*, pp. 10–17, Association for Computational Linguistics, Barcelona, Spain, 2004. 5, 119

Taher H. Haveliwala. Topic-sensitive PageRank. In *Proc. of the 11th International Conference on World Wide Web*, pp. 517–526, Honolulu, HI, 2002. DOI: 10.1145/511446.511513 87

Kaiming He, Xiangyu Zhang, Shaoqing Ren, and Jian Sun. Deep residual learning for image recognition. In *Proc. of the IEEE Conference on Computer Vision and Pattern Recognition*, pp. 770–778, Las Vegas, NV, 2016. DOI: 10.1109/cvpr.2016.90 39, 78

Shizhu He, Cao Liu, Kang Liu, and Jun Zhao. Generating natural answers by incorporating copying and retrieving mechanisms in sequence-to-sequence learning. In *Proc. of the 55th Annual Meeting of the Association for Computational Linguistics*, pp. 199–208, Vancouver, Canada, 2017. DOI: 10.18653/v1/p17-1019 51

Karl Moritz Hermann, Tomas Kocisky, Edward Grefenstette, Lasse Espeholt, Will Kay, Mustafa Suleyman, and Phil Blunsom. Teaching machines to read and comprehend. In C. Cortes, N. D. Lawrence, D. D. Lee, M. Sugiyama, and R. Garnett, Eds., *Advances in Neural Information Processing Systems 28*, pp. 1693–1701, Curran Associates, Inc., 2015. 6, 104, 119, 120

Sepp Hochreiter and Jürgen Schmidhuber. Long short-term memory. *Neural Computation*, 9(8):1735–1780, 1997. DOI: 10.1162/neco.1997.9.8.1735 30, 71

Eduard Hovy and ChinYew Lin. Automated text summarization in SUMMARIST. In *Intelligent Scalable Text Summarization*, 1997. 5

Jeremy Howard and Sebastian Ruder. Universal language model fine-tuning for text classification. *CoRR*, abs/1801.06146, 2018. DOI: 10.18653/v1/p18-1031 136

Wan-Ting Hsu, Chieh-Kai Lin, Ming-Ying Lee, Kerui Min, Jing Tang, and Min Sun. A unified model for extractive and abstractive summarization using inconsistency loss. In *Proc. of the 56th Annual Meeting of the Association for Computational Linguistics*, pp. 132–141, Melbourne, Australia, 2018. DOI: 10.18653/v1/p18-1013 86, 87, 91

Gao Huang, Zhuang Liu, Laurens van der Maaten, and Kilian Q. Weinberger. Densely connected convolutional networks. In *Proc. of the IEEE Conference on Computer Vision and Pattern Recognition*, pp. 2261–2269, Honolulu, HI, 2017. DOI: 10.1109/cvpr.2017.243 78

Nancy Ide, Collin Baker, Christiane Fellbaum, and Rebecca Passonneau. The manually annotated sub-corpus: A community resource for and by the people. In *Proc. of the ACL Conference Short Papers*, pp. 68–73, Association for Computational Linguistics, Uppsala, Sweden, 2010. 126

Kentaro Inui, Atsushi Fujita, Tetsuro Takahashi, Ryu Iida, and Tomoya Iwakura. Text simplification for reading assistance: A project note. In *Proc. of the 2nd International Workshop on Paraphrasing*, pp. 9–16, Association for Computational Linguistics, Sapporo, Japan, 2003. DOI: 10.3115/1118984.1118986 7

Sergey Ioffe and Christian Szegedy. Batch normalization: Accelerating deep network training by reducing internal covariate shift. *CoRR*, abs/1502.03167, 2015. 39

Glorianna Jagfeld, Sabrina Jenne, and Ngoc Thang Vu. Sequence-to-sequence models for data-to-text natural language generation: Word- vs. character-based processing and output diversity. In *Proc. of the 11th International Conference on Natural Language Generation*, pp. 221–232, Association for Computational Linguistics, Tilburg University, The Netherlands, 2018. DOI: 10.18653/v1/w18-6529 53

Tomáš Jelínek. Improvements to dependency parsing using automatic simplification of data. In *Proc. of the 9th International Conference on Language Resources and Evaluation*, pp. 73–77, European Language Resources Association, Reykjavik, Iceland, 2014. 7

Hongyan Jing and Kathleen R. McKeown. Cut and paste based text summarization. In *Proc. of the 1st North American chapter of the Association for Computational Linguistics conference*, pp. 178–185, Seattle, WA, 2000. 20

Juraj Juraska, Panagiotis Karagiannis, Kevin Bowden, and Marilyn Walker. A deep ensemble model with slot alignment for sequence-to-sequence natural language generation. In *Proc. of the Conference of the North American Chapter of the Association for Computational Linguistics: Human Language Technologies*, pp. 152–162, New Orleans, LA, 2018. DOI: 10.18653/v1/n18-1014 51

Mijail Kabadjov, Martin Atkinson, Josef Steinberger, Ralf Steinberger, and Erik Van Der Goot. NewsGist: A multilingual statistical news summarizer. In *Proc. of the Joint European Conference on Machine Learning and Knowledge Discovery in Databases*, pp. 591–594, Springer, Berlin, Heidelberg, 2010. DOI: 10.1007/978-3-642-15939-8_40 5

Nal Kalchbrenner, Edward Grefenstette, and Phil Blunsom. A convolutional neural network for modelling sentences. In *Proc. of the 52nd Annual Meeting of the Association for Computational Linguistics*, pp. 655–665, Baltimore, MD, 2014. DOI: 10.3115/v1/p14-1062 27, 68

David Kauchak. Improving text simplification language modeling using unsimplified text data. In *Proc. of the 51st Annual Meeting of the Association for Computational Linguistics*, pp. 1537–1546, Sofia, Bulgaria, 2013. 124

David Kauchak and Regina Barzilay. Paraphrasing for automatic evaluation. In *Proc. of the Human Language Technology Conference—North American Chapter of the Association for Computational Linguistics*, pp. 455–462, New York, 2006. DOI: 10.3115/1220835.1220893 6

James D. Keeler, David E. Rumelhart, and Wee Kheng Leow. Integrated segmentation and recognition of hand-printed numerals. In R. P. Lippmann, J. E. Moody, and D. S. Touretzky, Eds., *Advances in Neural Information Processing Systems 3*, pp. 557–563, Morgan Kaufmann, 1991. 88, 89

Chloé Kiddon, Luke Zettlemoyer, and Yejin Choi. Globally coherent text generation with neural checklist models. In *Proc. of the Conference on Empirical Methods in Natural Language Processing*, pp. 329–339, Association for Computational Linguistics, Austin, TX, 2016. DOI: 10.18653/v1/d16-1032 53

Yoon Kim. Convolutional neural networks for sentence classification. In *Proc. of the Conference on Empirical Methods in Natural Language Processing*, pp. 1746–1751, Association for Computational Linguistics, Doha, Qatar, 2014. DOI: 10.3115/v1/d14-1181 27, 68, 131

Yoon Kim, Yacine Jernite, David Sontag, and Alexander M. Rush. Character-aware neural language models. In *Proc. of the 30th AAAI Conference on Artificial Intelligence*, pp. 2741–2749, Phoenix, AZ, 2016. 27, 68

Diederik P. Kingma and Jimmy Ba. Adam: A method for stochastic optimization. *CoRR*, abs/1412.6980, 2014. 39

Thomas N. Kipf and Max Welling. Semi-supervised classification with graph convolutional networks. In *Proc. of the 5th International Conference on Learning Representations*, Toulon, France, 2017. 75

Kevin Knight and Daniel Marcu. Statistics-based summarization—Step One: Sentence compression. In *Proc. of the 17th National Conference on Artificial Intelligence and 12th Conference on Innovative Applications of Artificial Intelligence*, pp. 703–710, AAAI Press, Austin, TX, 2000. 6, 20

Rik Koncel-Kedziorski, Dhanush Bekal, Yi Luan, Mirella Lapata, and Hannaneh Hajishirzi. Text generation from knowledge graphs with graph transformers. In *Proc. of the Conference of the North American Chapter of the Association for Computational Linguistics: Human Language Technologies*, pp. 2284–2293, Minneapolis, MN, 2019. 136

Ravi Kondadadi, Blake Howald, and Frank Schilder. A statistical NLG framework for aggregated planning and realization. In *Proc. of the 51st Annual Meeting of the Association for Computational Linguistics*, pp. 1406–1415, Sofia, Bulgaria, 2013. 134

Ioannis Konstas and Mirella Lapata. Unsupervised concept-to-text generation with hypergraphs. In *Proc. of the Conference of the North American Chapter of the Association for Computational Linguistics: Human Language Technologies*, pp. 752–761, Montréal, Canada, 2012a. 5, 6, 14

Ioannis Konstas and Mirella Lapata. Concept-to-text generation via discriminative reranking. In *Proc. of the 50th Annual Meeting of the Association for Computational Linguistics*, pp. 369–378, Jeju Island, Korea, 2012b. 5

Ioannis Konstas, Srinivasan Iyer, Mark Yatskar, Yejin Choi, and Luke Zettlemoyer. Neural AMR: Sequence-to-sequence models for parsing and generation. In *Proc. of the 55th Annual Meeting of the Association for Computational Linguistics*, pp. 146–157, Vancouver, Canada, 2017. DOI: 10.18653/v1/p17-1014 1, 2, 41, 45, 57, 58, 60, 74, 92

Alex Krizhevsky, Ilya Sutskever, and Geoffrey E. Hinton. ImageNet classification with deep convolutional neural networks. In F. Pereira, C. J. C. Burges, L. Bottou, and K. Q. Weinberger, Eds., *Advances in Neural Information Processing Systems 25*, pp. 1097–1105, Curran Associates, Inc., 2012. DOI: 10.1145/3065386 27, 68, 69

Taku Kudo and John Richardson. SentencePiece: A simple and language independent subword tokenizer and detokenizer for neural text processing. In *Proc. of the Conference on Empirical Methods in Natural Language Processing: System Demonstrations*, pp. 66–71, Association for Computational Linguistics, Brussels, Belgium, 2018. DOI: 10.18653/v1/d18-2012 132

Julian Kupiec, Jan Pedersen, and Francine Chen. A trainable document summarizer. In *Proc. of the 18th Annual International ACM SIGIR Conference on Research and Development in Information Retrieval*, pp. 68–73, Association for Computing Machinery, Seattle, WA, 1995. DOI: 10.1145/215206.215333 22

Wuwei Lan, Siyu Qiu, Hua He, and Wei Xu. A continuously growing dataset of sentential paraphrases. In *Proc. of the Conference on Empirical Methods in Natural Language Processing*, pp. 1224–1234, Association for Computational Linguistics, Copenhagen, Denmark, 2017. DOI: 10.18653/v1/d17-1126 128, 129

Irene Langkilde. Forest-based statistical sentence generation. In *Proc. of the 1st Meeting of the North American Chapter of the Association for Computational Linguistics*, 2000. 17

Irene Langkilde-Geary. An empirical verification of coverage and correctness for a general-purpose sentence generator. In *Proc. of the International Natural Language Generation Conference*, pp. 17–24, Association for Computational Linguistics, Harriman, New York, 2002. 17

Carolin Lawrence, Bhushan Kotnis, and Mathias Niepert. Attending to future tokens for bidirectional sequence generation. In *Proc. of the Conference on Empirical Methods in Natural Language Processing and the 9th International Joint Conference on Natural Language Processing*, pp. 1–10, Association for Computational Linguistics, Hong Kong, China, 2019. DOI: 10.18653/v1/d19-1001 137

Rémi Lebret, David Grangier, and Michael Auli. Neural text generation from structured data with application to the biography domain. In *Proc. of the Conference on Empirical Methods in Natural Language Processing*, pp. 1203–1213, Association for Computational Linguistics, Austin, TX, 2016. DOI: 10.18653/v1/d16-1128 5, 82, 88, 90, 113

Yann Lecun. Generalization and network design strategies. In R. Pfeifer, Z. Schreter, F. Fogelman, and L. Steels, Eds., *Connectionism in Perspective*, Elsevier, 1989. 27

Yann LeCun, Bernhard E. Boser, John S. Denker, Donnie Henderson, R. E. Howard, Wayne E. Hubbard, and Lawrence D. Jackel. Handwritten digit recognition with a back-propagation network. In D. S. Touretzky, Ed., *Advances in Neural Information Processing Systems 2*, pp. 396–404, Morgan Kaufmann, 1990. 68, 78

Tao Lei, Regina Barzilay, and Tommi Jaakkola. Molding CNNs for text: Non-linear, non-consecutive convolutions. In *Proc. of the Conference on Empirical Methods in Natural Language Processing*, pp. 1565–1575, Association for Computational Linguistics, Lisbon, Portugal, 2015. DOI: 10.18653/v1/d15-1180 68

Jure Leskovec, Natasa Milic-Frayling, and Marko Grobelnik. Impact of linguistic analysis on the semantic graph coverage and learning of document extracts. In *Proc. of the 20th National Conference on Artificial Intelligence*, pp. 1069–1074, AAAI Press, Pittsburgh, PA, 2005. 22

Chenliang Li, Weiran Xu, Si Li, and Sheng Gao. Guiding generation for abstractive text summarization based on key information guide network. In *Proc. of the Conference of the North American Chapter of the Association for Computational Linguistics: Human Language Technologies*, pp. 55–60, New Orleans, LA, 2018a. DOI: 10.18653/v1/n18-2009 91

Haoran Li, Junnan Zhu, Jiajun Zhang, and Chengqing Zong. Ensure the correctness of the summary: Incorporate entailment knowledge into abstractive sentence summarization. In *Proc. of the 27th International Conference on Computational Linguistics*, pp. 1430–1441, Association for Computational Linguistics, Santa Fe, NM, 2018b. 135

Jiwei Li, Thang Luong, and Dan Jurafsky. A hierarchical neural autoencoder for paragraphs and documents. In *Proc. of the 53rd Annual Meeting of the Association for Computational Linguistics and the 7th International Joint Conference on Natural Language Processing*, pp. 1106–1115, Beijing, China, 2015. DOI: 10.3115/v1/p15-1107 63, 70

Jiwei Li, Michel Galley, Chris Brockett, Jianfeng Gao, and Bill Dolan. A diversity-promoting objective function for neural conversation models. In *Proc. of the Conference of the North American Chapter of the Association for Computational Linguistics: Human Language Technologies*, pp. 110–119, San Diego, CA, 2016a. DOI: 10.18653/v1/n16-1014 106

Jiwei Li, Michel Galley, Chris Brockett, Georgios Spithourakis, Jianfeng Gao, and Bill Dolan. A persona-based neural conversation model. In *Proc. of the 54th Annual Meeting of the Association for Computational Linguistics*, pp. 994–1003, Berlin, Germany, 2016b. DOI: 10.18653/v1/p16-1094 58, 106, 107, 108, 109

Jiwei Li, Will Monroe, Alan Ritter, Dan Jurafsky, Michel Galley, and Jianfeng Gao. Deep reinforcement learning for dialogue generation. In *Proc. of the Conference on Empirical Methods in Natural Language Processing*, pp. 1192–1202, Association for Computational Linguistics, Austin, TX, 2016c. DOI: 10.18653/v1/d16-1127 101, 102, 103, 105

Wei Li, Xinyan Xiao, Yajuan Lyu, and Yuanzhuo Wang. Improving neural abstractive document summarization with explicit information selection modeling. In *Proc. of the Conference on Empirical Methods in Natural Language Processing*, pp. 1787–1796, Association for Computational Linguistics, Brussels, Belgium, 2018c. DOI: 10.18653/v1/d18-1205 91

Xiaodan Liang, Xiaohui Shen, Jiashi Feng, Liang Lin, and Shuicheng Yan. Semantic object parsing with graph LSTM. In *Proc. of the 14th European Conference on Computer Vision Computer Vision*, pp. 125–143, Amsterdam, The Netherlands, 2016. DOI: 10.1007/978-3-319-46448-0_8 75

Chin-Yew Lin and Eduard Hovy. The automated acquisition of topic signatures for text summarization. In *Proc. of the 18th International Conference on Computational Linguistics*, Association for Computational Linguistics, Saarbrucken, Germany, 2000. DOI: 10.3115/990820.990892 22

Chin-Yew Lin and Eduard Hovy. Automatic evaluation of summaries using n-gram co-occurrence statistics. In *Proc. of the Human Language Technology Conference of the North American Chapter of the Association for Computational Linguistics*, pp. 71–78, Edmonton, Canada, 2003. DOI: 10.3115/1073445.1073465 93, 97

Wang Ling, Isabel Trancoso, Chris Dyer, and Alan W. Black. Character-based neural machine translation. *CoRR*, abs/1511.04586, 2015. 53

Fei Liu, Jeffrey Flanigan, Sam Thomson, Norman Sadeh, and Noah A. Smith. Toward abstractive summarization using semantic representations. In *Proc. of the Conference of the North American Chapter of the Association for Computational Linguistics: Human Language Technologies*, pp. 1077–1086, Denver, CO, 2015. DOI: 10.3115/v1/n15-1114 3

Elena Lloret and Manuel Palomar. Finding the best approach for multi-lingual text summarisation: A comparative analysis. In *Proc. of the International Conference Recent Advances in Natural Language Processing*, pp. 194–201, Association for Computational Linguistics, Hissar, Bulgaria, 2011. 5

Annie Louis, Aravind Joshi, and Ani Nenkova. Discourse indicators for content selection in summarization. In *Proc. of the 11th Annual Meeting of the Special Interest Group on Discourse and Dialogue*, pp. 147–156, Association for Computational Linguistics, Tokyo, Japan, 2010. 22

Xiaofei Lu. Automatic analysis of syntactic complexity in second language writing. *International Journal of Corpus Linguistics*, 15(4):474–496, 2010. DOI: 10.1075/ijcl.15.4.02lu 133

Hans Peter Luhn. The automatic creation of literature abstracts. *IBM Journal of Research and Development*, 2(2):159–165, 1958. DOI: 10.1147/rd.22.0159 21

Thang Luong, Hieu Pham, and Christopher D. Manning. Effective approaches to attention-based neural machine translation. In *Proc. of the Conference on Empirical Methods in Natural Language Processing*, pp. 1412–1421, Association for Computational Linguistics, Lisbon, Portugal, 2015. DOI: 10.18653/v1/d15-1166 75, 78, 88, 89

Nitin Madnani and Bonnie J. Dorr. Generating phrasal and sentential paraphrases: A survey of data-driven methods. *Computational Linguistics*, 36(3):341–387, 2010. DOI: 10.1162/coli_a_00002 81

François Mairesse and Steve Young. Stochastic language generation in dialogue using factored language models. *Computational Linguistics*, 40(4):763–799, 2014. DOI: 10.1162/coli_a_00199 4, 59

Jonathan Mallinson, Rico Sennrich, and Mirella Lapata. Paraphrasing revisited with neural machine translation. In *Proc. of the 15th Conference of the European Chapter of the Association for Computational Linguistics*, pp. 881–893, Valencia, Spain, 2017. DOI: 10.18653/v1/e17-1083 6, 58, 82

Inderjeet Mani. *Advances in Automatic Text Summarization*. MIT Press, 1999. 20, 81

Christopher Manning, Mihai Surdeanu, John Bauer, Jenny Finkel, Steven Bethard, and David McClosky. The Stanford CoreNLP natural language processing toolkit. In *Proc. of 52nd Annual Meeting of the Association for Computational Linguistics: System Demonstrations*, pp. 55–60, Baltimore, MD, 2014. DOI: 10.3115/v1/p14-5010 29

Diego Marcheggiani and Laura Perez-Beltrachini. Deep graph convolutional encoders for structured data to text generation. In *Proc. of the 11th International Conference on Natural Language Generation*, pp. 1–9, Tilburg University, The Netherlands, 2018. DOI: 10.18653/v1/w18-6501 71, 75, 78

Diego Marcheggiani and Ivan Titov. Encoding sentences with graph convolutional networks for semantic role labeling. In *Proc. of the Conference on Empirical Methods in Natural Language Processing*, pp. 1506–1515, Association for Computational Linguistics, Copenhagen, Denmark, 2017. DOI: 10.18653/v1/d17-1159 75

Diego Marcheggiani, Joost Bastings, and Ivan Titov. Exploiting semantics in neural machine translation with graph convolutional networks. In *Proc. of the Conference of the North American Chapter of the Association for Computational Linguistics: Human Language Technologies*, pp. 486–492, New Orleans, LA, 2018. DOI: 10.18653/v1/n18-2078 75, 78

Rebecca Marvin and Tal Linzen. Targeted syntactic evaluation of language models. In *Proc. of the Conference on Empirical Methods in Natural Language Processing*, pp. 1192–1202, Association for Computational Linguistics, Brussels, Belgium, 2018. DOI: 10.18653/v1/d18-1151 63

Jonathan May and Jay Priyadarshi. Semeval-2017 task 9: Abstract meaning representation parsing and generation. In *Proc. of the 11th International Workshop on Semantic Evaluation*, pp. 536–545, Association for Computational Linguistics, Vancouver, Canada, 2017. DOI: 10.18653/v1/s17-2090 2, 4, 57, 58, 71, 81, 92, 117

Ryan McDonald and Joakim Nivre. Analyzing and integrating dependency parsers. *Computational Linguistics*, 37(1):197–230, March 2011. DOI: 10.1162/coli_a_00039 7

Kathleen McKeown, Sara Rosenthal, Kapil Thadani, and Coleman Moore. Time-efficient creation of an accurate sentence fusion corpus. In *Human Language Technologies: The Annual Conference of the North American Chapter of the Association for Computational Linguistics*, pp. 317–320, Los Angeles, CA, 2010. 6

Kathleen R. McKeown. Paraphrasing questions using given and new information. *Computational Linguistics*, 9(1):1–10, 1983. 20

Yishu Miao and Phil Blunsom. Language as a latent variable: Discrete generative models for sentence compression. In *Proc. of the Conference on Empirical Methods in Natural Language Processing*, pp. 319–328, Association for Computational Linguistics, Austin, TX, 2016. DOI: 10.18653/v1/d16-1031 51

Rada Mihalcea and Paul Tarau. Textrank: Bringing order into text. In *Proc. of the conference on Empirical Methods in Natural Language Processing*, pp. 404–411, Association for Computational Linguistics, Barcelona, Spain, 2004. 22, 64, 86

Tomas Mikolov, Ilya Sutskever, Kai Chen, Greg S. Corrado, and Jeff Dean. Distributed representations of words and phrases and their compositionality. In C. J. C. Burges, L. Bottou, M. Welling, Z. Ghahramani, and K. Q. Weinberger, Eds., *Advances in Neural Information Processing Systems 26*, pp. 3111–3119, Curran Associates, Inc., 2013. 31, 79

Simon Mille, Anja Belz, Bernd Bohnet, Yvette Graham, Emily Pitler, and Leo Wanner. The first multilingual surface realisation shared task: Overview and evaluation results. In *Proc. of the 1st Workshop on Multilingual Surface Realisation*, pp. 1–12, Association for Computational Linguistics, Melbourne, Australia, 2018. DOI: 10.18653/v1/w18-3601 2, 3, 45, 82, 118, 133

Volodymyr Mnih, Koray Kavukcuoglu, David Silver, Alex Graves, Ioannis Antonoglou, Daan Wierstra, and Martin Riedmiller. Playing Atari with deep reinforcement learning. In *Advances in Neural Information Processing Systems: Deep Learning Workshop*, 2013. 100

Amit Moryossef, Yoav Goldberg, and Ido Dagan. Step-by-step: Separating planning from realization in neural data-to-text generation. In *Proc. of the Conference of the North American Chapter of the Association for Computational Linguistics: Human Language Technologies*, pp. 2267–2277, Minneapolis, MN, 2019. 133

Bradford Mott, James Lester, and Luther Branting. Conversational agents. In *The Practical Handbook of Internet Computing*, 2004. DOI: 10.1201/9780203507223.ch10 1

Hiroko Nakanishi, Yusuke Miyao, and Jun'ichi Tsujii. Probabilistic models for disambiguation of an HPSG-based chart generator. In *Proc. of the 9th International Workshop on Parsing Technology*, pp. 93–102, Association for Computational Linguistics, Vancouver, British Columbia, 2005. DOI: 10.3115/1654494.1654504 17

Ramesh Nallapati, Bowen Zhou, Cicero dos Santos, Caglar Gulcehre, and Bing Xiang. Abstractive text summarization using sequence-to-sequence RNNs and beyond. In *Proc. of the 20th SIGNLL Conference on Computational Natural Language Learning*, pp. 280–290, Association for Computational Linguistics, Berlin, Germany, 2016. DOI: 10.18653/v1/k16-1028 45, 51, 57, 58, 70

Ramesh Nallapati, Feifei Zhai, and Bowen Zhou. SummaRuNNer: A recurrent neural network based sequence model for extractive summarization of documents. In *Proc. of the 31st AAAI Conference on Artificial Intelligence*, pp. 3075–3081, San Francisco, CA, 2017. 85, 87, 94

Courtney Napoles, Chris Callison-Burch, Juri Ganitkevitch, and Benjamin Van Durme. Paraphrastic sentence compression with a character-based metric: Tightening without deletion. In *Proc. of the Workshop on Monolingual Text-to-Text Generation*, pp. 84–90, Association for Computational Linguistics, 2011. 6

Courtney Napoles, Matthew Gormley, and Benjamin Van Durme. Annotated gigaword. In *Proc. of the Joint Workshop on Automatic Knowledge Base Construction and Web-Scale Knowledge Extraction*, pp. 95–100, Association for Computational Linguistics, Montréal, Canada, 2012. 5, 125

Courtney Napoles, Chris Callison-Burch, and Matt Post. Sentential paraphrasing as black-box machine translation. In *Proc. of the Conference of the North American Chapter of the Association for Computational Linguistics: Demonstrations*, pp. 62–66, San Diego, CA, 2016. DOI: 10.18653/v1/n16-3013 20

Shashi Narayan and Claire Gardent. Structure-driven lexicalist generation. In *Proc. of the 24th International Conference on Computational Linguistics*, pp. 2027–2042, The COLING Organizing Committee, Mumbai, India, 2012. 16

Shashi Narayan and Claire Gardent. Hybrid simplification using deep semantics and machine translation. In *Proc. of the 52nd Annual Meeting of the Association for Computational Linguistics*, pp. 435–445, Baltimore, MD, 2014. DOI: 10.3115/v1/p14-1041 3, 6, 19, 41, 93, 123

Shashi Narayan and Claire Gardent. Unsupervised sentence simplification using deep semantics. In *Proc. of the 9th International Natural Language Generation conference*, pp. 111–120, Association for Computational Linguistics, Edinburgh, UK, 2016. DOI: 10.18653/v1/w16-6620 6

Shashi Narayan, Siva Reddy, and Shay B. Cohen. Paraphrase generation from latent-variable PCFGs for semantic parsing. In *Proc. of the 9th International Natural Language Generation conference*, pp. 153–162, Association for Computational Linguistics, Edinburgh, UK, 2016. DOI: 10.18653/v1/w16-6625 20

Shashi Narayan, Nikos Papasarantopoulos, Shay B. Cohen, and Mirella Lapata. Neural extractive summarization with side information. *CoRR*, abs/1704.04530, 2017. 27, 69, 70

Shashi Narayan, Ronald Cardenas, Nikos Papasarantopoulos, Shay B. Cohen, Mirella Lapata, Jiangsheng Yu, and Yi Chang. Document modeling with external attention for sentence extraction. In *Proc. of the 56th Annual Meeting of the Association for Computational Linguistics*, pp. 2020–2030, Melbourne, Australia, 2018a. DOI: 10.18653/v1/p18-1188 27, 69

Shashi Narayan, Shay B. Cohen, and Mirella Lapata. Don't give me the details, just the summary! Topic-aware convolutional neural networks for extreme summarization. In *Proc. of the Conference on Empirical Methods in Natural Language Processing*, pp. 1797–1807, Association for Computational Linguistics, Brussels, Belgium, 2018b. DOI: 10.18653/v1/d18-1206 79, 82, 91, 121, 122, 123

Shashi Narayan, Shay B. Cohen, and Mirella Lapata. Ranking sentences for extractive summarization with reinforcement learning. In *Proc. of the Conference of the North American Chapter of the Association for Computational Linguistics: Human Language Technologies*, pp. 1747–1759, New Orleans, LA, 2018c. DOI: 10.18653/v1/n18-1158 27, 63, 68, 69, 70, 71, 85, 97, 99, 101, 103, 135

Neha Nayak, Dilek Hakkani-Tür, Marilyn Walker, and Larry Heck. To plan or not to plan? Discourse planning in slot-value informed sequence to sequence models for language generation. In *Proc. of the 18th Annual Conference of the International Speech Communication Association*, pp. 3339–3343, Stockholm, Sweden, 2017. DOI: 10.21437/interspeech.2017-1525 51

Ani Nenkova and Kathleen McKeown. Automatic summarization. *Foundations and Trends in Information Retrieval*, 5(2–3):103–233, 2011. DOI: 10.1561/1500000015 1, 81

Ani Nenkova and Kathleen McKeown. A survey of text summarization techniques. In *Mining Text Data*, pp. 43–76, Springer, 2012. DOI: 10.1007/978-1-4614-3223-4_3 20

Ani Nenkova and Lucy Vanderwende. The impact of frequency on summarization. *Technical Report*, Microsoft Research, Redmond, WA, 2005. 21

Ani Nenkova, Kathleen McKeown, et al. Automatic summarization. *Foundations and Trends® in Information Retrieval*, 5(2–3):103–233, 2011. DOI: 10.1561/1500000015 20, 21

Rodrigo Nogueira and Kyunghyun Cho. Task-oriented query reformulation with reinforcement learning. In *Proc. of the Conference on Empirical Methods in Natural Language Processing*, pp. 574–583, Association for Computational Linguistics, Copenhagen, Denmark, 2017. DOI: 10.18653/v1/d17-1061 101

Jekaterina Novikova, Ondřej Dušek, Amanda Cercas Curry, and Verena Rieser. Why we need new evaluation metrics for NLG. In *Proc. of the Conference on Empirical Methods in Natural Language Processing*, pp. 2241–2252, Copenhagen, Denmark, 2017a. DOI: 10.18653/v1/d17-1238 132

Jekaterina Novikova, Ondřej Dušek, and Verena Rieser. The E2E dataset: New challenges for end-to-end generation. In *Proc. of the 18th Annual SIGdial Meeting on Discourse and Dialogue*, pp. 201–206, Association for Computational Linguistics, Saarbrücken, Germany, 2017b. DOI: 10.18653/v1/w17-5525 2, 5, 59, 92, 118

Miles Osborne. Using maximum entropy for sentence extraction. In *Proc. of the Workshop on Automatic Summarization (including DUC 2002)*, pp. 1–8, Association for Computational Linguistics, Philadelphia, PA, 2002. DOI: 10.3115/1118162.1118163 22

Lawrence Page, Sergey Brin, Rajeev Motwani, and Terry Winograd. The PageRank citation ranking: Bringing order to the Web. In *Proc. of the 7th International World Wide Web Conference*, pp. 161–172, Brisbane, Australia, 1998. 87

Martha Palmer, Daniel Gildea, and Paul Kingsbury. The proposition bank: An annotated corpus of semantic roles. *Computational Linguistics*, 31(1):71–106, 2005. DOI: 10.1162/0891201053630264 4

Kishore Papineni, Salim Roukos, Todd Ward, and Wei-Jing Zhu. BLEU: A method for automatic evaluation of machine translation. In *Proc. of the 40th Annual Meeting of the Association for Computational Linguistics*, pp. 311–318, Philadelphia, PA, 2002. DOI: 10.3115/1073083.1073135 92

Ankur Parikh, Oscar Täckström, Dipanjan Das, and Jakob Uszkoreit. A decomposable attention model for natural language inference. In *Proc. of the Conference on Empirical Methods in Natural Language Processing*, pp. 2249–2255, Association for Computational Linguistics, Austin, TX, 2016. DOI: 10.18653/v1/d16-1244 105

Razvan Pascanu, Tomas Mikolov, and Yoshua Bengio. On the difficulty of training recurrent neural networks. In *Proc. of the 30th International Conference on International Conference on Machine Learning*, pp. 1310–1318, Atlanta, GA, 2013. JMLR.org 29

Ramakanth Pasunuru and Mohit Bansal. Multi-reward reinforced summarization with saliency and entailment. In *Proc. of the Conference of the North American Chapter of the Association for Computational Linguistics: Human Language Technologies*, pp. 646–653, Association for Computational Linguistics, New Orleans, LA, 2018. DOI: 10.18653/v1/n18-2102 58, 97, 104, 105

Romain Paulus, Caiming Xiong, and Richard Socher. A deep reinforced model for abstractive summarization. In *Proc. of the 6th International Conference on Learning Representations*, Vancouver, BC, Canada, 2018. 57, 58, 97, 101, 104, 105

Jeffrey Pennington, Richard Socher, and Christopher Manning. Glove: Global vectors for word representation. In *Proc. of the Conference on Empirical Methods in Natural Language Processing*, pp. 1532–1543, Association for Computational Linguistics, Doha, Qatar, 2014. DOI: 10.3115/v1/d14-1162 31, 79

Laura Perez-Beltrachini and Claire Gardent. Analysing data-to-text generation benchmarks. In *Proc. of the 10th International Conference on Natural Language Generation*, pp. 238–242, Association for Computational Linguistics, Santiago de Compostela, Spain, 2017. DOI: 10.18653/v1/w17-3537 133

Laura Perez-Beltrachini and Mirella Lapata. Bootstrapping generators from noisy data. In *Proc. of the Conference of the North American Chapter of the Association for Computational Linguistics: Human Language Technologies*, pp. 1516–1527, New Orleans, LA, 2018. DOI: 10.18653/v1/n18-1137 5, 60, 88, 89, 90, 97, 101, 106, 113, 114

Matthew Peters, Mark Neumann, Mohit Iyyer, Matt Gardner, Christopher Clark, Kenton Lee, and Luke Zettlemoyer. Deep contextualized word representations. In *Proc. of the Conference of the North American Chapter of the Association for Computational Linguistics: Human Language Technologies*, pp. 2227–2237, New Orleans, LA, 2018. DOI: 10.18653/v1/n18-1202 32, 79, 85, 135, 136

Emily Pitler. Methods for sentence compression. *Technical Report*, University of Pennsylvania, 2010. 6

Nima Pourdamghani, Kevin Knight, and Ulf Hermjakob. Generating English from abstract meaning representations. In *Proc. of the 9th International Natural Language Generation Conference*, pp. 21–25, Association for Computational Linguistics, Edinburgh, UK, 2016. DOI: 10.18653/v1/w16-6603 17

Richard Power. Towards a generation-based semantic web authoring tool. In *Proc. of the 12th European Workshop on Natural Language Generation*, pp. 9–15, Association for Computational Linguistics, Athens, Greece, 2009. DOI: 10.3115/1610195.1610197 1, 5

Ratish Puduppully, Li Dong, and Mirella Lapata. Data-to-text generation with content selection and planning. In *Proc. of the 33rd AAAI Conference on Artificial Intelligence*, pp. 6908–6915, Honolulu, HI, 2019. DOI: 10.1609/aaai.v33i01.33016908 91

Yevgeniy Puzikov and Iryna Gurevych. E2E NLG challenge: Neural models vs. templates. In *Proc. of the 11th International Conference on Natural Language Generation*, pp. 463–471, Association for Computational Linguistics, Tilburg University, The Netherlands, 2018. DOI: 10.18653/v1/w18-6557 51

Chris Quirk, Chris Brockett, and William Dolan. Monolingual machine translation for paraphrase generation. In *Proc. of the Conference on Empirical Methods in Natural Language Processing*, pp. 142–149, Association for Computational Linguistics, Barcelona, Spain, 2004. 20, 130

Alec Radford, Karthik Narasimhan, Tim Salimans, and Ilya Sutskever. Improving language understanding with unsupervised learning. *Technical Report*, OpenAI, 2018. 32, 79, 132, 136

Alec Radford, Jeffrey Wu, Rewon Child, David Luan, Dario Amodei, and Ilya Sutskever. Language models are unsupervised multitasl learners. *Technical Report*, OpenAI, 2019. 32, 79, 135, 136

Pranav Rajpurkar, Jian Zhang, Konstantin Lopyrev, and Percy Liang. SQuAD: 100,000+ questions for machine comprehension of text. In *Proc. of the Conference on Empirical Methods in Natural Language Processing*, pp. 2383–2392, Association for Computational Linguistics, Austin, TX, 2016. DOI: 10.18653/v1/d16-1264 105, 136

Ashwin Ram, Rohit Prasad, Chandra Khatri, Anu Venkatesh, Raefer Gabriel, Qing Liu, Jeff Nunn, Behnam Hedayatnia, Ming Cheng, Ashish Nagar, Eric King, Kate Bland, Amanda Wartick, Yi Pan, Han Song, Sk Jayadevan, Gene Hwang, and Art Pettigrue. Conversational AI: The science behind the Alexa prize. *CoRR*, abs/1801.03604, 2017. 106

Marc'Aurelio Ranzato, Sumit Chopra, Michael Auli, and Wojciech Zaremba. Sequence level training with recurrent neural networks. *CoRR*, abs/1511.06732, 2015. 40, 65, 91, 92, 93, 97, 98, 99, 100, 101

Sashank J. Reddi, Satyen Kale, and Sanjiv Kumar. On the convergence of Adam and beyond. In *Proc. of the 6th International Conference on Learning Representations*, Vancouver, Canada, 2018. 39

Byron Reeves and Clifford Nass. *The Media Equation: How People Treat Computers, Television, and New Media Like Real People and Places*. Cambridge University Press, New York, 1996. 106

Ehud Reiter. A structured review of the validity of BLEU. *Computational Linguistics*, 44(3):393–401, 2018. DOI: 10.1162/coli_a_00322 93, 132

Ehud Reiter and Anja Belz. An investigation into the validity of some metrics for automatically evaluating natural language generation systems. *Computational Linguistics*, 35(4):529–558, 2009. DOI: 10.1162/coli.2009.35.4.35405 132

Ehud Reiter and Robert Dale. *Building Natural Language Generation Systems*. Cambridge University Press, New York, 2000. DOI: 10.1017/cbo9780511519857 1

Ehud Reiter, Somayajulu Sripada, Jim Hunter, Jin Yu, and Ian Davy. Choosing words in computer-generated weather forecasts. *Artificial Intelligence*, 167(1):137–169, 2005. DOI: 10.1016/j.artint.2005.06.006 1, 5

Steven J. Rennie, Etienne Marcheret, Youssef Mroueh, Jarret Ross, and Vaibhava Goel. Self-critical sequence training for image captioning. *CoRR*, abs/1612.00563, 2016. DOI: 10.1109/cvpr.2017.131 65, 105

Leonardo Ribeiro, Claire Gardent, and Iryna Gurevytch. Enhancing AMR-to-text generation with dual graph representations. In *Proc. of the Conference on Empirical Methods in Natural Language Processing*, pp. 3174–3185, Association for Computational Linguistics, Hong Kong, China, 2019. DOI: 10.18653/v1/d19-1314 132

Korbinian Riedhammer, Dan Gillick, Benoit Favre, and Dilek Hakkani-Tür. Packing the meeting summarization knapsack. In *Proc. of the 9th Annual Conference of the International Speech Communication Association*, pp. 2434–2437, Brisbane, Australia, 2008. 23

Stefan Riezler, Alexander Vasserman, Ioannis Tsochantaridis, Vibhu Mittal, and Yi Liu. Statistical machine translation for query expansion in answer retrieval. In *Proc. of the 45th Annual Meeting of the Association of Computational Linguistics*, pp. 464–471, Association for Computational Linguistics, Prague, Czech Republic, 2007. 6

Alan Ritter, Colin Cherry, and William B. Dolan. Data-driven response generation in social media. In *Proc. of the Conference on Empirical Methods in Natural Language Processing*, pp. 583–593, Association for Computational Linguistics, Edinburgh, Scotland, UK, 2011. 106

Sascha Rothe, Shashi Narayan, and Aliaksei Severyn. Leveraging pre-trained checkpoints for sequence generation tasks. *CoRR*, abs/1907.12461, 2019. 137

David E. Rumelhart, Geoffrey E. Hinton, and Ronald J. Williams. Learning representations by back-propagating errors. *Nature*, 323:533–536, 1986. DOI: 10.1038/323533a0 39

Alexander M. Rush, Sumit Chopra, and Jason Weston. A neural attention model for abstractive sentence summarization. In *Proc. of the Conference on Empirical Methods in Natural Language Processing*, pp. 379–389, Association for Computational Linguistics, Lisbon, Portugal, 2015. DOI: 10.18653/v1/d15-1044 6, 19, 40, 45, 70, 125

Evan Sandhaus. The *New York Times* annotated corpus. Linguistic Data Consortium, Philadelphia, PA, 2008. 6, 104, 119, 121

Natalie Schluter. The limits of automatic summarisation according to rouge. In *Proc. of the 15th Conference of the European Chapter of the Association for Computational Linguistics: Short Papers*, pp. 41–45, Valencia, Spain, 2017. DOI: 10.18653/v1/e17-2007 93

Abigail See, Peter J. Liu, and Christopher D. Manning. Get to the point: Summarization with pointer-generator networks. In *Proc. of the 55th Annual Meeting of the Association for Computational Linguistics*, pp. 1073–1083, Vancouver, Canada, 2017. DOI: 10.18653/v1/p17-1099 40, 41, 50, 51, 53, 54, 55, 57, 58, 59, 64, 68, 74, 84, 85, 87, 92, 132

Rico Sennrich, Barry Haddow, and Alexandra Birch. Improving neural machine translation models with monolingual data. In *Proc. of the 54th Annual Meeting of the Association for Computational Linguistics*, pp. 86–96, Berlin, Germany, 2016. DOI: 10.18653/v1/p16-1009 132

Matthew Shardlow. A survey of automated text simplification. *International Journal of Advanced Computer Science and Applications, Special Issue on Natural Language Processing*, 2014. DOI: 10.14569/specialissue.2014.040109 1

Shiqi Shen, Yong Cheng, Zhongjun He, Wei He, Hua Wu, Maosong Sun, and Yang Liu. Minimum risk training for neural machine translation. In *Proc. of the 54th Annual Meeting of the Association for Computational Linguistics*, pp. 1683–1692, Berlin, Germany, 2016. DOI: 10.18653/v1/p16-1159 101

Anastaisa Shimorina, Claire Gardent, Shashi Narayan, and Laura Perez-Beltrachini. The WebNLG challenge: Report on human evaluation. *Report*, 2017. 115

Anastasia Shimorina and Claire Gardent. Handling rare items in data-to-text generation. In *Proc. of the 11th International Conference on Natural Language Generation*, pp. 360–370, Association for Computational Linguistics, Tilburg University, The Netherlands, 2018. DOI: 10.18653/v1/w18-6543 51

Anastasia Shimorina and Claire Gardent. Surface realisation using full delexicalisation. In *Proc. of the Conference on Empirical Methods in Natural Language Processing and the 9th International Joint Conference on Natural Language Processing*, pp. 3077–3087, Association for Computational Linguistics, Hong Kong, China, 2019. DOI: 10.18653/v1/d19-1305 133

Huang Shudong, David Graff, and George Doddington. Multiple-translation Chinese corpus (ldc2002t01). Linguistic Data Consortium, Philadelphia, PA, 2002. 130

Advaith Siddharthan. An architecture for a text simplification system. In *Proc. of the Language Engineering Conference*, pp. 64–71, IEEE Computer Society, 2002. DOI: 10.1109/lec.2002.1182292 7, 18

Advaith Siddharthan. Text simplification using typed dependencies: A comparison of the robustness of different generation strategies. In *Proc. of the 13th European Workshop on Natural Language Generation*, pp. 2–11, Association for Computational Linguistics, Nancy, France, September 2011. 18

Advaith Siddharthan. A survey of research on text simplification. *Recent Advances in Automatic Readability Assessment and Text Simplification, Special issue of International Journal of Applied Linguistics*, 165(2), 2014. DOI: 10.1075/itl.165.2.06sid 1

Advaith Siddharthan, Ani Nenkova, and Kathleen McKeown. Syntactic simplification for improving content selection in multi-document summarization. In *Proc. of the 20th International Conference on Computational Linguistics*, pp. 896–902, COLING, Geneva, Switzerland, 2004. DOI: 10.21236/ada457833 6

H. Gregory Silber and Kathleen F. McCoy. Efficiently computed lexical chains as an intermediate representation for automatic text summarization. *Computational Linguistics*, 28(4):487–496, 2002. DOI: 10.1162/089120102762671954 22

David A. Smith and Jason Eisner. Quasi-synchronous grammars: Alignment by soft projection of syntactic dependencies. In *Proc. of the HLT-NAACL Workshop on Statistical Machine Translation*, pp. 23–30, Association for Computational Linguistics, 2006. DOI: 10.3115/1654650.1654655 19

Kaitao Song, Xu Tan, Tao Qin, Jianfeng Lu, and Tie-Yan Liu. MASS: Masked sequence to sequence pre-training for language generation. In Kamalika Chaudhuri and Ruslan Salakhutdinov, Eds., *Proc. of 36th International Conference on Machine Learning*, 97:5926–5936, Proceedings of Machine Learning Research, 2019a. 137

Linfeng Song, Xiaochang Peng, Yue Zhang, Zhiguo Wang, and Daniel Gildea. AMR-to-text generation with synchronous node replacement grammar. *CoRR*, abs/1702.00500, 2017. DOI: 10.18653/v1/p17-2002 1, 17

Linfeng Song, Yue Zhang, Zhiguo Wang, and Daniel Gildea. A graph-to-sequence model for AMR-to-text generation. In *Proc. of the 56th Annual Meeting of the Association for Computational Linguistics*, pp. 1616–1626, Melbourne, Australia, 2018. DOI: 10.18653/v1/p18-1150 71, 72, 74

Linfeng Song, Daniel Gildea, Yue Zhang, Zhiguo Wang, and Jinsong Su. Semantic neural machine translation using AMR. *Transactions of the Association for Computational Linguistics*, 7:19–31, 2019b. DOI: 10.1162/tacl_a_00252 3

Alessandro Sordoni, Michel Galley, Michael Auli, Chris Brockett, Yangfeng Ji, Margaret Mitchell, Jian-Yun Nie, Jianfeng Gao, and Bill Dolan. A neural network approach to context-sensitive generation of conversational responses. In *Proc. of the Conference of the North American Chapter of the Association for Computational Linguistics: Human Language Technologies*, pp. 196–205, Denver, CO, 2015. DOI: 10.3115/v1/n15-1020 106

Karen Spärck Jones. Automatic summarising: The state of the art. *Information Processing and Management*, 43(6):1449–1481, 2007. DOI: 10.1016/j.ipm.2007.03.009 81

Nitish Srivastava, Geoffrey Hinton, Alex Krizhevsky, Ilya Sutskever, and Ruslan Salakhutdinov. Dropout: A simple way to prevent neural networks from overfitting. *Journal of Machine Learning Research*, 15(1):1929–1958, 2014. 39

Ilya Sutskever, Oriol Vinyals, and Quoc V. Le. Sequence to sequence learning with neural networks. In *Advances in Neural Information Processing Systems*, pp. 3104–3112, 2014. 25, 33, 45, 70, 106

Richard S. Sutton and Andrew G. Barto. *Reinforcement Learning: An Introduction*. MIT Press, 1998. 91, 96

Krysta Marie Svore, Lucy Vanderwende, and Christopher J. C. Burges. Enhancing single-document summarization by combining RankNet and third-party sources. In *Proc. of the Joint Conference on Empirical Methods in Natural Language Processing and Computational Natural Language Learning*, pp. 448–457, Association for Computational Linguistics, Prague, Czech Republic, 2007. 94

Kai Sheng Tai, Richard Socher, and Christopher D. Manning. Improved semantic representations from tree-structured long short-term memory networks. In *Proc. of the 53rd Annual Meeting of the Association for Computational Linguistics and the 7th International Joint Conference on Natural Language Processing*, pp. 1556–1566, Beijing, China, 2015. DOI: 10.3115/v1/p15-1150 75

Jiwei Tan, Xiaojun Wan, and Jianguo Xiao. Abstractive document summarization with a graph-based attentional neural model. In *Proc. of the 55th Annual Meeting of the Association for Computational Linguistics*, pp. 1171–1181, Vancouver, Canada, 2017. DOI: 10.18653/v1/p17-1108 49, 63, 64, 65, 68, 86, 87, 132

Kapil Thadani and Kathleen McKeown. Supervised sentence fusion with single-stage inference. In *Proc. of the 6th International Joint Conference on Natural Language Processing*, pp. 1410–1418, Asian Federation of Natural Language Processing, Nagoya, Japan, 2013. 6

Masaru Tomita. *Efficient Parsing for Natural Language: A Fast Algorithm for Practical Systems*. The Springer International Series in Engineering and Computer Science, Springer U.S., 1985. 7

Kristina Toutanova, Chris Brockett, Ke M. Tran, and Saleema Amershi. A dataset and evaluation metrics for abstractive compression of sentences and short paragraphs. In *Proc. of the Conference on Empirical Methods in Natural Language Processing*, pp. 340–350, Association for Computational Linguistics, Austin, TX, 2016. DOI: 10.18653/v1/d16-1033 xix, 6, 84, 125, 126, 127

Bayu Distiawan Trisedya, Jianzhong Qi, Rui Zhang, and Wei Wang. GTR-LSTM: A triple encoder for sentence generation from RDF data. In *Proc. of the 56th Annual Meeting of the Association for Computational Linguistics*, pp. 1627–1637, Melbourne, Australia, 2018. DOI: 10.18653/v1/p18-1151 51, 71, 74, 75, 76

Zhaopeng Tu, Zhengdong Lu, Yang Liu, Xiaohua Liu, and Hang Li. Modeling coverage for neural machine translation. In *Proc. of the 54th Annual Meeting of the Association for Computational Linguistics*, pp. 76–85, Berlin, Germany, 2016. DOI: 10.18653/v1/p16-1008 53, 54

Jenine Turner and Eugene Charniak. Supervised and unsupervised learning for sentence compression. In *Proc. of the 43rd Annual Meeting on Association for Computational Linguistics*, pp. 290–297, Sydney, Australia, 2005. DOI: 10.3115/1219840.1219876 20

Chris van der Lee, Thiago Castro Ferreira, Emiel Krahmer, and Sander Wubben. Tilburg university models for the WebNLG challenge. *Technical Report*, Tilburg University, 2017. 51

Ashish Vaswani, Noam Shazeer, Niki Parmar, Jakob Uszkoreit, Llion Jones, Aidan N. Gomez, Łukasz Kaiser, and Illia Polosukhin. Attention is all you need. In I. Guyon, U. V. Luxburg, S. Bengio, H. Wallach, R. Fergus, S. Vishwanathan, and R. Garnett, Eds., *Advances in Neural Information Processing Systems 30*, pp. 5998–6008, Curran Associates Inc., 2017. 32, 79, 134, 135, 136

Erik Velldal and Stephan Oepen. Statistical ranking in tactical generation. In *Proc. of the Conference on Empirical Methods in Natural Language Processing*, pp. 517–525, Association for Computational Linguistics, Sydney, Australia, 2006. DOI: 10.3115/1610075.1610147 17

David Vickrey and Daphne Koller. Sentence simplification for semantic role labeling. In *Proc. of the 46th Annual Meeting of the Association for Computational Linguistics: Human Language Technology*, pp. 344–352, Columbus, OH, 2008. 7

Oriol Vinyals and Quoc Le. A neural conversational model. *CoRR*, abs/1506.05869, 2015. 106

Oriol Vinyals, Meire Fortunato, and Navdeep Jaitly. Pointer networks. In C. Cortes, N. D. Lawrence, D. D. Lee, M. Sugiyama, and R. Garnett, Eds., *Advances in Neural Information Processing Systems 28*, pp. 2692–2700, Curran Associates Inc., 2015. 50

Xiaojun Wan, Jianwu Yang, and Jianguo Xiao. Manifold-ranking based topic-focused multi-document summarization. In *Proc. of the 20th International Joint Conference on Artifical Intelligence*, pp. 2903–2908, Hyderabad, India, 2007. 87

Alex Wang and Kyunghyun Cho. BERT has a mouth, and it must speak: BERT as a Markov random field language model. In *Proc. of the Workshop on Methods for Optimizing and Evaluating Neural Language Generation*, pp. 30–36, Association for Computational Linguistics, Minneapolis, MN, 2019. 137

Alex Wang, Amanpreet Singh, Julian Michael, Felix Hill, Omer Levy, and Samuel Bowman. GLUE: A multi-task benchmark and analysis platform for natural language understanding. In *Proc. of the EMNLP Workshop BlackboxNLP: Analyzing and Interpreting Neural Networks for NLP*, pp. 353–355, Association for Computational Linguistics, Brussels, Belgium, 2018. DOI: 10.18653/v1/w18-5446 136

Dingding Wang, Shenghuo Zhu, Tao Li, and Yihong Gong. Multi-document summarization using sentence-based topic models. In *Proc. of the Joint Conference of the 47th Annual Meeting of the Association for Computational Linguistics and the 4th International Joint Conference on Natural Language Processing*, pp. 297–300, Suntec, Singapore, 2009. DOI: 10.3115/1667583.1667675 21

Willian Massami Watanabe, Arnaldo Candido Junior, Vinícius Rodriguez Uzêda, Renata Pontin de Mattos Fortes, Thiago Alexandre Salgueiro Pardo, and Sandra Maria Aluísio. Facilita: Reading assistance for low-literacy readers. In *Proc. of the 27th ACM International Conference on Design of Communication*, pp. 29–36, New York, 2009. DOI: 10.1145/1621995.1622002 7

Tsung-Hsien Wen, Milica Gasic, Nikola Mrkšić, Pei-Hao Su, David Vandyke, and Steve Young. Semantically conditioned LSTM-based natural language generation for spoken dialogue systems. In *Proc. of the Conference on Empirical Methods in Natural Language Processing*, pp. 1711–1721, Association for Computational Linguistics, Lisbon, Portugal, 2015. DOI: 10.18653/v1/d15-1199 4, 45, 54, 56, 59

Michael White. Reining in CCG chart realization. In *Proc. of the 3rd International Conference on Natural Language Generation*, pp. 182–191, Brighton, UK, 2004. DOI: 10.1007/978-3-540-27823-8_19 16

Michael White. CCG chart realization from disjunctive inputs. In *Proc. of the 4th International Natural Language Generation Conference*, pp. 12–19, Association for Computational Linguistics, Sydney, Australia, 2006. DOI: 10.3115/1706269.1706274 16

John Wieting and Kevin Gimpel. ParaNMT-50M: Pushing the limits of paraphrastic sentence embeddings with millions of machine translations. In *Proc. of the 56th Annual Meeting of the Association for Computational Linguistics*, pp. 451–462, Melbourne, Australia, 2018. DOI: 10.18653/v1/p18-1042 127, 128

John Wieting, Mohit Bansal, Kevin Gimpel, Karen Livescu, and Dan Roth. From paraphrase database to compositional paraphrase model and back. *CoRR*, abs/1506.03487, 2015. DOI: 10.1162/tacl_a_00143 6, 128

Adina Williams, Nikita Nangia, and Samuel Bowman. A broad-coverage challenge corpus for sentence understanding through inference. In *Proc. of the Conference of the North American Chapter of the Association for Computational Linguistics: Human Language Technologies*, pp. 1112–1122, New Orleans, LA, 2018. DOI: 10.18653/v1/n18-1101 105

Ronald J. Williams. Simple statistical gradient-following algorithms for connectionist reinforcement learning. *Machine Learning*, 8(3–4):229–256, 1992. DOI: 10.1007/978-1-4615-3618-5_2 65, 88, 91, 97, 98, 101, 104

Sam Wiseman, Stuart Shieber, and Alexander Rush. Challenges in data-to-document generation. In *Proc. of the Conference on Empirical Methods in Natural Language Processing*, pp. 2253–2263, Association for Computational Linguistics, Copenhagen, Denmark, 2017. DOI: 10.18653/v1/d17-1239 1, 5, 45, 82, 91, 113, 115, 116

Kam-Fai Wong, Mingli Wu, and Wenjie Li. Extractive summarization using supervised and semi-supervised learning. In *Proc. of the 22nd International Conference on Computational Linguistics*, pp. 985–992, Coling Organizing Committee, Manchester, UK, 2008. DOI: 10.3115/1599081.1599205 22

Kristian Woodsend and Mirella Lapata. Automatic generation of story highlights. In *Proc. of the 48th Annual Meeting of the Association for Computational Linguistics*, pp. 565–574, Uppsala, Sweden, 2010. 94

Kristian Woodsend and Mirella Lapata. Learning to simplify sentences with quasi-synchronous grammar and integer programming. In *Proc. of the Conference on Empirical Methods in Natural Language Processing*, pp. 409–420, Association for Computational Linguistics, Edinburgh, Scotland, UK, 2011. 6, 19, 20, 123, 124

Kristian Woodsend, Yansong Feng, and Mirella Lapata. Title generation with quasi-synchronous grammar. In *Proc. of the Conference on Empirical Methods in Natural Language Processing*, pp. 513–523, Association for Computational Linguistics, Cambridge, MA, 2010. 20

Xianchao Wu, Ander Martinez, and Momo Klyen. Dialog generation using multi-turn reasoning neural networks. In *Proc. of the Conference of the North American Chapter of the Association for Computational Linguistics: Human Language Technologies*, pp. 2049–2059, New Orleans, LA, 2018. DOI: 10.18653/v1/n18-1186 106

Yonghui Wu, Mike Schuster, Zhifeng Chen, Quoc V. Le, Mohammad Norouzi, Wolfgang Macherey, Maxim Krikun, Yuan Cao, Qin Gao, Klaus Macherey, Jeff Klingner, Apurva Shah, Melvin Johnson, Xiaobing Liu, Lukasz Kaiser, Stephan Gouws, Yoshikiyo Kato, Taku Kudo, Hideto Kazawa, Keith Stevens, George Kurian, Nishant Patil, Wei Wang, Cliff Young, Jason Smith, Jason Riesa, Alex Rudnick, Oriol Vinyals, Greg Corrado, Macduff Hughes, and Jeffrey Dean. Google's neural machine translation system: Bridging the gap between human and machine translation. *CoRR*, abs/1609.08144, 2016. 132

Sander Wubben, Antal van den Bosch, and Emiel Krahmer. Paraphrase generation as monolingual translation: Data and evaluation. In *Proc. of the 6th International Natural Language Generation Conference*, 2010. 6

Sander Wubben, Antal van den Bosch, and Emiel Krahmer. Sentence simplification by monolingual machine translation. In *Proc. of the 50th Annual Meeting of the Association for Computational Linguistics*, pp. 1015–1024, Jeju Island, Korea, 2012. 6, 19, 123

Kelvin Xu, Jimmy Lei Ba, Ryan Kiros, Kyunghyun Cho, Aaron Courville, Ruslan Salakhutdinov, Richard S. Zemel, and Yoshua Bengio. Show, attend and tell: Neural image caption generation with visual attention. In *Proc. of the 32nd International Conference on Machine Learning*, pp. 2048–2057, Lille, France, 2015a. 27, 68

Wei Xu, Alan Ritter, Chris Callison-Burch, William B. Dolan, and Yangfeng Ji. Extracting lexically divergent paraphrases from Twitter. *Transactions of the Association for Computational Linguistics*, 2:435–448, 2014. DOI: 10.1162/tacl_a_00194 128, 129

Wei Xu, Chris Callison-Burch, and Courtney Napoles. Problems in current text simplification research: New data can help. *Transactions of the Association for Computational Linguistics*, 3:283–297, 2015b. DOI: 10.1162/tacl_a_00139 6, 124

Wei Xu, Courtney Napoles, Ellie Pavlick, Quanze Chen, and Chris Callison-Burch. Optimizing statistical machine translation for text simplification. *Transactions of the Association for Computational Linguistics*, 4:401–415, 2016. DOI: 10.1162/tacl_a_00107 93, 97, 102, 124

Kenji Yamada and Kevin Knight. A syntax-based statistical translation model. In *Proc. of the 39th Annual Meeting of the Association for Computational Linguistics*, pp. 523–530, Toulouse, France, 2001. DOI: 10.3115/1073012.1073079 19

Mark Yatskar, Bo Pang, Cristian Danescu-Niculescu-Mizil, and Lillian Lee. For the sake of simplicity: Unsupervised extraction of lexical simplifications from Wikipedia. In *Human Language Technologies: The Annual Conference of the North American Chapter of the Association for Computational Linguistics*, pp. 365–368, Los Angeles, CA, 2010. 123

David Zajic, Bonnie J. Dorr, Jimmy Lin, and Richard Schwartz. Multi-candidate reduction: Sentence compression as a tool for document summarization tasks. *Information Processing and Management*, 43(6):1549–1570, 2007. DOI: 10.1016/j.ipm.2007.01.016 20

Wojciech Zaremba and Ilya Sutskever. Reinforcement learning neural turing machines. *CoRR*, abs/1505.00521, 2015. 98

Matthew D. Zeiler. ADADELTA: An adaptive learning rate method. *CoRR*, abs/1212.5701, 2012. 39

Wenyuan Zeng, Wenjie Luo, Sanja Fidler, and Raquel Urtasun. Efficient summarization with read-again and copy mechanism. *CoRR*, abs/1611.03382, 2016. 51

Renxian Zhang, Wenjie Li, and Dehong Gao. Towards content-level coherence with aspect-guided summarization. *ACM Transactions on Speech and Language Processing*, 10(1):2, 2013. DOI: 10.1145/2442076.2442078 22

Tianyi Zhang, Varsha Kishore, Felix Wu, Kilian Q. Weinberger, and Yoav Artzi. BERTScore: Evaluating text generation with BERT. *CoRR*, abs/1904.09675, 2019. 133

Xiang Zhang, Junbo Zhao, and Yann LeCun. Character-level convolutional networks for text classification. In C. Cortes, N. D. Lawrence, D. D. Lee, M. Sugiyama, and R. Garnett, Eds., *Advances in Neural Information Processing Systems 28*, pp. 649–657, Curran Associates, Inc., 2015. 27, 68

Xingxing Zhang and Mirella Lapata. Chinese poetry generation with recurrent neural networks. In *Proc. of the Conference on Empirical Methods in Natural Language Processing*, pp. 670–680, Association for Computational Linguistics, Doha, Qatar, 2014. DOI: 10.3115/v1/d14-1074 45

Xingxing Zhang and Mirella Lapata. Sentence simplification with deep reinforcement learning. In *Proc. of the Conference on Empirical Methods in Natural Language Processing*, pp. 584–594, Association for Computational Linguistics, Copenhagen, Denmark, 2017. DOI: 10.18653/v1/d17-1062 6, 58, 97, 101, 102, 105, 123, 135

Ying Zhang, Mohammad Pezeshki, Philemon Brakel, Saizheng Zhang, César Laurent, Yoshua Bengio, and Aaron C. Courville. Towards end-to-end speech recognition with deep convolutional neural networks. *CoRR*, abs/1701.02720, 2017. DOI: 10.21437/interspeech.2016-1446 27

Shiqi Zhao, Cheng Niu, Ming Zhou, Ting Liu, and Sheng Li. Combining multiple resources to improve SMT-based paraphrasing model. In *Proc. of the 46th Annual Meeting of the Association for Computational Linguistics: Human Language Technologies*, pp. 1021–1029, Columbus, OH, 2008. 20

Liang Zhou and Eduard Hovy. A web-trained extraction summarization system. In *Proc. of the Conference of the North American Chapter of the Association for Computational Linguistics on Human Language Technology*, pp. 205–211, Edmonton, Canada, 2003. DOI: 10.3115/1073445.1073482 22

Qingyu Zhou, Nan Yang, Furu Wei, and Ming Zhou. Selective encoding for abstractive sentence summarization. In *Proc. of the 55th Annual Meeting of the Association for Computational Linguistics*, pp. 1095–1104, Vancouver, Canada, 2017. DOI: 10.18653/v1/p17-1101 82, 83, 84, 91, 135

Jie Zhu, Junhui Li, Muhua Zhu, Longhua Qian, Min Zhang, and Guodong Zhou. Modeling graph structure in transformer for better AMR-to-Text generation. *CoRR*, abs/1909.00136, 2019. DOI: 10.18653/v1/d19-1548 136

Zhemin Zhu, Delphine Bernhard, and Iryna Gurevych. A monolingual tree-based translation model for sentence simplification. In *Proc. of the 23rd International Conference on Computational Linguistics*, pp. 1353–1361, Coling Organizing Committee, Beijing, China, 2010. 6, 19, 122, 123

Authors' Biographies

SHASHI NARAYAN

Shashi Narayan is a research scientist at Google in London. Prior to joining Google, he was a post-doctoral researcher at the University of Edinburgh. This book was written while he was still at the University of Edinburgh. He received his Ph.D. from the University of Lorraine. His research focuses on natural language generation understanding and structured predictions. The questions raised in his research are relevant to various natural language applications such as question answering, paraphrase generation, semantic and syntactic parsing, document understanding and summarisation, and text simplification. His research has appeared in computational linguistics journals (e.g., *TACL*, *Computational Linguistics*, and *Pattern Recognition Letters*) and in conferences (e.g., ACL, EMNLP, NAACL, COLING, EACL and INLG). He was nominated to the SIGGEN board (2012–14) as a student member. He co-organised the WebNLG Shared Task, a challenge on generating text from RDF data. He served as an area co-chair for Generation at NAACL HLT 2018 and ACL 2020, and for Summarisation at ACL and EMNLP 2019.

CLAIRE GARDENT

Claire Gardent is a research scientist at CNRS, the French National Center for Scientific Research. Prior to joining the CNRS, she worked at the Université de Clermont-Ferrand (France), Saarbrücken Universität (Germany), Utrecht, and Amsterdam Universiteit (The Netherlands). She received her Ph.D. from the University of Edinburgh and her M.Sc. from Essex University. She was nominated Chair of the EACL and acted as program chair for various international conferences, workshops, and summer schools (EACL, ENLG, SemDIAL, SIGDIAL, ESSLLI, *SEM). She served on the editorial board of the journals *Computational Linguistics*, *Journal of Semantics* and *Traitement Automatique des Langues*, recently headed the WebNLG project (Nancy, Bolzano, Stanford SRI), and acted as chair of SIGGEN, the ACL Special Interest Group in Natural Language Generation. She also co-organised the WebNLG Shared Task, a challenge on generating text from RDF data. Her research interests include executable semantic parsing, natural language generation, question answering, dialogue and the use of computational linguistics for linguistic analysis.

Printed in the United States
by Baker & Taylor Publisher Services